HASHI MOHAMED arrived in Britain as a child refugee, and is now a Barrister at No5 Chambers in London. A contributor to the *Guardian*, *The Times* and *Prospect*, he has explored class and mobility for the BBC. He presented *Adventures in Social Mobility* (April 2017) and *Macpherson: What Happened Next* (2019).

'A vital work of courage and hope, by a truly remarkable individual.' Philippe Sands, author of *East West Street*

'A penetrating book about the dilemmas of social mobility in Britain, intelligently conceived, powerfully argued. Don't expect a comfortable read. Hashi Mohamed challenges those who think that we are doing OK, as well as those who know we aren't but look for more extreme solutions. It deserves a wide audience.' Jonathan Sumption, author of *Trials of the State: Law and the Decline of Politics*

'He is an unconventional figure, and a key strength of his book is his refreshing willingness to address controversial issues with candour.' *Sunday Times*

'An extraordinary memoir-cum-polemic, beautifully written and powerfully argued, *People Like Us* is essential reading, expertly challenging the stories we tell ourselves about social mobility in the twenty first century.' The Secret Barrister

'I found myself nodding in agreement with every word of *People Like Us*. Hashi Mohamed has written a moving, shocking and clear-eyed account of the increasingly rare phenomenon of social mobility. Using his own extraordinary story as a spine he has written an analysis, how-to-guide and pole..
Britain today..........................
Descent of M.....

'Hashi Mohamed powerfully exposes the alienating and segregating effect of social immobility in this country. Beautifully written, *People Like Us* makes a deeply personal case for a world in which anybody can reach success, but doesn't have to leave a part of themselves behind to achieve it.' David Lammy MP

'Mohamed's is an impressive tale, but he turns it into something much larger and far more resonant in his finely written memoir ... a rather ambitious and far-ranging attempt to rethink the whole stalled project of social mobility. A careful and affecting study of personal struggle, social mobility and international migration that brings a fresh and well-informed voice to the debate.' *Observer*

'Even those who do not daily rub up against British class distinctions will find Mohamed's achievements extraordinary; those well acquainted with the wider themes will find themselves challenged by his conclusions ... [he uses] his new social status to deliver a few home truths.' *Financial Times*

People Like Us

What it Takes to Make it in Modern Britain

Hashi Mohamed

PROFILE BOOKS

This paperback edition published 2020

First published in Great Britain in 2020 by
Profile Books Ltd
29 Cloth Fair
London
ECIA 7JQ

www.profilebooks.com

1 3 5 7 9 10 8 6 4 2

Typeset in Berling Nova Text by MacGuru Ltd
Printed and bound in Great Britain by
CPI Group (UK) Ltd, Croydon CRO 4YY

A CIP catalogue record for this book is available from the British Library.

ISBN 978 1 78816 113 8
eISBN 978 1 78816 111 4
Audio ISBN 978 1 78283 681 0

To my late father, who never saw the man I became.
And to his mother, who did so much to make me the man I am.

Contents

Introduction

Say not, 'I have found the truth,' but rather, 'I have found a truth.'

Kahlil Gibran, *The Prophet*

I had to learn the hardest way. But it didn't have to be like that.

That's what this book is about.

It is a book that seeks to understand why what I went through on my own journey from poverty to privilege was necessary. It is a form of therapy, but, more importantly, I hope it is a way for me to pass on what I have learned along the way. It contains a world about which most people know very little; but for many people like me the reality of it was – and still remains – remarkably unremarkable.

My name is Hashi Mohamed Hashi. I was born in Kenya to Somali parents and my name follows the tradition of Somali names in which, instead of having surnames, you list a series of forenames that trace your lineage back to your clan forefathers: Hashi was my grandfather's name, which is why it appears twice. I come from a nomadic, oral tradition, in which historical records were preserved through poetry and in the memory of generations instead of on parchments and vellum: relatives often claim to 'meet you' at your seventh or eighth listed name, tracing back many generations. My father had little formal education and left his family to seek his fortunes in Kenya in the late 1970s. A few years later, he met my mother, a divorcee with six children from her previous marriage, who had come to Kenya alone in 1980 to seek a new beginning. She was never formally educated and has never learned how to read and write. She and my father had another six children, five of whom survived and of whom I am the second. There has never been a point at which all of my siblings have lived in the same place at the same time. Again, for many people like me this is quite normal.

Thirteen years after my parents met, the Somali state collapsed following a brutal civil war. The whole of my family still remaining in Somalia was uprooted and rendered stateless in Kenya. At the same time, my father died in a car crash in Kenya, and I ended up in North West London with some of my siblings. Our mother had stayed behind.

I was nine years old.

Today, twenty-five years later, I am a barrister and broadcaster – and now, as you read these words, I am an author, too. This was, frankly, a very unlikely outcome. I grew up in some of the most deprived areas of London, attended failing schools (when I bothered to turn up at all) and was raised exclusively on state benefits. With the benefit of full scholarships, I went on to study law and French at the University of Hertfordshire, do a postgraduate degree at St Antony's College, Oxford, and soon after took a Bar School vocational qualification from City Law School. At twenty-seven, I became a member of the Bar of England and Wales, and a lifetime member of The Honourable Society of Lincoln's Inn – one of the four Inns of Court, established in 1422, to which barristers belong. I practise out of No5 Chambers, the largest set of chambers in the country, specialising in planning and environment law, and commercial litigation.

I say all this not to boast, but because mine has been the unlikeliest of journeys; and even from the inside it is hard to understand what shaped and powered it. The trajectory for most of my siblings and family has been very different, and yet I have had no discernible advantage over any of them. I am left to wonder 'why me?'

It was partly in search of answers that, in April 2017, I made a radio documentary for BBC Radio 4 entitled *Adventures in Social Mobility*. The documentary charted my journey from arriving in the UK as a young unaccompanied child refugee, to becoming a barrister practising in England and Wales. Though the programme was short, the issues I touched upon, the lessons I picked up along the way, the people I met and the challenges I had overcome seemed to strike a chord with many people. Parents wrote to tell me how encouraging my broadcast was to them as they worked out how best to raise their sons. Teachers confided to me that they had been unsure about whether they were doing the right thing, unsure about their efforts and how much of an impact they were making. It was reassuring to know that they found something to take away from the story that I told. Men shared with me intimate details about what it meant for them to have grown up without a father. At one point, not knowing who I was, someone at a party recommended 'an incredible podcast about social mobility' to me. I was inundated with messages and invitations to discuss the issues at schools, at community centres and at various institutions. It was both humbling and daunting when people spoke to me as though I could explain how to navigate journeys that many before me had struggled to complete, as if I had the map to the Promised Land.

Just after the documentary aired, *Private Eye* ran a cartoon depicting two men in a pub. One is an older gentleman with silver hair, formally dressed, nursing what looks like a gin and tonic. He offers: 'Yes, I was listening to a documentary about social mobility on Radio 4.' The response from his younger, shaven-headed companion, who is casually dressed, has a beer in front of him and a bemused look on his face, is: 'What's Radio 4?' I realised that, if I really wanted to make a difference, I should find a way to bring this story to a much wider audience. What the cartoon pointed out was that the people who were most affected by the lack of social mobility in Britain, despite the number who had been in touch with me, were not necessarily the ones I was reaching. To put it bluntly, the demographic that listens to Radio 4 documentaries about inequality are perhaps the least affected by it. But it also touched on an essential truth about social mobility: that is, what one group considers essentially familiar, part of the furniture of everyday life, can to someone else be entirely foreign. We just don't know what we don't know about how others live in our own country.

My story is also, like all life stories, unique. It is not a template or a blueprint. With such specific and individual twists and turns, how could it be? Instead, by exploring my own journey so far, I hope to answer a simple but important question: what does it take for you to do better in life and improve on what was accomplished by those who came before you? As you read this book, I hope that your starting point is not as difficult or as marked with grief and struggle as my own; but I hope that you're able to connect with some of what I describe in these pages. I recognise the need to tell this story to young people: never underestimate the power of seeing someone who looks like you – someone with whom you share a similar background, someone whose struggles you may relate to – occupying a place where you hope to be one day. Perhaps most importantly, I recognise that very few people are in a position to tell this story as I can. And unless you have been there, experienced the difficulties and struggle and disillusionment of a journey from the bottom to the top, what can you really say about the matter?

* * *

It also felt to me that such a book was timely. Always obsessively interested in matters of class, British society seems suddenly awake to the fact that, in the last decade or so, social mobility has entered a state of paralysis. Three weeks before I signed my contract for this book, the entire board of the government's own Social Mobility Commission resigned, apparently in despair at a lack of government commitment to solving any of the problems it had been set up to investigate. 'I have little hope of the current government making the progress I believe is necessary to bring about a fairer Britain,' was the parting shot of its chair, Alan Milburn. Hardly a day goes by without a deluge of articles about school exam performances, the rising number of children living in poverty, or the shockingly small number of Black and Minority Ethnic (BAME)* students offered places at Oxbridge. We are frequently reminded of the domination of the top professions by a small minority of people who are privately educated; the ways in which privilege is maintained through an effortless natural order of the well connected and well educated.

---

*The designation BAME (Black and Minority Ethnic) is somewhat problematic, given the fundamental inadequacy of any collective term for so many distinct communities. However, it continues to be used widely by government departments, public bodies and across the media, and I have retained it here.

It can sometimes feel as if one mentoring programme a week is born out of a well-intended desire to help, but the execution can often be misguided or cack-handed – and ultimately likely to do more harm than good. Employers and companies are keen to highlight their latest 'diversity and inclusion' initiatives; but while they may move the dial at the entry level, albeit slightly, it's often a very different story a few years down the line, or in the upper reaches of the organisation.

This concern is justified: Britain is a deeply divided nation. After twenty years of improvement, poverty levels are on the rise again. Social mobility has flatlined. The upper reaches of our industries and institutions are sclerotic and riven with privilege: 'a closed shop at the top', as the Social Mobility Foundation put it.[1] Only 7 per cent of the British population attend independent fee-paying schools. And yet in my own profession, 71 per cent of barristers have attended independent schools, and only 29 per cent are state educated. Although only 1 per cent of the population is educated at Oxbridge, 78 per cent of the Bar attended those universities.[2] It is not a coincidence that these worlds mirror each other so closely, with barristers able to move seamlessly from one stone-built, green-lawned 'quad' to the next, their colleagues and mentors people who have glided through the same ancient institutions, with remarkably similar mindsets and outlooks.[3]

The military recruits nearly three-quarters (71 per cent) of its officers from the privately educated. Over half (51 per cent) of journalists were educated at independent schools, as were 61 per cent of senior doctors, despite medicine having traditionally attracted a wider spectrum of society.[4] In government, 49 per cent of MPs attended private schools, and, at the time of writing, 64 per cent of the cabinet did (with 36 per cent attending private schools *and* Oxbridge).[5] What is it about these schools that apparently leads to a much more successful life in modern-day Britain? What precisely is holding back the 88 per cent of our population, who are currently educated at comprehensive schools, from these top positions in society? This book is partly an attempt to understand how, and why, we find ourselves in this shocking situation in a society like Britain, which claims to value fair play and opportunity for all. It is important to be clear that my own story marks me out as an anomaly in terms of social mobility. In many ways, the part of this book that draws on my own experiences is a series of truly unlikely events over which, at the beginning, I had no control, but which have shaped my life and the man I am today.

It is a story of hope and despair, tragedy and trauma, luck and ambition; a story of death and survival. It is about what it means to arrive in Britain with little understanding of the culture, the language, the political context, or really anything at all. It is a story of navigating through all of this, of the sustained resilience required, and of the deep search for meaning amidst the suffering and indignities. It explores how I have ended up where I am today, at the time of writing, working in one of the elite and ancient professions, and supposedly now part of the 'establishment'. So, yes, this is a book about social mobility and how to dream of a different destiny, but it is also about life, choices and opportunities, or lack of them. Above all, it is a story which continues to unfold and which (I hope) has its longest chapters yet to be written.

* * *

The term social mobility can mean different things to different people, depending on the context. It's often held up as an ultimate good: a reward for 'strivers', ambitious hard workers, the deserving poor. It can carry negative connotations: accusations of naked ambition, of climbing the greasy pole, disowning your 'heritage' and 'culture' for the promise of a better life or higher position in society. In purely sociological terms, it relates to the particular movement of the social position of groups or individuals when compared to a defined starting point. These movements are usually assumed to be upwards, but they could just as easily be downwards. In the UK, the conversations are typically defined in class terms. People talk about having 'working class' roots or might identify as 'middle class' compared to their parents or grandparents. The definition of social mobility therefore tends to revolve around the socio-economic status of parents compared to their children – or, put bluntly, are you doing better than the previous generation? An indication of 'moving up the ladder' might be home ownership, traditionally considered to be a marker of middle-class status (though that is becoming less and less typical), but it could also be being the first in your family to have gone to university.

Sociologists often use the terms 'absolute' and 'relative' mobility. Put simply, absolute mobility can relate to the significant changes in the living standards of a society as a whole, and any movement is judged against how far someone has come from their parents' starting point. An example of a change in absolute mobility would be the major social shifts that occurred after the Second World War, where the percentage of people with higher (or significantly improving) incomes, or professional positions, markedly increased. The post-war shifts were primarily a result of society being in flux, allowing for more movement in income distribution and the narrowing of inequality, rather than, for example, the proliferation of grammar schools, as is often suggested. Crucially, absolute mobility is not a zero-sum game. In theory, it allows for society as a whole to improve. If there is an increase in opportunities and an expansion of top-end jobs, then the people at the top get to stay there and there are more places for those seeking entry.[6]

Relative mobility is the more commonly used term, and it is what politicians are talking about when you hear them discuss social mobility. It refers to the degree to which you can predict how far someone is likely to go in life, depending on their starting point. For example, if your mother held a minimum-wage, unskilled job and never went to university, and you are a doctor with a postgraduate degree, earning a six-figure salary, you have experienced significant relative social mobility. Relative mobility *is* a zero-sum game: it assumes that there are a finite number of places 'at the top', that the best-positioned members of society will flourish, and that the remainder will stay where they are – or move downwards. As one wealthy mother, who wanted her children to get into a prestigious school in Highgate, put it to a friend of mine who was tutoring her children: 'It is not enough for my children to succeed. The children of other parents also have to fail.'

This is the dark truth behind social mobility, which is rarely verbalised: in our current society, not everyone will – or can – 'make it'. The many parents who desperately want to see their children get on in life, or even just maintain their position in society, know that to do so they will need an edge over others. In this book, while my main aim is to try to map out a different future, one that takes us away from these definitions and depressing realities, it is impossible to ignore these facts. Therefore, when I refer to my own story and my journey, I am talking about relative mobility. When attempting to think about the bigger picture, however, and what governments can do to create the right opportunities in both school and in employment in order to access more opportunities 'at the top', I will be referring to absolute mobility.

Almost everyone you speak to believes in upward social mobility; how could you not? No one can disagree with the proposition that your talent and hard work should take you as far as it can in life. Yet in order to *really* believe in this idea, we must confront its opposite: downward mobility. While some parents may work hard to better the lives of their children, other parents work just as hard to ensure that their children do not 'regress towards the mean'.[7] They pay for private education. They hand over flat deposits. They fund their offspring when, as new graduates, they take on the unpaid internships that are the gateway to many industries – and they get out the address book to see who could help Sophie or Oliver get their foot in the door of their chosen career. To that end, to borrow a phrase coined by former government adviser Richard Reeves, they construct a 'glass floor' below which their children cannot fall. This is the missing and unspoken link in this whole debate. It is for this reason that it is critical to understand that, without fundamental social change, when we buy into this idea of relative social mobility we have to be prepared to accept the consequences, namely that there will be movement downwards as well as upwards.

We also need to look at how we measure social mobility. For too long, we've viewed it through the prisms of class structure and material wealth, or through the persistent British obsession with measuring people's worth through metrics like the school you went to, the accent you speak in, or the part of town you grew up in. What does personal and institutional progress increasingly look like in modern-day Britain? In some ways, my own story is a classic tale of relative social mobility: my parents were barely educated and, by any standards, badly off. I went to university, I have a high-status, lucrative job and I own a house. Is the ideal situation one in which everyone follows my example? No – I am lucky in that my particular set of talents and skills allowed me to flourish at university and in an 'elite' professional field. Not everyone is suited to being a barrister. And nor would everyone want to be one.

The truth is that we have idealised a particular standard towards which people should be aiming: the round hole. Despite the fact that people come in all shapes and sizes, we are constantly forcing individuals – through our schooling system, culture, parenting and expectations – into the standard round hole. The idea that each child's ambition (almost certainly set by someone else), is to become a doctor, a lawyer, an accountant, or whatever other nice middle-class career looks like progress, must be revisited – and the measure against which we judge 'success' and what it means to have 'made it' must also be re-examined. This is not to undermine the ambition or aspiration of those who do want to enter those professions (and unless they are supported in their attempts we will be leaving the arena to the few who dominate it today). Instead, we must find new ways of motivating our children to work harder, to aspire to discover what they're good at and enjoy, in so far as it is possible, otherwise we will only set them up for failure.

True social mobility, in fact, may involve changing the way in which we value and remunerate jobs. The columnist and author Owen Jones has argued that, as a society, we should pay more attention to the social worth of working-class jobs, with the aim of improving the pay and conditions of those workers, instead of obsessing over a kind of social mobility that will only elevate a few individuals while leaving an unfair system in place.[8] Social mobility, he thinks, is a busted flush: 'It's the idea of creaming off a small minority of able working-class kids and catapulting them into the middle classes. You accept the class system, merely offering ladders for some to escape the bottom.' It's a position I agree with: but I also think that if we're waiting for the class system to be dismantled then we'll be waiting a long time. This book will also offer advice for young people trying to make it right now, and who are dealing with the system as it is rather than as it could be.

In fact, there is a tension running throughout this book. On the one hand, I want to advise those beginning their social mobility journey about the best way to deal with the world as they find it. But I also don't want to pretend that that world is anything other than imperfect, unfair and unpredictable. Succeeding within it means both learning its rules and learning to bend them. We should never be content with the status quo, for we know how inadequate, unjust and excluding it is; but it's also true that you will be much better placed to change things from the inside, to make a difference to someone just like you one day, than if you stand on the outside simply waiting for the world around you to change. You will be unnecessarily sacrificing yourself for little reward. Don't be a martyr, but don't let go of the burning desire for change, be mindful of the power that you *do* have. This is my view and I am comfortable with it. Make your own decision and be content with it; anything else would only make you feel resentful.

* * *

Education is often cited as the answer to the social mobility problem. It is true that any successful society must seek to educate its population to be literate and numerate, to broaden people's minds and prepare them for the modern world. Yet, in terms of how education affects the individual's chances of moving up the social ladder, a cruel paradox is at work. Education is vital for social mobility, but being highly educated does not guarantee that you will be socially mobile. In other words, although leaving school at sixteen, not going to university, or being NEET (not in education, employment or training) have a marked effect on your chances, having A Levels and a degree does not necessarily free you from the effects of disadvantage. For example, by the time they are in their early thirties, graduates from wealthy backgrounds earn significantly more than their graduate peers from working-class families. Clearly something is at work that education itself does not resolve.

The persistent narrative – promoted by politicians and successive governments – that education, on its own, has the answer, or even the *main* answer, to addressing deep inequalities and lack of access to top universities and professions has distorted the discussion. Of course, education should be pursued for its own sake (and I will talk later about the role that cultural capital – access to art, music, literature – plays in social mobility), but the intense focus on, and expectations of, our schooling institutions and teachers has not moved the dial much. It may have led to more people passing more exams, breaking the link between poor attainment and class or wealth, but it has piled pressure on to teachers and students, making the experience of education profoundly stressful and often unrewarding. At the same time, little space has been left for 'soft skills' such as art, acting, music, presenting – all of which can confer a surprising advantage in later life.

I do not pretend that any of this is easy; I do not expect to see it resolved in my lifetime. Some of the more serious obstacles in our way are values and attitudes underpinned by centuries-old customs and mindsets, which are for the most part designed and meticulously maintained to ensure that everyone 'knows their place'. This deep conditioning is unlikely to be shifted either easily or quickly. The first step, though, must be to call it out. As a relatively recent entrant into British society, and someone who has been able to observe it from the perspective of both deprivation and privilege, I can see the situation that confronted my family when we arrived for what it was. I have been able to navigate through it, and can also identify the attitudes – from outright racism to more subtle forms of prejudice against accents or social presentation – that perpetuate inequalities, and that remain the obstacle to our society harnessing all of the talents it contains. From the cradle onwards, towards whichever fulfilling career you desire, there are many hurdles to clear, some more visible than others: some are determined by an accident of birth, and some you may be able to resist, but most are beyond your immediate control.

* * *

When I first met David Johnston, the chief executive of the Social Mobility Foundation, to interview him about this topic, I began by saying, 'Don't worry, this is not a story about how I lifted myself up by the bootstraps.' He sighed in relief.

It's an exchange that represents our mutual frustration at how simplistic the discussion about social mobility has become over the years. In the UK, there are several narratives we employ when we think about social mobility – different models, if you like, for how people can do 'better'. One is the 'pulling yourself up by your bootstraps' storyline, beloved of self-made millionaires, where your own hard work and vision take you from rags to riches. It's an account that all too often omits crucial details, details that would place the story in its rightful context and would undermine the idea that all that is needed is hard work and dedication. Another model contends that intrinsic value is recognised and cherished early on – when a child from a deprived background wins a scholarship to Eton, for instance, this is often how it is framed.[9] But perhaps the most deeply entrenched model is the one in which an earlier generation slaves and sacrifices so that their children can do what they themselves could not: social mobility as a shared project carried out over decades.

None of these narratives is entirely false; nor are any of them the full truth. In the UK, it has been the case historically that a complete transformation of circumstances is usually possible only over a number of generations, with no guarantee of progress. You might see a first-generation immigrant work multiple menial jobs, or pour their energy into a small business, in effect choosing a different form of self-fulfilment: that of improving the lot of their children. Each generation passes on not only a little more comfort and stability, but tales of struggle and perseverance too. As each cohort, armed with knowledge and focus, clears away more of the debris left by ignorance, they may skip along a path that increasingly looks like it's paved with gold. But this is not always guaranteed, and in some instances social movement may slow as the imperative of escaping grim circumstances becomes less pressing.

Again, all things being equal, this has been an achievable dream for many generations, in many places around the world: it's the American dream, but it's also the Indian dream, and the Mexican dream and the ... you get the picture. But even this model, which requires extraordinary sacrifice and years of work, necessitates luck. Not all parents have the ability – or desire – to provide for their children in this way. This was my own experience: the adults who brought me up had no formal education, and were themselves at sea in a foreign country that they never properly understood. They didn't speak the language, and for a long time their immigration status didn't allow them to work. They were focused on day-to-day survival, and as a result they couldn't plan a future for me and my siblings. Aside from an individual's family circumstances, there's a wider social context that complicates these straightforward narratives of 'striving', 'sacrificing' and 'shining'. The so-called 'millennial generation' (broadly, those born between 1980 and 1996), of whom I am one, face challenges that make them the first generation to do worse than their parents, despite being more likely to go to university. The resources available to their parents, such as affordable housing, free tertiary education and secure employment, are either scarce or non-existent.

I am confident that, as you read this book, examples will come to mind of people you know who have 'made it' out of disadvantageous circumstances, and of disadvantaged millennials who now own houses and have pensions; indeed, I am one myself. But we are the exceptions who prove the rule, and to extrapolate from our stories a narrative of 'anything is possible' would be a cruel joke. As we have seen, your chances of success in UK society are directly correlated with arbitrary starting circumstances – the economic situation of your parents, the economic situation of the country as a whole, and the kind of school you attended. Of course, innate abilities will play a part, but so does a less discussed but just as important factor – luck.

Luck: a term that is hard to define and impossible to quantify. Although it can sometimes appear like a bolt from the blue – a chance meeting, a misdirected letter – in general, luck is the relationship between a set of circumstances, hard work and the right opportunity at the right time. We have to be in a position to seize the opportunity when it arrives, but luck always has as much to do with factors beyond our control as within it, and it's often only possible to appreciate its effect on our daily lives with the benefit of hindsight. In my own experience, for example, I am convinced that it is in part luck that allowed me to realise, very young (and without being dispirited), both the limitations of the cards life had dealt me and the possibilities offered by them as well. It was my luck, again, to have had the intellectual capacity, the physical health and the absence of immediate pressure to ruthlessly focus on creating a better future for me and my family. I was lucky, also, to meet a series of mentors who guided me through the new worlds in which I found myself. I was lucky when I was offered a fully funded postgraduate place at Oxford, and I was lucky again when I was accepted into a pupillage at the Bar, picked from a sea of equally well-qualified, ambitious and hard-working candidates.

To put it another way, if I genuinely believed that what I have achieved and overcome was possible for anyone, then I would have profoundly misunderstood the overarching lesson of my life. Therefore, if you, or someone you know, has succeeded against all the odds, please let go of the idea that all that's required is some hard work and determination for others to do the same. Many factors are beyond your control: your own family circumstances remain the overarching indicator of how well you're likely to do, and whether you will realise your potential and/or fulfil your dreams. Where you come from is also likely to have shaped your worldview, the values against which you conduct yourself and judge others, and above all how you view the question of social mobility. That means that 'failure to succeed' cannot be placed wholly at the door of the individual, which is what is implied when we frame social mobility as a question of 'aspiration' or 'ambition'. Neither is the answer simply asking institutions to change, for institutions are only as capable of doing so, or of recognising the issues in the first place, as the individuals who run them.

* * *

So, without holding myself up as an example (in fact, the reverse – I want you to learn from my mistakes), this book aims to explain the hurdles I have overcome, identifying the personal and individual steps required for a social mobility journey, but outlining, too, the institutional barriers I have crossed (a more arduous process than it should have been). If you, as I once did, look at your life and think, *'I want something better'*, then I want you to benefit from these lessons, to avoid my mistakes, to do what I have done quicker, better, and be able to pass on the lessons to others. I want you to see the bigger picture in a new way; to understand where the fault lines lie, and even articulate for yourself for the first time something you've known all along.

Certain things are far from obvious, just as that cartoon from *Private Eye* illustrates. Inhabiting the contrasting worlds that I now do, at work and at home, in elite institutions and in the same difficult neighbourhoods where I grew up and still live, in the legal profession and at the BBC, in the deprived and isolated communities and with the well-off second-homers, both of whom use my services at planning inquiries, I am constantly amazed by, and reminded of, the huge gulf that exists in our society. There is a vast divide between the different starting points and outlooks, the different realities, expectations, and hopes and dreams. As I navigate between these worlds, and through the lives of friends and family, my day-to-day life has served as a constant reminder to never assume that anything is obvious to somebody else.

Class barriers are also consciously and unconsciously enforced by individuals who conform to certain rules, or who stick to codes on how 'people like them' ought to behave, look or even think. What I am talking about is often subtle: get rid of the antiquated wig and gown in the legal profession and I very much doubt that all will fall into place in terms of equal access and fundamental change. The aesthetic props that represent the status quo are rarely the problem; it is the groupthink that automatically, and sometimes aggressively, seeks to exclude what it doesn't find familiar. It is the way in which the recruitment process, which in theory is a rigorous exercise in finding the best possible candidate, in practice leads to interviewers selecting the person who is 'the best fit' – or the most like the interviewer. It is the way we judge intelligence and ability by the way people express themselves, or the way that applicants for a job who have a 'white' surname like Smith or Jones are nearly 50 per cent more likely to be called to interview than a Begum or an Ahmed.[10] I am absolutely convinced that *most* people, although they want the best for themselves and their children, also want a fairer society. These two objectives can sometimes be mutually exclusive, and people often see the question of access as a zero-sum game, that opening up a place for those from deprived communities will inevitably mean a place lost for another family's child.

* * *

So, what am I saying? It's all hopeless and you might as well

19

quit? What should you tell your children about the sort of world they find themselves in? How can you prevail against odds like these? How can you, if you're reading this from a privileged position, make a difference? Well, if these are the questions you are now asking, we are heading in the same direction together. What I seek to explore in this book, and what is sorely needed, is a new way of seeing the same intractable issues; to recast how we see deprivation and inequality, and to then think anew about the possibilities of affecting change, measuring success in a different way, and leveraging all the talents society has to offer.

If there was an easy answer we would have found it by now. This book is probably not the one you have been waiting for all your life; it will not make you 'socially mobile' overnight, nor will you find the answers to all your questions. But what I hope you find is a new way of connecting the dots; a new way of seeing the world, which in turn may inspire you to look at the problems you've been staring at for so long. What you might find here, maybe for the first time, is the articulation of something you've thought all along but couldn't describe. I believe that, at an instinctual level, we all understand that society could be more fair, and that one day soon we will develop a new set of attitudes, the building blocks for transformation. I hope that this will inject us all with a new sense of urgency about how we teach and train people, what we expect from various institutions, and how we recruit and mentor others; an urgency that will, ultimately, guide us towards creating a society that's more inclusive than the current one.

Above all, we need a society that creates the environment for every child and adult to test their own abilities, to truly discover what they are good at, what they like and dislike, no matter their starting point; to acquire the possibility to imagine a different world for themselves and those around them, whatever that may be. We deserve better than to be confronted by a congested society, one that lacks the fluidity needed for everyone to find their place and play their role, in whatever posture suits their stature. Society is just us – each of us together – but it is also so much greater than the sum of its parts. It is up to us to encourage, support and challenge each other – in good faith – to provide that environment, that open and flexible space for human flourishing.

Finally, this is not a memoir; it doesn't tell the *whole* story. When people hear my story, they often make a joke along the lines of, 'At least it will be smooth sailing from here!' I smile along, but privately, my response is something along the lines of '... and there's still plenty of time to mess this up'. Social mobility is not, and never has been for me, a destination – it's a journey, and a process of transformation, a process of renewal that could take a lifetime. I am still travelling that road, learning as I go. This book is a call to action, a demand that we do better. Everything that we need is within us and around us. We do not need to start from the beginning of time, we just need to start right now.

Happy Reading.

1

Three Hashis: Origins and Starting Points

> We do owe something to parentage and patronage. The
> people who stand before kings may look like they did
> it all by themselves. But in fact they are invariably the
> beneficiaries of hidden advantages and extraordinary
> opportunities and cultural legacies that allow them to learn
> and work hard and make sense of the world in ways others
> cannot. It makes a difference where and when we grew up.
> The culture we belong to and the legacies passed down to
> our forebears shape the patterns of our achievement in ways
> we cannot begin to imagine. It's not enough to ask what
> successful people are like, in other words. It is only by asking
> where they are *from* that we can unravel the logic behind
> who succeeds and who doesn't.
>
> Malcolm Gladwell, *Outliers*

It is hard to talk about social mobility without talking
about our lived experiences, and in particular our family
and childhood. Our past shapes who we are to begin
with, and who we end up becoming later; our destinies
are forged by the circumstances in which we are born, by
who our parents are, by when and where the story begins.
My own story is not a linear one: it has involved movement across countries and continents, and it is peppered
by tragedy, trauma and confusion, by deep ruptures, major

adjustments, false starts and continual renewal. Because of this, I want to start at the beginning of my own family's recent history.[1]

I begin with my grandfather.

My grandfather and namesake, Hashi Omar Guled, was born around 1930 in a place called Ceelbuur, 377 kilometres north of Mogadishu, the capital of Somalia. He was born to a nomadic family in the wilderness of what was then an Italian colony, in a community of camel and goat herders. His father died when he was ten and together with his three siblings, he was raised solely by his mother. In Somalia at that time (and in some ways even today among nomadic Somalis), wealth was measured in camels and livestock, without which it was an uphill struggle to earn respect even within your own group of kin. And my grandfather's family weren't rich.

In 1948, at the age of eighteen, he married my grandmother, an extraordinary woman by the name of Mumina Hassan Abdulle. She had not been to school and could not read or write. This wasn't unusual; very few Somalis knew how to read and write back then, and in fact the language was not even written down until 1974. But speech and folklore were valued currency and she excelled at both.

But Hashi was restless: this was not the destiny he saw for himself or his new wife. He made a decision that socially mobile people have made throughout history, and still do across the world: he upped sticks and moved to the big city. In the big town of Beledweyne, Hashi was lucky, being quickly recruited into the Italian colonial police force, where he would be trained in what was a civil service job, learning Italian as part of the teaching programme. In 1950, he was settled enough to send for his wife to join him. Two years later, on 10 September 1952,[2] they had a son, Mohamed Hashi Omar: my father.

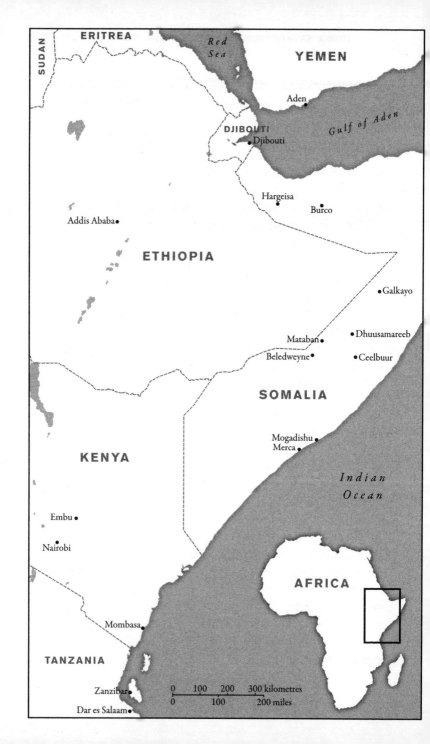

In 1962, two years after Somalia became independent, my grandfather, who had by that point reached the senior rank of inspector, left the police force and opened his first shop in Beledweyne. Five years later, he moved the family again, some 40 kilometres away, this time closer to the city of Mataban. There, they opened an all-purpose store, selling basic groceries like sugar, rice, maize and other cereals, as well as clothing; and they also had a sewing machine, which generated a good portion of the income. But sourcing material and the goods needed involved many journeys on treacherous roads down to Mogadishu and north to Hargeisa and Berbera port. Accidents were common.

My father's brother Ibrahim, my uncle, was at school in Beledweyne. On 19 July 1971, while home on school holidays, he was manning a mobile shop near Mataban, providing goods to the more rural and isolated communities. My grandfather had gone with a large shipment, moving goats and sheep to sell at a lucrative animal market. Ibrahim was listening to the radio: it's a family habit, and to this day my grandmother constantly has the BBC Somali Service on. My uncle had been listening to Radio Hargeisa, and at the end of the afternoon news there was an announcement that caught his attention. A lorry had crashed near the town of Burro' and there were four fatalities. The presenter then began to announce the names of those who had died. My uncle was hardly listening until the last name was announced. It was Hashi Omar Guled.

In line with Islamic tradition, the funeral was arranged immediately, and he was buried in the company of tribal clansmen linked to our community, his 'representatives' in the northern part of the country where he had died. My grandmother and Ibrahim travelled for two days to reach the place where he was buried. On arrival, they found a small heap of earth marking the place. My grandfather, like my father and me, was a very tall man. He was well built and handsome, with an authoritative bearing; and this was all that was left of him.

My teenaged father was now, as the eldest male in a deeply patriarchal society, the head of the household. He had shared a special bond with my grandfather, in whose eyes my father could do no wrong. As a consequence, my father had developed from an early age into a precocious leader, someone unafraid to try new ways of living. But he was also a wanderer, a young man not yet ready to assume his responsibilities. He would often disappear for days, ostensibly on family business to neighbouring cities, but would usually return with little to show for his escapades.

By most accounts, my father was not much of a planner, but rather an impulsive man who more often than not followed his gut instincts. He was proactive, always volunteering for things, trying out new ideas, travelling to new places, always keen to meet new people. At the same time he was responsive: always adjusting, reacting, improving, dodging, and evolving when his impulsive decisions went wrong. Little fazed him; even though the majority of his life had chaos at its centre. I don't think he ever read a book beyond the elementary text books he had had as a child, but he had developed a deep knowledge of Somali and East African culture. He was a great linguist and a great speaker, captivating audiences with stories, proverbs and poetry. He was generous with any money he may have had, and he was generous with his time, with how he helped someone out of a sticky situation. His word was always his bond: when he promised to do something he never failed to deliver, usually to the detriment of himself and his family (some weeks he returned home with only half of his earnings). Although living in a deeply tribal society and community, he was never one to look inward and focus on his own tribal allegiances. He was outward-looking, with friendships outside his own community, beyond Somalis or Africans.

Following the death of my grandfather, he uprooted the family from where they had settled in Mataban to Balanballe (see map on page 24), 30 kilometres to the north-west. On this occasion, his impulsive decision paid off: Somalia, just eleven years into independence and in the throes of a new military revolution, was developing quickly, financed by Cold War proxy wars. The town of Balanballe had major wells and water facilities, and what was once a small village soon became a major hub for a nomadic community that required their animals to graze, drink water, and stop on their way to other major cities. Elementary and intermediate schools were built, which allowed my father's younger siblings to continue studying. The decision to move had placed the family and its fortunes at the heart of a transforming society.

I want to point out that my family and especially my father were not particularly interested in status. Our tribe are known to be troublemakers, warriors who were said to be independently minded, always ready for battle and vengeance, and, of course, deeply proud. But at the same time, we didn't take our reputation too seriously, and often mocked it among ourselves as a backward way of thinking, especially when, for example, the particular qualities that individuals were supposed to be endowed with were usually conspicuous by their absence. But, for as long as I can recall, my family never sought the approval of others, or respectability in the eyes of outsiders. For my father's generation, and, more recently, my own, the main focus has been survival, as we battled through bereavement, hardship, injury, war. Beyond survival was self-sufficiency; we thought that success could be measured by the relatively unambitious metric of not needing to rely on something or someone else, whether that be state hand-outs or begging someone for help (and, when we moved to England, we conspicuously failed our own test). We never thought about how we would like to be seen in the 'Somali community's eyes' or by British society. Sometimes, when people hear my story, they remark that my family 'must be so proud of what you've done'. And I usually reply that my mother is just happy that I didn't end up dead, in jail or on drugs – 'everything else is just a bonus!' It's partly self-deprecation – but mostly truth. Of course they're proud of me, and my aunt, who travels a great deal, goes around bragging about me as the 'only known Somali British bar-rister'. But the truth is that we continue to be surprised that we have even made it this far, still less that we are doing what we are doing in the places we have been fortu-nate enough to find ourselves.

* * *

Back in Balanbelle, business was booming, and the family fortunes began to turn. My father was able to send his younger brother Ibrahim away to boarding school, which cost 336 Somali shillings per term (at the time quite expen-sive: a little more than $120 USD per year).

The school transformed Ibrahim's life: he would later get a scholarship to go to Italy, which led to an academic post in Ferrara University. In 1994, he would get a lucrative post as a chemical engineer with the Italian multinational oil giant Agip (ENI), where he still works today. All his children benefited from private education in Italy, and his youngest – also Hashi – is an undergraduate in chemical engineering at Cambridge University. After my father's death, Ibrahim was the male role model we all looked up to. His was the first example I had of the transformative effect of education, and it was one he didn't hesitate to ram home himself. He bribed many of us to do well in school, explaining that without education we had little to show for life. If it didn't always have the intended effect, we always felt at the back of our minds that we had the capability – if only we'd act on it.

Having stabilised the family finances somewhat, my father, like his father before him, became restless. He wanted to travel, and he found a way in the long-distance trucks, then becoming huge business, that were moving material across the African continent. In late 1973, my uncle Ibrahim recalls accompanying him on one of those trips during the school holidays, where he noticed my father's shrewd ability to make a quick buck – and to lose it just as fast. The people he met on his long journeys told my father about faraway places that he burned to explore, and so, in 1974, he set out seeking fortunes beyond Somalia. From this point, communication between my father and his family was sporadic, and it would be months before his news would reach the family, from someone, who had met someone else, who had had tea with him months earlier. Sometimes, they would hear news from him just once in a year. He was not the kind of man whose education was advanced enough, or whose personality was sentimental enough, to write letters recounting his romantic road trips across Africa, and later the Middle East and Asia. He started as a driver adjutant – an administrative assistant to the driver – on the trans-haulage of goods from Kenya to Uganda, to Rwanda and Burundi, and as far away as Mozambique. He quickly picked up the trade and, even more quickly, the languages he required to get by. My mother tells me that he had mastered not only Kiswahili but many of the dozens of local tribal languages spoken in

Kenya, allowing him to talk with strangers and gain their trust. At one point news reached the family that he had gone to Saudi Arabia and didn't particularly like it: he did the Hajj and quickly returned to Kenya. I have seen pictures of him in Mumbai – or Bombay as it was then – with businessmen he barely knew.

Then, in the summer of 1982 my mother, Fatuma Ahmed Sudi, turned up in Somalia heavily pregnant with her first child with my father, her seventh child, when she came to see the children from her previous marriage. On 20 August 1982, my brother Ali was born in Mogadishu. Soon afterwards, my mother left for Kenya without her infant son, having left him with my maternal grandmother. My brother would stay in Somalia for eight years before he would meet his own father (and me, his younger brother).

* * *

I know a lot less about my mother's side of the family. Both my mother's parents were also born in Ceelbuur, the same place as Hashi, my paternal grandfather. My maternal grandfather was called Ahmed and my maternal grandmother is called Asli. Both my maternal grandparents were born in complete wilderness, in the bush, the nomadic pastoral world. There were no hospitals; no records of any sort were kept. No one knows precisely when they were born.

My maternal grandparents had two children: my mother, who was also born in Ceelbuur around 1952, although no one can say the exact month or year, and her younger brother. The family ended up in Mogadishu, where my mother's brother died very young. Soon after, my grandparents divorced, when my mother was around ten years old, and she remained with her mother, Asli. In early 1980, my mother came to Kenya for the first time, working, transporting potatoes in a planned venture with one of her brothers. As I understand it, she came alone. By this point, having married at sixteen and had six children, my mother was divorced and had left the children with relatives in Mogadishu. She married my father, and the new couple soon moved to a small suburb of Nairobi called Eastleigh.

On 10 September 1983, exactly thirty-one years after my father's birth, I was born in the Radiant Health Clinic in Nairobi, Kenya. I was the first child in my whole family's lineage to be born outside of Somalia. I enjoyed two uninterrupted years of undivided attention from both my parents (something which, incidentally, my father had also enjoyed). After this, our neighbours in Eastleigh never referred to my parents by their names. They were henceforth known as the 'mother of Hashi' and the 'father of Hashi'. This was not necessarily affectionate: according to my family, I would run riot in shops nearby, taking things from shelves and never paying, later discovering that each storekeeper kept a ledger, which every few days my mother or father would settle.

Two years after me, my sister Shukri was born, and two years after that came Hamdi, my youngest sister, then Ibrahim, named after my uncle, who, sadly, died as a toddler. And then my youngest and final sibling, my brother Abdi. Though we were very poor I remember it as an idyllic time spent in a small community where I knew everybody and everybody knew me. School lasted a total of about three or so years; you had to pay to go to school in Kenya then (and it remains the case in places today), and it cost even more to bribe teachers to ensure that your child got extra attention. I vividly remember the cold early mornings: we had to be at school at 7 a.m., assembling in the large courtyard in neat single file to watch the Kenyan flag being hoisted up as we all sang the national anthem.

Classrooms were generally crowded, with basic equipment, and there was a cane in the hand of most teachers. Looking back, I realise that my classmates and I were abjectly poor by modern standards, but I never felt it. I don't remember ever going hungry; I don't remember missing the basics. It must be said, though, that I don't recall ever getting anything I wanted either (and perhaps that was the root of my infant shoplifting).

Then, in 1991, civil war broke out in Somalia. By 1992, the state had collapsed, and everyone who could do so fled to the neighbouring countries of Ethiopia and Kenya for safety. My father's family came to Nairobi, and for the first time in my life, I met my aunt, my grandmother and Ali, my oldest brother. We were united at last, but in terrible, disorientating circumstances – and not for long. A vast wave of people was sweeping out of Somalia, searching for any place where they thought they could seek asylum: Ethiopia, Canada, America, Sweden, Britain. It soon carried away most of my newly integrated family, but my father was adamant that we would not leave: we had built a stable life here in Eastleigh, and we didn't need help from anyone else.

And so we would have continued, had not another disaster struck us: in April 1993, my father was killed in a car accident in Embu. It was a catastrophe, and one that shaped the rest of all of our lives. By this point, almost everyone who had been displaced had left Kenya or was in the process of doing so; we no longer had any source of income or any family who could help us, and staying in Eastleigh wasn't an option. The decision was made to split the family, and for me and my three oldest siblings to seek asylum elsewhere. And so, in 1993, aged nine, and knowing nothing at all about Britain, I found myself on a plane to London with Shukri, Hamdi and Ali.

When we arrived, we were settled with my aunt, who had left just months before, and her six children. She was newly widowed: her husband had been killed while she was waiting for him to join her in Kenya. The following year, my grandmother – my father's mother – joined us, and after that we lived as a large family group, in the London borough of Brent. All of us were lost in grief, completely adrift: mourning not only our lost loved ones, but our homes and everything we'd ever known.

It's a terrible story, but, again, a remarkably unremarkable one: pick any Somali who arrived in Britain in the 1990s and they'll tell you a similar tale. Decades later, the legacy of this trauma – exacerbated both by a lack of available help and a reluctance on the part of the community to seek it – is still deeply felt, in wounds that manifest themselves in myriad ways, from mental health problems to family rifts, from poor school results to gang membership. Being black and Muslim in Britain is not easy, nor is being a refugee, nor starting out as a recent immigrant in a context of abject poverty, little continuity with the past, and a sense of extreme precariousness. Some of us have been lucky enough to strike out beyond the survival zone and thrive. Others continue their gentle creep towards the light; some may never make it that far.

But at the same time, I often look at our lives today and wonder at how far we have come. As I was beginning this book in April 2018, my sister Shukri had just given birth to her first baby, a boy called Hashi. Twenty-five years to the month after our father's death in Nairobi, his first grandson was born in London, England – something that he, wild dreamer though he was, surely couldn't have imagined.[3] This new Hashi's beginning is as unlike his grandfather's as it is possible to be: he will grow up in a world of internet searches and social media profiles, of cheap international air travel and touchscreens, of endless choice and enormous opportunity. He will grow up a Londoner, an inhabitant of a vast and global city, and a British citizen. Like all babies, his future contains countless possibilities: librarian, chef, doctor, architect, artist, journalist, astronaut, gymnast, geneticist. Perhaps he will find fulfilment in something that none of us, reading today, can even imagine: when he is the same age as me, the world may be as different from ours today as this moment is from the world that my great-grandfather was born into. And yet, as he takes his first steps into it, he carries with him all the gifts and difficulties bequeathed to him by the story of his family, the family whose story I have told to you.

* * *

Your family's history is important because when we want to work out who someone is, we often ask where they come from. Rightly or wrongly, we assume that your life story, and the story of your family, tells us something about who *you* are: it gives you a context. My story tells you (and me) that I come from a line of people who began as nomadic herders living in harsh conditions; who were illiterate or, at best, school dropouts; who had many children, sometimes with different partners; who lived difficult lives consistently disrupted by sudden tragedy and death. My story also tells you that I come from a line of deeply proud and resilient survivors; of quick learners, of people who rarely stay down for long, of ambitious entrepreneurs who seized opportunities when they came along, adapting to circumstances wherever they found themselves; of talented linguists and sharp minds; of travellers, wanderers and explorers, and of people never afraid to leave what was familiar in search of new horizons. A line of people who were always prepared to try their hand at something, no matter how difficult it might first appear. This is my context.

And we are right to assume that context is key: research into social mobility has shown that nothing has a more profound impact on your destination than your starting point. For most of human history, it would have seemed something of a self-evident truth: the idea that you might move beyond your social origins at all is something of a modern phenomenon. We still talk of 'blue blood' or 'good stock', and those phrases reflect the historical idea that the aristocracy was fundamentally different from the common man: entitled to power, respect and wealth through the genetic inheritance of special qualities. To live in Britain in 2020 is to live under a hereditary constitutional monarchy: a system that at its heart holds that the ability and right to rule over every other member of that society can be passed down from parent to child, like blue eyes or big ears. And we like it: a recent YouGov poll found that 68 per cent of the people polled thought the monarchy was 'good for Britain'; only 9 per cent thought it was 'bad'. But that we are so comfortable with our royals says something about how we feel about equality: as the journalist and author Afua Hirsch points out, 'The very concept of the royal family is the antithesis of diversity.' These divisions are not simply social, either. As Hirsch notes, 'blue blood' comes from a Spanish term, *sagre azul*, 'coined in the late 1500s to distinguish between the racially superior white Christian nobility (with pale skin revealing blue veins) and the Jews, Muslims and West Africans whom Europeans were increasingly ousting from their continent.'[4]

The fact that – far from being left behind in ancient history – these ideas are very current, was amply illustrated by the response to the marriages of Prince William, second in line to the British throne, and his younger brother Harry, sixth in line to the throne. When William got engaged to his long-term girlfriend Kate Middleton, there was fevered speculation in the media about her status as a 'commoner' and the fact that her mother had worked as an air hostess. When her younger sister Pippa married a hedge fund millionaire several years later, a rumour did the rounds in the press that both women had been known in 'aristocratic circles' as the Wisteria Sisters: 'highly decorative, terribly fragrant and with a ferocious ability to climb.'

This was despite the fact that Kate Middleton was a white, upper-middle-class woman from a wealthy family who was educated at Marlborough, a prestigious public school. When Harry announced his relationship with Meghan Markle, a biracial American actress, in 2017, the reaction was so severe that Kensington Palace, who represent Prince Harry, put out an official announcement announcing that 'a line has been crossed' by the media, and complaining of 'a wave of abuse and harassment' with 'racial overtones'. Like Middleton, Markle was perceived as a sharp-eyed social climber – a variety of social mobility which is almost always viewed with intense suspicion in Britain – but the narrative of her ascension up the social scale was also inextricably linked to her racial origins. Whereas Middleton was seen as 'decorative, fragrant', and ultimately only guilty of being a bit nouveau riche, Markle was linked to slavery ('Now that's upwardly mobile! How in 150 years, Meghan Markle's family went from cotton slaves to royalty')[5] and gang violence and social deprivation ('Harry's girl is (almost) straight outta Compton: Gang-scarred home of her mother revealed)'[6].

Of course, few of us will (or will want to) marry into the royal family. But the way that Middleton and especially Markle were treated says something about the way we think about class, origins and value in modern Britain. The furore that still surrounds Markle has its origins in a deep anxiety about social mobility, and a desire to police existing institutions against intruding forces: the common, the non-white, the poor. It also says a lot about how an individual's worth is often perceived as linked to their family origins, reinforcing the idea that the existing social structure is based not on arbitrary divisions and deeply rooted inequalities, but is an expression of differing abilities.

The idea that people like me are not represented in the elite tiers of society not because of a want of opportunity but because they fundamentally lack qualities present in the middle and upper classes is still very much with us (as are similar ideas relating to women and ethnic minorities). The controversial right-wing journalist and education campaigner Toby Young, 'who has never disguised his view that IQ is both higher among the socially advantaged and appears to be passed between generations'[7] got into hot water in 2017 when he proposed something he called 'progressive eugenics' as a solution to intergenerational inequality. Musing on potential gene-editing technology that would allow 'parents to screen embryos in vitro and select the most intelligent one to implant' he asks: 'why not offer it free of charge to parents on low incomes with below-average IQs? Provided there is sufficient take-up, it could help to address the problem of flat-lining intergenerational social mobility.'[8] In other words, the solution to stagnant social mobility lies in manipulating the genetic make-up of the children from disadvantaged backgrounds, who don't achieve like their privileged peers because they *can't*: they just don't have the same capacities. But we could solve the problem by allowing disadvantaged parents to selectively 'breed out' an inherited tendency towards low IQ: armed with their new, 'middle-class standard' genetic inheritance, their children would be able to storm up the social hierarchy.

Whether Young was deliberately evoking it or not (and I would argue that if he's not aware of the connotations then he shouldn't be anywhere near the education sector), eugenics and social class have a deep and dark history together. While it has its roots in Darwin's theory of natural selection – that organisms which had adapted to their environment by developing certain favourable characteristics would be most likely to breed and thus pass down those characteristics to their offspring – the term 'eugenics' was first coined by Darwin's cousin, Francis Galton, in 1883. Eugenics acknowledged the fact that qualities (like eye colour or, as Galton believed, intelligence) could be passed down from parent to child, and sought to improve society as a whole by selective breeding to promote 'good' genes and suppress 'bad' ones. Perhaps not such a bad idea on the surface: as Galton said when presenting his ideas in 1904 at the London School of Economics, 'All creatures would agree that it is better ... to be good rather than bad specimens of their kind.'[9] But from its earliest beginnings, eugenics was intimately entwined with anxieties about race and class: in his book *The Gene*, the doctor and author Siddhartha Mukherjee writes of how Galton 'like many members of the Victorian elite ... [was] chilled by the fear of race degeneration'.[10] But it was class that really loomed large in the imaginations of Galton and his followers. Galton firmly believed that the upper classes were genetically superior, and had in fact begun his research by making 'pedigrees' of distinguished families in an attempt to show that 'eminence ... was inherited'.[11] But the turn of the century was also a period of social upheaval in Britain. Working-class men had recently gained the right to vote, and the relatively new Labour Party – which explicitly aimed to represent the interests of the urban working class – had established a significant presence in the government in the 1906 election. Slowly, but clearly, the times were changing, and Galton's ideas struck a chord among the old ruling classes who were terrified of being overwhelmed by the teeming, genetically inferior masses.

As well as defending their own interests, there was also a sense in which Galton's followers thought that eugenics might be better for *everyone*. The Eugenics Society, founded in 1907 by Galton's followers and originally known as the Eugenics Education Society, consisted of middle- and upper-class biologists, social scientists and activists, many of whom saw themselves as liberals who were working for the betterment of society as a whole through the removal of 'undesirable' traits. At the time and in the following decades, members of the Society campaigned to legalise voluntary sterilisation and promoted birth control because they saw 'feeble-mindedness' or 'weakness' (in practice this often meant merely being poor) as a biological defect that could be removed. In 1908, a leading psychiatrist, Sir James Crichton-Brown, told the Royal Commission on the Care and Control of the Feeble-Minded that the mentally ill were 'our social rubbish' who should be sterilised in order to protect the rest of society: 'We pay much attention to the breeding of our horses, our cattle, our dogs and poultry, even our flowers and vegetables; surely it's not too much to ask that a little care be bestowed upon the breeding and rearing of our race.'[12]

Despite the influence of Galton's ideas on contemporary thinking, thankfully, sterilisation never really caught on in Britain in practice. But the legacy of eugenics was grim: as it fanned out across the globe, it was put into practice in forced sterilisations and internments in America, Canada and Europe. Between 1924 and 1962 the US State of Virginia sterilised over 7,500 individuals deemed to be 'feeble-minded' or 'antisocial' (including prostitutes, criminals and unwed mothers), their deficiencies assumed to be the result of their biology, and compounded by their social origins. But the most famous – and egregious – manifestation of eugenics was as part of Nazi Germany's 'applied eugenics', a 'genetic final solution',[13] which saw the wholesale murder of disabled children, Jewish children and adults, prisoners, the 'degenerate', and people who were deaf, gay or mentally ill.

Despite his choice of the term eugenics, it's perhaps fairer to call Young a biological determinist: a proponent of the idea that your intellectual capacity and abilities, even your behaviour, are set in stone in your genetic code. For biological determinists, privilege starts before the moment of conception: whether you're able to take advantage of the opportunities offered by, for example, the education system, is determined by what abilities your parents are able to pass on. Professor Alison Pilnick put it like this. 'Any individual may succeed, but whether they do so or not is the result of their biological endowments rather than' their economic or social resources. This transmission of 'good' genes by the genetically advantaged and successful to their children – something that's fairly likely because 'successful people tend to have children with people of the same status' – means that the social hierarchy is the 'natural result of biological differences rather than differences in access to cultural or material resources'. This leads inevitably to certain conclusions: that inequalities in society are the direct result of an individual's inherited traits, and that 'social inequalities are both inevitable and fair, because they are *natural*'.[14]

But this is, in my view, both a convenient untruth and a fundamental error of logic: it is the same mistake that

Galton and his followers made, and for the same reasons. When Galton plotted out his elite pedigrees, he was guilty of a basic scientific error, that is seeking to prove a hypothesis that he already believed in. As Mukherjee notes, 'his anxieties about class and status were so deep that he could not bear the thought that his own "intelligence" might merely be the by-product of privilege and opportunity.'[15] Just as Galton's ideas soothed and reinforced his own ideas of class superiority, the universally white, middle-class, privileged modern advocates of 'it's all in the genes' clutch at straws to justify their own position as due to intrinsic worth rather than privilege. In claiming that it's nature, not nurture, that makes the difference, they free themselves from all obligation to change the fundamental structure of society. After all, there's no point blaming societal issues, lack of resources, structural inequality and so on if your fate was sealed when you were born. The way society is, therefore, is both fair and inevitable, and it's simply an unfortunate coincidence that those inequalities work to the advantage of the upper middle classes, the social tier to which advocates of this argument belong.

* * *

Biological determinism is an argument that feels personal to me. I often wonder how my illiterate mother, on her eighth child, me, would have been treated in another place and time. My poor, black ancestors would certainly not have been perceived as likely to pass on a 'superior' genetic inheritance. But while the heyday of eugenics, when mainstream scientists and geneticists argued that the rich, privileged and white are genetically superior, may be behind us – its legacy lingers on. It lingers on most visibly in the chants of 'You will not replace us' at white supremacist rallies, and in the 'white genocide' conspiracy theories circulated by the resurgent far-right, but also, more subtly, in the complaints about the size of immigrant families, welfare and NHS pressures, and 'super-sized benefits families ... who cost the taxpayer thousands'. The implication is that individuals who have grown up in circumstances like my own are unlikely to go on to contribute in a meaningful way, but there's also a tinge of the existential fear felt by the Eugenic Society's members at being overrun by freely breeding, genetically defective paupers. Of course, we also hear about the 'feckless' offspring of millionaires or the 'idle rich': but any critique of their lifestyles or behaviour – which, even if spoilt, destructive or entitled, is often reported with an overtone of envious admiration – is not linked to their genetic inheritance or fundamental value to society. Indeed, in 2019, multiple newspapers ran articles claiming that having five children was now 'the ultimate middle-class status symbol'.[16]

* * *

It was Galton who coined the phrase 'nature versus nurture' to describe the tension between your genes and your environment in determining who you are. And, awkwardly, despite the flawed science and troubled history of biological determinism, it is clear that we cannot discount the role of genetics in social mobility entirely: scientific studies have shown that there *is* a link between achievement and genetics. A study carried out in July 2017, for example, found that 'half of the differences between whether families were socially mobile or not, can be attributed to genetic differences between them'. [17]

So, are the biological determinists on to something after all? The answer is: probably not. After all, if half of your social mobility is down to your parents, then half is down to your environment, and it seems likely that it is that half that makes the difference. As Dr Sophie von Stumm, one of the authors of the study, made clear: 'genetics can only play a significant role for children's educational attainment if their environmental opportunities are relatively equal.' In other words, how much an influence or role our genetic make-up plays is largely dependent on whether we are all on the same footing to start off with. Other academics have argued that human behaviour cannot be straightforwardly divided between nature and nurture, that if we 'reduce societies to individuals, and individuals to their genes, we cannot put the pieces back together again and expect to understand them, for we deny the interaction between genes and the environment, the individual and their interaction with society'.[18] To me, the real question is: who gets the chance to develop their genetic potential? And who is shielded from the consequences of theirs?

This, to me, is the real reason that, as sociologists Sam Friedman and Daniel Laurison put it 'the link between people's origins and destinations remains doggedly persistent in contemporary Britain'.[19] And persistent it is: in Britain today, the single best predictor of what your job will be is the occupation of your parents. This doesn't mean, of course, that if you're born as, say, the child of two semi-illiterate parents, only one of whom was in employment, and you were raised in deprivation entirely on benefits, you cannot succeed in life. I'm the proof of that. Statistics only tell the story of society as a whole, and they mean nothing to the individual: there are always outliers. But still, the statistics paint a bleak picture: only 3.3 per cent of working-class and under-privileged people will end up in elite occupations like medicine, law or finance.[20]

Quite how powerful the 'nurture' part of the equation

is can be seen from a quick overview of what it means to grow up in poverty, as I did, and as 4.6 million children[21] are in the UK today.[22] No period of your life is as important as your first four years: it's when the basic structure of your brain is formed, shaping your capacities for language, reasoning and for interacting with others and with your environment. Your early years set the course for the rest of your life, a course that it is extremely hard to correct later on.[23] And deprivation begins in the womb: children born into poverty are more likely to be born prematurely, and are more likely to have low birth weight and receive less nutrition in the womb, all factors associated with poorer future health. They are also at a higher risk of infant mortality.[24] They are more likely, too, to have mothers who suffer from post-natal depression and stress during pregnancy, something that can affect the way in which their genes are expressed. As babies and young children, they often live in inadequate housing, and are part of families that struggle to afford enough food and heating, stressful situations that rewire their brains to make them anxious and jumpy.

Poverty is not just about material deprivation, although that is part of it. It means not just the food you eat and the clothes you wear but the words you hear, and how many of them: a US study showed that by the age of four 'a child from a professional family will hear 45 million words, a working-class child 26 million, and a child on welfare only 13 million', *a gap of 30 million words*.[25] It means a fundamental lack of choice and control over your own life, even in the smallest decisions. When we initially settled in Britain, we received food stamps: these meant that we weren't starving, that we were being looked after, but the stamps were only good for milk or bread – we couldn't exercise the smallest choice about what we ate. Later on, we were almost as constrained by what we could spend: the only way to afford enough calories to keep eight hungry boys quiet was chicken or kebabs from the chicken shop, with nothing left over for fruit or vegetables. It means social isolation: nearly one in ten people in poverty 'rarely or never feel close to others',[26] while a report by the Joseph Rowntree Foundation in 2015 found that people in poverty are less likely to have mixed, diverse social networks, as well as being less likely to have a majority of friends who are in employment.[27] And it means geographical isolation too: though we lived in one of the most rich and cultured cities in the world, we never left our immediate neighbourhood. Being poor seeps into everything, and shapes every thought you have: it lowers your horizons, making you unable to see beyond your immediate situation, and the stress it puts you under makes it difficult to plan ahead, think clearly or make the right decisions: one study found that 'financial stress ... had the effect of making [a participant's] IQ drop by between 13 and 14 per cent. That is the same impact as going without a night's sleep.'[28]

The effect of deprivation on children is so severe that the NHS classes 'growing up in poverty' as a form of 'childhood adversity', grouped together with other 'Adverse Childhood Experiences' (ACEs) such as emotional, physical and sexual abuse, neglect, and having a carer who is an addict or in prison. While ACEs are reported across the entire social spectrum, being born into poverty also appears to put you at higher risk of other ACEs, such as neglect or having a parent who is mentally ill. Unsurprisingly, childhood trauma is strongly associated with difficulties in adult life: the effects can include attachment disorders, learning difficulties, impulsiveness, problems controlling emotions and with social skills,[29] and issues with trust as well as conditions such as PTSD and depression.

Of course, not all children who grow up in poverty are

irredeemably traumatised by it, and doomed to failure and mental illness as adults. But it is extremely hard to escape unscathed: the uprooting and separation of my family, the deaths of our parents and family members, and the severe deprivation we experienced when we settled in England all left a mark on me and my siblings (some of whose lives are indeed closer to the pattern described by NHS guidelines). I vividly remember the mould and the rats that infested our first flat, the shame and confusion we felt when we engaged with authorities, and the horror of knowing as a nine-year-old that my adult relatives – who we relied on to look after us in our strange and challenging new world – were just as lost and confused as we were.

* * *

As we will see in later chapters, in the conversation about social mobility huge weight is placed on the role of education, which is sometimes described as 'the great leveller': a way of flattening the playing field so that the talented poor have a chance against their better-off peers. I will discuss this in more detail in Chapter 3, but the short story is this: there is only so much the education system can do to balance the scales when so much of the damage to a poor child's chances has already been done by the time they start school. By the age of five – the point at which children start school in the UK – children born into poverty are already a year behind the expected level of development. In the long term, children from deprived backgrounds who score highly on cognitive tests at twenty-two months fall behind peers from higher socio-economic groups, and while children of wealthy and educated parents who score poorly initially tend to catch up, those from poorer groups fail to do so. The damage sustained is long term. According to the authors of the study, 'There is no evidence that entry into schooling reverses this pattern.'[30]

Of course, you don't have to be brought up in the kind of poverty that blighted my childhood to want to move up the social scale and feel frustration at your way being blocked: far from it. Being working class does not – of course – mean a life of deprivation: and even if your class circumstances happen to coincide with material deprivation, your parents may be able to compensate in different ways. I was lucky, for instance, in the fact that, although my childhood was in some ways extremely challenging, my crucial early years were stable, and I had two years of uninterrupted attention from both of my parents. Even after we moved to London, I never remember going to bed hungry or cold, and I knew that, however difficult our lives, the adults in the family were trying their best.

But regardless of the circumstances of the individual family you're born into, your early years will still be shaped by your origins in a particular social class and milieu. That parenting styles differ between social classes is well established, both by academic studies that seek to explore the social implications and, more informally, by the way that stereotypes of middle-class parenting, such as the latte-wielding, bugaboo-pushing 'yummy mummy' or the anxious, piano-teacher-on-speed-dial 'helicopter parent', have entered the cultural consciousness. The work of American sociologist Annette Lareau has been particularly influential in this area. Her research into the lives of young children in America showed that 'upper-middle-class parents (those with professional jobs and university degrees) approached raising their children as a project in "concerted cultivation"',[31] which involved help with homework, conversations over the dinner table, asking children for their opinion or involving them in decisions, trips to museums or cultural events, and being encouraged to engage with and challenge authority figures like teachers.[32] By contrast, Lareau found that parenting among working-class parents – which she dubbed the 'accomplishment of natural growth' – to be much less interventionist. Instead of constant monitoring and engagement, the parents prioritised independence, did not tend to involve children in mutual decisions, and were less actively involved in the child's relationship with their school. Instead of the 'frenetic' schedule of activities their middle-class peers experienced, working-class children had a lot of free, unstructured time in which they invented games,[33] 'played outside with cousins and watched television'.[34] This was undoubtedly partly because things like piano lessons and museum visits cost money, but it also reflects some fundamentally different ideas about what childhood is for. Middle-class parents seemed to see childhood as a sort of intensive training period for success in adulthood, whereas their working-class compatriots were, as one academic put it 'emotionally and practically engaged in helping their children negotiate disadvantages and challenges that were considerably less likely to trouble middle-class children or their parents'.[35]

Neither style is 'right' or 'wrong': as Lareau said herself 'working-class and poor parents care for their children, love them, and set limits for them ... both [styles] have strengths and weaknesses.'[36] Middle-class children are often worn out by their intense schedules, in which 'things are so hectic that the house sometimes seems to become a holding pattern between activities',[37] and Lareau also noted that their families tended to spend less time together. But when 'concertedly cultivated' children reach adulthood, they have one great advantage: they are entering a system that is designed by people like their parents, for people like them.[38] One aspect of this is that, in universities and professional environments, a store of 'cultural capital' – the wealth of experiences, reference points and tastes carefully inculcated during those museum trips and excursions to the theatre – is an enormous advantage. But another is that when middle-class parents encourage their children to speak up for themselves – to talk to authority figures like teachers or doctors about what they want – they give their children what Lareau calls 'an emerging sense of entitlement', that in adulthood expresses itself as a feeling of belonging and comfort, and a willingness to ask for what the individual wants or needs: special treatment, advice, a pay rise. Working-class children, whose parents are less likely to have positive experiences with authority, don't develop the same sense that the adults they interact with, for example teachers or doctors, might be in charge but are ultimately there to help them achieve what they want. Instead, they develop an 'emerging sense of constraint', a feeling that places, roles and opportunities 'aren't for the likes of them'.

In his book *Dream Hoarders*, the writer and former government adviser Richard Reeves points out a phenomenon known as 'opportunity hoarding'. Because these days social mobility generally means relative, rather than absolute, mobility, there are only a limited number of places at the top. Conferring an advantage on your own child, therefore, probably means that another child will miss out. And a lot of middle- and upper-class parenting is – consciously or unconsciously – about opening up opportunities for their children, which, eventually, will put that child on the inside track to success, wealth and status. An extreme example is the college admissions scandal, code-named Operation Varsity Blues, which broke in 2019, when it was revealed that a number of wealthy Americans – including celebrities, CEOs and private equity millionaires – had been using the services of two firms that promised to get their children into elite academic institutions by artificially inflating test scores and bribing officials. Of course, very few parents have either the inclination or the resources (up to $250 million was allegedly paid to the firms) to break the law in this way. But at the same time, it's hard to deny that opportunity hoarding is rife in modern Britain: from paying for private school, which, as we will see, confers an enormous advantage well into adulthood, or private tutoring, to helping with homework or arranging work experience. Even things that seem to be simply good parenting, like reading your child a bedtime story every night, will enlarge their vocabulary and reading skills, reinforcing them for success at school.

The problem of social mobility, as the philosopher Kwame Anthony Appiah recognises, is that it 'conflict[s] with a force in human life as inevitable and as compelling as the idea that some individuals are more deserving than others, namely, the desire of families to pass on advantages to their children'.[39] When middle-class parents propel their children through Mandarin classes and Montessori schools, their intention isn't necessarily to perpetuate inequality and block working-class children from opportunity. But they desperately want the best for *their* child: they want to make sure that they aren't left behind, locked out, moving downward. And, usually, they have the inside knowledge and the resources to stop that happening: the knowledge to equip their child with the tools they need to navigate elite tiers of society, the money to provide them with a rich and varied cultural hinterland, and the social and economic clout to compensate for any problems their child might come across, from dyslexia to a failing local school. This is what has been termed the 'glass floor', as mentioned earlier: the ability of well-off parents to use their resources to ensure that their children cannot fall below their own level. Individually, the glass floor is intended to protect an individual child. But collectively, it forms an impenetrable barrier that prevents movement up from below: what Friedman and Laurison term a 'class ceiling'.

Of course, as we have seen, the interaction between a person's beginnings and their social mobility is complicated, and not due to one factor – it would be unfair to blame middle-class parents for the structural inequalities in society that create and perpetuate poverty, or the war that separated my family and brought us to a foreign country, or the government cuts to programmes such as Sure Start, which tried to bridge the gap in circumstances between poor and middle-class families. But the knotty problem remains, and will dog us throughout the rest of this book: that for some children to move up, other children must move down. And while parents might *aspire* to better for their child, they will fight tooth and nail to stop them losing what they already have.

* * *

In November 2013, Boris Johnson, then Mayor of London, gave a speech on the subject of meritocracy. 'It is surely relevant to a conversation about equality', he said, 'that as many as 16 per cent of our species have an IQ below 85, while about 2 per cent have an IQ above 130.' Of course, he said, he wasn't suggesting that everyone in the clever 2 per cent was getting a fair deal, and he suggested some educational reforms to make it easier for them: 'The harder you shake the pack, the easier it will be for some cornflakes to get to the top.'[40]

Johnson's speech – as he surely hoped it would – ignited a furore. The *Daily Mirror* reported it with the headline

'Boris Johnson: Millions of people too STUPID to get on in life'.[41] But the meritocratic worldview that Johnson propounded to his City audience is a common one, and one that lies beneath a lot of thinking about social mobility. Some children, it goes, are naturally bright – and some are naturally not so bright. Of course, not all the bright ones are getting the opportunity to thrive – but if you can just find that clever 2 per cent, you can move them into the sunlit glow of a better school or a scholarship programme, and they can flourish. Social mobility, from this perspective, is a matter of finding the deserving bright sparks – the ones who can make the most of their lives – and moving them up. The others, well ... they were never destined for greatness. Indeed, as Johnson went on to say, 'some measure of inequality is essential for the spirit of envy ... that is, like greed, a valuable spur to economic activity'.

Of course, you will already have identified the problem with this: meritocracy assumes a level playing field, and that is exactly what we don't have in Britain today. Despite this, it has become something of a political obsession in modern Britain. In a speech given in September 2016, Theresa May talked about building 'a truly meritocratic Britain that puts the interests of ordinary, working-class people first'.[42] Her words recalled Tony Blair's statement in 1997 that 'the Britain of the elite is over. The new Britain is a meritocracy.' Campaigning to become party leader in 2005, David Cameron styled himself as a 'believer in meritocracy', while in 2010, ex-prime minister Gordon Brown wrote in *The Guardian* that 'Our values demand a genuine meritocracy for all British people'.[43] The idea that a meritocracy is the ideal society – fair, equal, rewarding merit not advantage – has become so ingrained in our public discourse that we rarely question what it actually means, or whether it's really working for us.

And yet the man who coined the term, Michael Young, did so in the context not of an ideal society but of a dystopia. Young's enormously influential book on the subject *The Rise of the Meritocracy*, was published in 1958. It popularised the term: but it was also a dire warning against a society that judged its inhabitants purely on merit. Even a fully functioning meritocracy, Young suggested, would still in effect be a system of class: even if you were able to shake up society sufficiently to release the talented cornflakes at the bottom of the packet, once they reached the top they would still form a well-off, well-remunerated layer sitting on top of their fellow bits of breakfast cereal. These worse-off cornflakes would not even have the right to complain: 'the eminent know that success is a just reward for their own capacity, their own efforts ... As for the lower classes, the situation is different. ...They are tested again and again ... If they have been labelled "dunce" repeatedly, they cannot any longer pretend.'[44]

Presumably this isn't what politicians have in mind when they extol the virtues of meritocracy (or perhaps it is). But in fact the problem with meritocracy is less what would happen if we put it into practice, and more that we are light years away from being able to put it into practice. Johnson's description reveals a belief – which we've seen in the context of biological determinism – that clever people are clever because they just *are*, in the way that some cornflakes are bigger than others. But as I hope I have demonstrated, talent and potential aren't inborn: they are carefully searched for and nurtured, shaped to fit existing institutions and environments, supported and given space to grow through a vast range of parental resources and techniques. The business boardrooms and think tanks that Johnson referenced in his speech are indeed stuffed with hard-working, clever people (though not all of them will be as hard-working or as clever as they think they are) – but not because they are a naturally occurring intellectual elite. With some exceptions they will have been nourished, tended to and encouraged in ways that are denied to other children. They have had opportunities to develop and demonstrate 'merit' that for others were denied before they were even born. And this says nothing of those often referred to as the 'middle attainment group', some of whom have difficulty enough in attaining C grades or equivalent, and who, in the presence of other variables, may fail to achieve even that.

* * *

There are, I hope, two messages to this chapter. The first is that if, in Britain, we wish to do something to break the link between someone's origins and their destination, we must begin with inequality, and as early as we can. But the second, and perhaps less obvious message is that nothing is simple. Everyone's story is important, and everyone's origins define them. But that definition is not two-dimensional, and a statistical probability is not the same as a cast-iron certainty. I'm proud of my own story, and I know from experience that what you might lose in museum visits or tennis lessons you gain in resilience, in the richness of coming from more than one culture, and in the pride of knowing that you survived. By coincidence, the profession that I have chosen is one in which the link between parents and children is particularly strong: the children of lawyers are seventeen times more likely to become lawyers than are children not connected to the profession.[45] When I ask some of my colleagues about their childhoods, they describe growing up in houses full of books, heated debates over the dinner table, perhaps even an exciting excursion to watch Mum or Dad perform in court. That's not my story. But when I am in court, wearing the wig and gown that mark me out as a member of one of the oldest professions in my country's history (perhaps even, whisper it, a member of the *establishment*), I think of the people who came before me: my grandfather, who started all this when he left the wilderness to build a new future for his family; my father, fluent in the many languages of the people whose paths he crossed in his travels; my mother, who gave birth to so many children over the course of her most formative years; and my grandmother, sitting in our overcrowded council flat in Wembley, sitting so far away from where she started, spinning a golden web of proverbs, simile and metaphor as she told me the story of our family. The story I have just shared with you.

2

Getting On and Getting Along: Race and Class

> When it rains in Mogadishu, the umbrellas go up in Minnesota.
>
> Nuruddin Farah

On 22 April 1993, in Eltham in South East London, just a few months before my own arrival in England, a young black teenager was stabbed to death in a racially motivated attack while waiting for a bus. It is hard to overstate the impact of the murder of Stephen Lawrence. Britain was different after it, as, propelled by the courageous determination of the Lawrence family to pursue justice at enormous personal cost, the country finally confronted the racism and prejudice deeply embedded in its social fabric and institutions. It was a seminal moment for any young black man growing up in London at the time. For us, new arrivals to the country and mostly young boys in households where the only adults were women – mothers, grandmothers and sisters – well, we were paying attention. I remember my aunty, my father's only sister, a real matriarch and the mother of six boys, laying down some new rules: we go to school, we play football (or whatever sport we were currently obsessed with), and *we come home straight afterwards*. No hanging around in the streets like we used to in

Eastleigh, no wasting time outside, because 'they kill black boys in this country'. It was my first experience of being a minority: in Kenya, race wasn't an issue. We, and everyone we knew, were black. For the first time, we were coming to see ourselves as different, and realising that in our strange new country, the way we looked marked us out, and made us vulnerable.

* * *

None of us is just one thing: all of us are composed of constellations of overlapping identities that together form 'who we are'. We might see ourselves simultaneously as a brother, a fiancé, an uncle, a Liverpool fan, a bookworm, a graduate, a petrolhead, a Scouser, a Virgo, a millennial ... the list is potentially endless. But over all these infinite variations loom two great categories that shape our identities and our futures like no other in modern Britain: race and class.

'England', George Orwell wrote, 'is the most class-ridden country under the sun. It is a land of snobbery and privilege, ruled largely by the old and silly.' And it is certainly true that class pervades every aspect of British society: it shapes the lives of its members in ways that are both profound and ordinary, from their life expectancy to their brand of teabags. It is both strictly codified and somewhat vague, although many British people will have internalised it to such an extent that they will reflexively be able to 'sort' a stranger by such details as where they live, what they order in the pub, and what sort of dog they have. I find these complex webs of taboos and rules, of unspoken agreements and secret codes, endlessly fascinating, sometimes funny and often infuriating. It took me, for example, a long time to work out that when someone from an upper-class background talked of 'having been at school near Slough' or owning 'a little cottage in the country', they did not mean that their school was near Slough or that they were the owner of a small dwelling in a rural location: they meant that they went to Eton and have a second home in the Cotswolds or Cornwall, probably quite a big one with an orchard or a pool. As Orwell pointed out, to outsiders these rules can seem impenetrable, and the divisions so subtle as to be invisible: 'Somehow these differences fade away the moment that any two Britons are confronted by a European. ... Looked at from the outside, even the cockney and the Yorkshireman have a strong family resemblance.'[1] My family, arriving not from neighbouring Europe but from a poverty-stricken suburb of Nairobi, were dropped into the middle of a vastly complex, rigidly structured society that we didn't understand and which itself had trouble categorising us. We were definitely poor, but we knew nothing of British working-class culture or history. We lived in London, but we weren't Londoners: we were from somewhere else. Apart from the colour of our skin, we didn't have much in common with other, more established ethnic groups like Nigerians or Pakistanis. We also had no way to tell other people where we belonged: we barely spoke English, so the difference between 'napkin' and 'serviette' was lost on us, and we liked to drink our tea with cardamom, pepper and clove as well as milk or sugar. We were that vaguely defined yet much-discussed group in modern Britain: the recent immigrant.

* * *

Since the late 1990s Britain has experienced high levels of migration. Whatever your personal view – that this represents a vital infusion of young workers and vibrant new cultures, or an uncontrolled wave of potential benefit fraudsters and NHS-waiting-list-blockers – the fact remains that, between 2004 and 2017, the foreign-born population in the UK nearly doubled, increasing from around 5.3 million to just under 9.4 million. Consequently, this has meant that Britain has become more diverse, with the number of people in England and Wales who identified as 'White British' falling by 7 per cent between the 2001 and 2011 censuses.[2] This still left a country that was overwhelmingly white, however (especially as some of the shortfall was made up by immigration from 'White Other' groups): 80.5 per cent of the UK population is White British, and the next largest ethnic group, Asians, make up 7.5 per cent of the population, followed by black ethnic groups at 3.3 per cent. But the effect on the national psyche was such that, during this period, immigration became one of British society's most sensitive issues: depending on who you asked it is either an unmitigated boon or an unmitigated disaster, a disastrous act of misguided generosity that the country can ill afford, or an apologetic hand extended to the occupants of countries destroyed by the legacy of British colonialism. Such is the emotional pitch of the debate that it is unsurprising that we are consistently bad at estimating the actual *level* of immigration: a poll taken just prior to the EU referendum in 2016 showed that, on average, we think that EU citizens make up 15 per cent of the total UK population (10.5 million people), when in reality it is 5 per cent (around 3.5 million people).[3] Again predictably, those who intended to vote leave overestimated EU immigration more; they thought that 20 per cent of the UK population are EU immigrants.

But despite the fact that these immigrant and ethnic minority groups face many of the same obstacles and difficulties experienced by disadvantaged white Britons – and despite a growing body of evidence that coming from an ethnic minority puts you at *greater* risk of poverty and disadvantage – a fault line between race and class has opened up in our national conversation. Although British society, as we have seen, has changed significantly in the thirty years since my arrival, our image of the British working class has, like a dusty 'Welcome to Blackpool' figurine on a high shelf, remained untouched since the middle of the last century. In the words of the economist and activist Faiza Shaheen and journalist Ellie Mae O'Hagan, 'When we think of the average working-class person, we ... picture a sooty white man emerging from a coal-mine as the Hovis theme tune plays in the background.'[4] It's a vision that's sorely in need of updating: like my own family, immigrants tend to join British society in the lower ranks (and in fact, if they don't, they'll be known to Brits as 'expats'). In other words, the working class has changed. No longer ethnically monochrome, stably employed in factories or service jobs, and voting Labour, the working class is ethnically diverse, working in the gig economy, and increasingly voting Conservative.[5]

Nonetheless, there is a persistent tendency in British society to behave as if race and class are different categories, or worse, mutually exclusive and competing ones. Like the election of Donald Trump in America, the result of the 2016 EU referendum was widely seen as the 'revenge of the white working class': a roar of defiance from communities whose jobs had been destroyed by globalisation and who'd long been marginalised by a contemptuous metropolitan elite who had ignored their suffering while at the same time rushing to promote the causes of immigrants and minorities. Across the media, commentators rushed to position the vote as the inevitable result of decades of hurt visited upon a forgotten and unfashionable minority.

The lines of battle that were subsequently drawn were often demarcated by attitudes to class and immigration: the Europhile defenders of free movement against the self-appointed Eurosceptic defenders of the 'white working class'.

The idea that there is a fundamental separation between minorities and the 'white working class', and that the interests of those two groups are in direct conflict, is nothing new: it is now over fifty years since the Conservative MP Enoch Powell delivered his 'Rivers of Blood' speech to his local Birmingham Conservative Association, in which he sought to describe the change taking place in the country in the wake of the arrival of the 'Windrush generation' from the Caribbean. In one of the most frequently quoted sections, as Powell tells it, one of his constituents – 'an ordinary working man' – confides that he wished his family to settle overseas because 'In this country in fifteen or twenty years' time the black man will have the whip hand over the white man.' Powell knew, he said that repeating this would provoke a 'chorus of execration', but he felt duty bound to do so: 'I do not have the right not to ... here is a decent, ordinary fellow Englishman, who in broad daylight in my own town says to me, his Member of Parliament, that his country will not be worth living in for his children.' Britain was, he concluded, 'a nation busily engaged in heaping up its own funeral pyre'.

After the speech, Powell was sacked from his position as shadow minister for defence by Edward Heath, who condemned the speech for being 'racialist in tone'. But the impact of Powell's words was deep and long-lasting: a poll taken shortly afterwards showed that 74 per cent of respondents agreed with him. It solidified a particular perspective on class and race that still informs the way we see the working class today, and how immigrants see themselves in relation to the country they call home. Powell's 'ordinary decent Englishman', deserving, but overwhelmed and out-competed by an influx of immigrants who are taking the resources he had counted on for his family's survival, has remained a persistent social stereotype. He's the person who we hear about being pushed down housing queues and NHS waiting lists – one of the forgotten majority who, in Powell's words, find 'their wives unable to obtain hospital beds in childbirth, their children unable to obtain school places, their homes and neighbourhoods changed beyond recognition, their plans and prospects for the future defeated'. But the very idea that the Windrush immigrants were seen as competing for the same jobs and resources – as people like them still are today – reveals the fact that they were in similar situations themselves. If we define 'working class' not in terms of culture and behaviour (or even skin tone) but in terms of lack of opportunity, access to resources or social and cultural capital, then they too were part of the working class: the 'black working class', a term that always sounds strange to me, because I hear it rarely, if at all. But the working class has always been more diverse than our image of it, and in terms of the challenges they faced securing a decent life and opportunities for themselves, Powell's white constituents probably had more in common with their black neighbours than with the middle-class white people with whom they shared a heritage and a skin tone.

When I see the legacy of Powell's speech – the headlines about immigrants taking homes and jobs away from British people, the shouts of 'go home' aimed at black and Asian people after the Brexit vote – I despair. Far from holding 'the whip hand', there is little evidence that immigrants or ethnic minorities do better than their white British contemporaries in similar circumstances. My family, for instance, had absolutely no idea that there *was* a queue for basic housing, let alone how to jump one. In fact, black and Asian households are the most likely of any sector of society to be in persistent poverty and receive income-related benefits: where the figure was one in ten for white households, in black households it was one in five and a shocking one in four for Asian households.[6] Ethnic minorities – especially those of black, Pakistani and Bangladeshi origin – are more likely to live in areas of deprivation,[7] and while around one in twenty-five white British people is unemployed, the figure climbs to one in ten for those from black, Pakistani, Bangladeshi or mixed-race backgrounds.[8] Neither do immigrants or minorities appear to ascend the socio-economic ladder faster than their white British peers: while BAME students are going to university in high numbers, a white British student is still 16 per cent more likely to be accepted to the elite Russell Group universities than a black African student with the same grades.[9] And even when BAME students do enter higher education, they are less likely to graduate with a first-class degree, less likely to be employed subsequently, and, if they are, they earn less.[10] Immigrants, and in particular refugees, are more likely to move down the social ladder than the disadvantaged white British: even middle-class BAME groups in Britain seem less able to convert their social background into economic success in the labour market and are more vulnerable to seeing their children experience downward social mobility.[11]

Racism is certainly a factor in why immigrants and minorities experience such limited social mobility. But the fact that disadvantage correlates with ethnicity hides the fact that it also correlates with class: class cuts across racial categories, distributing disadvantage in such a way that the educational success of a working-class white boy on free school meals is much closer to an Afro-Caribbean boy than a middle-class white boy (who is an astonishing 135 per cent more likely to gain five good GCSEs). Class also accounts for many of the large and significant differences within BAME communities, explaining why pupils of Chinese and Indian heritage, who are far more likely to have parents from professional backgrounds, do better at school than their peers of Bangladeshi or Pakistani origin, who are overwhelmingly less likely to come from privileged backgrounds.[12] If you come from an Indian or a Chinese background, you're *more* likely than a disadvantaged white person to end up in an elite occupation, but if you're Bangladeshi, you're only half as likely to do so.[13] These differences are sometimes attributed to 'culture' through a sort of 'positive racism' (if such a thing exists), which sees the Chinese and Indians as 'good immigrants': striving, hardworking, education-focused, upwardly mobile. But clearly, they are really about class. Chinese and Indian immigrants, like the Nigerian and Ugandan immigrants who arrived in the UK in the 1980s and whose children also perform well at school, were often from the middle classes, while Pakistani and Bengali immigrants often came from the equivalent of the working class.[14] It's ironic that, in the endless circling conversation around 'diversity', the fact that the ethnic population of Britain is just that – diverse – is often ignored completely.

This isn't to say that ethnicity isn't important: the challenges posed by your socio-economic status can be *compounded* by your ethnicity. This is what is meant by the term intersectionality: the idea that our separate identities do not operate independently but in fact interact to produce unique benefits or challenges. For example, I am a tall black man in my thirties. At the weekend, or if I'm on my way back from the gym, I might wear a hoody. And if

I get on the tube like this, I quite often notice the person next to me pull their bag tighter towards them or move it from the floor to their lap. To put it plainly, either consciously or unconsciously, something about me makes them think I might steal their possessions. But it's not just being black, or being a young man, or even my clothes that trigger the response. The same thing doesn't happen when I'm coming home from court wearing a suit, and my middle-class white friends seem able to use public transport while wearing a tracksuit without being treated like potential muggers. So the particular form of racism I'm experiencing is to do with being black *and* young *and* male *and* wearing clothes that people associate with a particular section of society: my different identities together unite to form a new kind of identity that disadvantages me. Coming from the working class is one kind of disadvantage in terms of social mobility. Being BAME is another, as is being a woman, as is being disabled, which is another aspect of personal identity or experience that appears to disadvantage you in the workplace, and disproportionately affects working-class people.[15] Faith matters: as a Muslim in Britain today, the challenges you face in seeking to realise your full potential are immense.[16] British Muslims, like myself, often grow up in the most deprived wards in the country: not just the worst-off cities or towns, but the worst-off wards within those worst-off places.[17] Naturally, the schools catering to these wards are also likely to be the most impoverished and the least nurturing places. As we have seen, unemployment is significantly higher among Muslim minorities, like those of Pakistani or Bangladeshi origin: the likelihood that there are two working adults in such households is quite low, and if a wage is being brought in, it will be at the lowest end of the scale.[18] These groups are vulnerable not just to racism, but to Islamophobia, and

Muslim women who wear a visible symbol of their religion are particularly vulnerable, and are subject to sexism both from within their communities and wider society.

* * *

Despite the fact that I have been liberally using the term throughout this book, class is notoriously hard to define. It's not about money, though economic resources are certainly part of it, and it's not entirely about status either: Sir Philip Green, the owner of the vast Arcadia Group, is both a knight of the realm and a billionaire, but you'll rarely see a newspaper profile of him that misses the chance to point out his humble origins as a market trader or dwell on the vulgarity of his super-yacht or displays of temper. Jobs are an important marker of class, but a university lecturer might proudly boast of their working-class roots, while a plumber might send their children to private school, holiday in the Mediterranean, and display many familiar middle-class signifiers. Immigrants and (especially) refugees often lose significant social status when they leave their original country, but not always in a straightforward way. In Somalia, my family had been connected to a well-established and respected clan, and although in England we were very much the bottom of the heap, among the Somali community in London we retain a certain cachet.

To my mind, the best way to define class – if we are not to get mired in endless academic divisions of economic potential or nuances of etiquette – is not in terms of behaviour, status or self-identification, but instead in terms of access to privilege, opportunities, and representation in elite institutions and professions. Viewed like this, it becomes clear that the 'bottom tier' of society – what the independent race equality think tank Runnymede terms the 'left-behind people' – have much more in common with each other than with people of their own ethnicity further up the social scale. Working-class jobs are done by both the white working class and the BAME working class: they face similar barriers of resources, send their children to the same schools, and are affected by similar kinds of prejudice and the same paralysing lack of knowledge about how to get on. In the years after our arrival in London, I would often walk with my aunt or grandmother to a place called Mahatma Gandhi House, in the London Borough of Brent, where we would ask for the family to be rehoused in decent accommodation. Regardless of who we met or what we said to them, we were sent from pillar to post, moved from one substandard accommodation infested with rodents and cockroaches to the next. The sort of disdainful look housing officers would give us when we desperately tried to explain our predicament, and the constant humiliation of being told to sit back down with a dismissive hand wave, only to wait there the whole day and later to be told to return the next day, or next month, is seared on my memory. But, obediently, we always did as we were told. Our fellow travellers, with whom we shared both the waiting rooms and our predicament, were a diverse bunch: white Londoners whose families had lived in the area for generations, newly arrived Somalis, second-generation Bangladeshis and Jamaicans. We were not – as certain parts of the media might have it – in fierce competition with each other, but at the mercy of a dysfunctional and uncompassionate system. In creating a narrative that pits them endlessly against minorities, a disservice has been done to the white working class, who are all too often portrayed as racist, intolerant and jealous. But Omar Khan and Faiza Shaheen point out in a report for the Runnymede think tank:

It's not the white working class who make people with African and Asian-sounding surnames send in twice as many CVs; it's not the white working class who award white British graduates nearly three times as many firsts as Black British graduates; it's not the white working class who have eliminated targets for child poverty, which is highest among British Bangladeshi and Pakistani households; and it's not the white working class who design budgets that make the poorest Black and Asian women some £2,000 worse off, and the wealthiest white men slightly better off.[19]

Addressing these deeply rooted ideas is a huge task. But what we have at the moment works for no one except the privileged – it stops us from reaching out to others who share our experience and could give us advice or support, and it allows bad-faith politicians to promote dangerous, harmful agendas, to spread dissent between groups, and disguise the fact that the source of the problem lies not in competition between the deserving 'traditional' working class and the less-deserving incomers, but in a fundamental inequality in our society that harms us all. I hope that we will be able to build a greater solidarity between the 'left-behinds' in our society: that we can put aside the idea that the only interest of the white working class is the revival of a departed cultural past, recognising that this is a bankrupt narrative offering no real policy solution other than mass deportation of British subjects. Instead, we must ensure the equal voice and dignity of every citizen. If we can acknowledge that what we have in common cuts across our difference, focus on the common enemy of economic inequality and pull together, we can perhaps begin to turn our society in the right direction.

* * *

There is no one 'immigrant experience': every new arrival faces their own particular set of challenges, although there may well be shared touchstones. My family, fleeing war-torn Somalia, arrived in England weighed down with the baggage of trauma (and light on actual baggage: one of the many problems that afflict refugees is the fact that you often arrive lacking vital documents, diplomas, birth certificates and so on). Even in a pre-9/11 world, being black and Muslim was its own particular challenge, and each of these problems was made worse by the language barrier and a general failure to integrate. But, despite all this, in many ways the Britain we found in the early 1990s was an easier place to be an immigrant than it had been before, or is now, come to that. I know that this may seem hard to believe, but it really was: on arrival, once it was verified that you were ethnic Somalis, being granted asylum was a mere formality, and even if it took some time to get through the system and be granted citizenship, we never questioned the fact that we would eventually get there (something that is far from the case for asylum seekers today). The compassion we encountered from the British people we met, in the early stages at least, was real and tangible. I will always remember, for instance, the teacher who assigned us some homework about the Second World War. Realising that, unlike most of the other children at the school, we didn't have grandparents or relatives who'd lived through it, he found us an elderly couple who lived nearby and who we could interview instead. In the end, we stayed in touch with them for about two years. Perhaps it was because I was a child, and shielded to some extent from the reality of our situation, but despite the struggles we faced, and the humiliation that would follow, Britain felt like a welcoming place. Certainly, it was a safer, more tranquil place than the one we had come from. We were aware that we stood out, but it didn't always feel like a bad thing: there was some kind of novelty to it, a kind of fascination with other people's fascination. As time went on and – as happened to many of us – we were randomly attacked in the streets and harassed by the police, the fascination would come to seem less benign, but these were my first impressions of Britain.

Undoubtedly, we found Britain like this because our path had been smoothed to an extent by the battles fought by earlier immigrants and ethnic minorities. We didn't have to face down the National Front at the height of its power in the 1980s, or endure the worst kind of daily street harassment because others had gone before us and had prevailed, changing society for the better. I am always conscious of myself as the direct beneficiary of those who campaigned tirelessly to fight prejudice everywhere, by marching, standing for elections, organising, voting for the other guy, fighting for the right legislation, and finding new ways to show people just how much we have in common. I still experienced my fair share of unjustified and humiliating stop-and-searches as a teenager and young man, but the pursuit of justice by people like Doreen and Neville Lawrence, and, ultimately, the willingness of British society as a whole to change, allowed me to grow up as a black man, not untouched by discrimination and bigotry, but, crucially, unscarred by it.

* * *

A funny story was once told to me by a Somali friend whose family settled in the Netherlands. She said that the Dutch had a camp where new arrivals would be housed for some time. While they were there, they would be taught about the country's produce of cheese and milk, and the new immigrants would be taught other essential parts of Dutch culture, such as the importance of canals and how to ride a bike. Grown Somali women who had never ridden a bike before were expected to learn – and learn they did. It conjured up an amusing picture, all these newly arrived refugees having clogs, tulips and windmills earnestly explained to them. Of course, from another perspective, it could also seem patronising or oppressive. But I think it was a great idea, because if there's one thing people underestimate about being a new immigrant from an entirely different culture, it's how little you know about your new home.

When we arrived, our fundamental problem was a complete and utter lack of knowledge and information. We knew absolutely nothing about Britain, and the most basic facts about life here were entirely new to us: a few weeks after we arrived, I knocked myself unconscious by walking into a lamppost. I simply wasn't expecting it to be there: there wasn't street lighting in Eastleigh and I'd never seen one before. We were much less prepared for our new life than, for example, the Windrush generation, who mainly came to Britain to work, and who already had strong – if complicated and painful – connections to the country, either through the historical atrocities of the slave trade or more broadly through the ties of the Commonwealth and empire. The Windrush generation, especially those from the Caribbean, shared a common language with the inhabitants of their new country and – for the most part – a common faith. They faced intense and corrosive racism, and in many ways a harsher environment in which to build a life for themselves, but they at least did not arrive in a completely unfamiliar place, not speaking the language, here not because you chose to leave your home but because you had to, and with no real idea how to start making another.

We groped about in total darkness, helpless to do anything about it. Unlike me, some of my siblings had had direct and traumatic experiences fleeing war, without either of our parents: but where to seek help or support in dealing with this was completely beyond us. This, the frustration of not knowing what you need, where to get it, who to speak to and how best to go about improving on last week or last month, was the defining experience of our early years in Britain. We relied on those who arrived a few months before, thinking that, after all they must know more than we did having *just* arrived? In reality, garbled or half understood information would trickle down, delivered with a certainty that often led to more chaos and confusion. We were extremely vulnerable to exploitation, in particular from the dodgy lawyers who preyed on people like us, trying to spin out immigration cases for as long as possible in order to collect the legal aid fees. All of this made it impossible to properly understand our rights, still less our responsibilities, in a society that was clearly not set up to absorb new arrivals unaccustomed to the language, culture and customs. At home, we were desperate to maintain some sort of identity in the best way we knew how, by clinging on to our Somali-ness, just as you would expect of any proud people in order to survive the daily humiliations that came our way. We learned only through our mistakes, and it was a slow and painstaking business.

Given all this, it's not surprising that there has been, for the best part of two decades, a persistent narrative of return among Somali refugee communities, from Minnesota to Copenhagen, Melbourne to Cardiff. From the moment of arrival, we hoped that Somalia would one day be peaceful again, and soon. And when she rises from the ashes, we told each other, she will seek out her sons and daughters, even if most of them now do not speak the language and have never set foot in the country. We nurtured a hope of one day being in the majority instead of the minority. The idea of making a permanent home in Europe felt like a sort of betrayal of Somalia. Why, we reasoned, should a Western nation, and one that had a hand in destabilising most of the African continent, benefit from the fruits of our labour? Why should it keep the best and brightest of our children, who are desperately needed elsewhere? This was compounded by the sense that, having taken us in, Britain was now leaving us to fend for ourselves, and leaving its new arrivals to flail about in search of their place in society.

This mindset is instantly recognisable to many different immigrant communities who've come to make Britain their home. It's the misplaced hope of a peaceful return, and the connected need of keeping the old culture alive. This hope has as its currency rose-tinted memories of better times, still vivid in the minds of those telling compelling but ultimately incomplete stories. But, understandable though it is, I think it has profoundly negative effects on the lives of immigrants: it creates friction and division between generations, and prevents families from setting down the roots they need to progress and improve their circumstances. As the latest generation of Somalis have grown up, they have found themselves confused by stories from a nomadic culture to which they can barely relate, in a language they barely understand, and they fail to understand the intransigence of the older generation in the face of the only culture the younger ones have ever known. Some of these failures of communication are literal: Somali is an extremely difficult language to learn unless you are completely immersed in it. Unlike me, many of my nieces, nephews and cousins were born and bred in Britain and are native English speakers. Unless second-generation Somalis have grown up in a household where Somali is spoken fluently (invariably by a grandmother) they're unlikely to learn their 'mother tongue' proficiently. This is a problem if you're attempting to understand your history, your context, where you have come from and your legacy: but it also makes for practical misunderstanding and miscommunications between youngsters and elders. The parents, if they are able to speak English, won't necessarily have the range needed to be able to communicate with their children, or the ability to understand their worldview – and often deep and damaging conflict arises out of simple frustration. And, of course, like any other teenagers, Somali teenagers are in the tortuous process of trying to forge an independent identity, one that may have little to do with their parents' expectations or desires. But in their case the normal misunderstandings are intensified by a language barrier within the family and a difference in outlook that might span not just generations but vastly different cultures.

These experiences, I believe, are common to many immigrant communities. And the situation is compounded by the fact that young second-generation immigrants are not only told by their families that their 'real' home is not the country where they were born and brought up, but also that the quiet drumbeat of not-quite-belonging is matched by an insistent narrative from the rest of society, which also tells them that they don't really belong here, that, yes, perhaps they should 'go back home'. In this way, British children, born and raised in this country, are repeatedly told, by society, by their own family, by the national media, by their own daily experiences, that this is not their home. Even someone like me – a 'success story', a higher-rate

taxpayer, an Oxford graduate, a member of an elite profession – is often reminded in subtle, and (if I were to be
generous), unintentional ways, that I don't quite belong
here. The question 'but where are you from *really*?' often
stems from curiosity rather than hostility, and probably
seems fairly harmless to the questioner: but it reveals the
underlying assumption that, regardless of whether you've
said Croydon or Leeds or Portsmouth, you're *really* from
somewhere else; you don't belong here. But when you do
go back to visit the homelands, whether that's Somalia or
Pakistan, Ghana or Jamaica, the chances are that you'll feel
like a foreigner there too. You won't speak the language,
and you won't fit into the culture. You don't fit in here, and
you don't fit in in Blighty either.

The feeling that we immigrants often have of walking
on a knife edge, only a slip away from disaster, is not just
the existential angst of not 'really' belonging: it is sometimes a real and present danger. When, in 2019, the Home
Secretary Sajid Javid stripped a nineteen-year-old girl from
East London of her British citizenship as punishment for
her decision to travel to Syria to join Islamic State, it sent
a shiver down my spine, and not simply because the girl,
Shamima Begum, was stranded in a refugee camp with
her newborn baby. Javid's reasoning was that – although
it is illegal under international law to render somebody
stateless – Begum was entitled to Bangladeshi citizenship
through her parents. Begum had never been to Bangladesh,
and, as Bangladesh made clear, they didn't especially want
to grant a traumatised and heavily indoctrinated British
teenager citizenship. The mere fact that Begum was rendered stateless by her own government was profoundly dis-
turbing, but there was also another, more subtle, message
behind it. In her interviews with the media, Begum came
across as unlikeable and unrepentant, prone to tone-deaf

comments like 'people should have sympathy towards me for everything I've been through'. She seemed entitled and ungrateful – and that is the one thing immigrants are not allowed to be in Britain. As the columnist Caitlin Moran pointed out, Begum's behaviour – eye-rolling, defensive, self-absorbed – wasn't out of line with normal teenage behaviour, albeit in extreme circumstances: being entitled and 'unlovably defensive about massively screwing up' is 'kind of their thing ... however, until now their citizenship wasn't subsequently based on how much they'd got everyone's back up – or this country would be looking a lot emptier, and older, right now.'[20] Whether you see Shamima Begum as a young and silly girl who was groomed, lured to a war zone and then deeply traumatised, or as a selfish and unrepentant member of a ruthless and criminal organisation, the fact remains that what happened to her would not have happened to somebody who didn't come from an immigrant family. Javid's ruling underscored something all immigrants half-suspected: you might be a citizen, you might have a passport, you might have been born and brought up here: but if you don't toe the line, you'll find out pretty quickly how much that counts for.

Gratitude is, accordingly, a complicated concept for immigrants. I am grateful for the *literal* assistance given to us as a family when we arrived on these shores fleeing war and dire circumstances. I am incredibly grateful for – and proud of now contributing to – a welfare state that gave me and my family a lifeline. I am extremely grateful for the opportunities I was given to rise through British society: for the scholarships that funded me through Oxford and Bar School, and for the helping hands extended by British people across the social spectrum, without which I would not be where I am today. But I am also extremely angry that it had to be so painful, and sad that it wasn't available for others, and that the same helping hand isn't extended to people like me today. I have no idea what would have happened to us if we'd been forced to contend with the chaos of Universal Credit,[21] or what I would have done without the Education Maintenance Allowance (EMA), an income-assessed weekly allowance of £30 to help students with the cost of further education. This sort of help made a huge difference to me and my family, but EMA is no longer available in England.[22] I am furious that so many others have been left behind through no fault of their own, when there is plenty of wealth to go round in our country. And I am also angry that, while I am expected to be (as I am) grateful, if I want to express my more negative feelings it's a different story. When people of colour or minority communities raise their voices about the shortcomings of our society, a chorus goes up, the subtext of which always is: be grateful that we let you live here. When the British-born grime artist Stormzy commented on his government's response to the Grenfell Tower fire ('Yo, Theresa May, where's the money for Grenfell?'), the *Daily Mail* columnist Amanda Platell wrote: 'Is it asking too much that he show a scintilla of gratitude to the country that offered his mother and him so much?'[23] You're here and we accept you – as long as you behave yourself and toe the line. But neither should you partake too enthusiastically of the opportunities offered to you by your new home. The American novelist Dina Nayeri, whose family moved first to England and then to America as refugees from Iran in the 1980s, picked out the exhausting contradictions and constraints faced by immigrants in their new countries in her book *The Ungrateful Refugee*: 'The refugee has to be less capable than the native, needier; he must stay in his place. That's the only way gratitude will be accepted.' On the one hand, the refugee or immigrant must not compete with her new countrymen, must stay in a position of humble gratitude to the people who took her in. But if you're too dependent you become a scrounger, a parasite: as Nayeri says, 'one can go around in this circle forever, because it contains no internal logic. You're not enough until you're too much. You're lazy until you're a greedy interloper.'[24]

As a black British man, it's tough to hear this. And it's also profoundly damaging, because if you don't have the kind of stake in society that gives you the right to criticise it, you can't commit to building a future here either. And each time you hear the subliminal message that this is a society not entirely for you or people like you, it hardens that impression: it will make it harder for those people to reimagine a different future for themselves in the here and now, and much harder to find their rightful place in the near future. I felt it as a young boy, as we made our way around council offices and job centres, often feeling like we were an imposition or somehow in the way, or failing some kind of obscure test that we didn't even realise we were taking. And I feel it now, as a Muslim man in a society that all too often asks people of my faith to apologise for the actions of suicide bombers and mass murderers, as if by sharing a religion we are all guilty by association. But if my family's immigrant experience was partly one of alienation and anxiety, it also co-existed with a feeling of belonging that – when we did experience it – was intoxicating.

In 1987, Diane Abbott, Keith Vaz, Bernie Grant and Paul Boateng broke huge barriers to become the first people of colour elected to the House of Commons. Paul Boateng, who is of Ghanaian and Scottish heritage, was our MP. Although I didn't know it when our paths crossed in the early 2000s, he was a lawyer by training and had a distinguished record fighting injustice and representing many left behind by the system. At that time, my family's immigration status was precarious, and we'd had little luck with our attempts to rally dodgy lawyers and a non-responsive Home Office to our cause. I was fifteen at the time, and, in a last-ditch attempt to get some help, I attended a constituency surgery in Harlesden library. This was long before it got its most recent revamp and, carrying a plastic bag full of papers, I sat patiently on the staircase waiting for my turn to be seen, not quite sure what to expect. At the surgery there were three tables, each with a pair of individuals, including one table where Paul Boateng sat alongside a member of staff. It was the luck of the draw if your turn came when his table was free, and, as it turned out, I didn't get to speak to him directly – but I did manage to catch his eye, and he returned an acknowledgement. It was a tiny moment, but one that mattered enormously to me: from that point on, a sense of place and of direction slowly became a reality, a sense that this representative – this man who looks like me – is here to help me, help us, towards belonging here; towards citizenship and proper roots in this country. His staff members promised me that he'd write a letter to the Home Office to get things speeded up; something that had a miraculous effect. I was supremely impressed with this: how could one letter have transformed our situation? I would later find out that this is actually quite common: a letter from an MP is often enough to push your case to the top of a Home Office official's in tray. But for us it was extraordinary, and I remember thinking that this power to transform lives is magical, and that the ability to make a difference to your own community in this tangible way was admirable.

This experience – along with a few others – instilled in me a growing sense of belief in where I was, what I could one day be in this society, and gave me the strength not to be disheartened, not to give up on life and what it may offer. It was impossible to be unaffected by some of our experiences, but, having arrived at a relatively young age, I was resilient, and the effects were not deep or long-lasting for me. For most of my older siblings the experience was different. Over the years, resentment, lack of hope, lack of self-belief and despair has taken its toll – sometimes in intensely destructive ways. Perhaps, looking back, I have the luxury of reviewing the past from a standpoint of having made a 'success of it'. But as I grew older, and learned to believe in my belonging, I came to see the setbacks and bigotry for what they were: pure ignorance based on warped views of the world and other people. From a young age I taught myself to recognise obstacles and prejudice, but to never allow the rot of bitterness to set in. Controlled rage about the status quo, yes. But rancour, never. I don't mean to suggest that this is easy, or for everyone: but I think it protected me. I grew up seeing others crushed by racism and deprivation, which scarred their souls and made these experiences the prism through which they saw themselves, the country, and society at large. It's tragic – but also understandable.

* * *

You may have noticed that I've been dancing around a subject that has a particularly vexed history in British society: integration. The idea of integration has been used as a stick to beat immigrants with for many decades. For Enoch Powell, integration meant 'to become for all practical purposes indistinguishable from other members' of your society, and it was the refusal of immigrant communities to do so that provoked him to use the doom-laden quote from the *Aeneid* that gave the speech its name:

immigrant communities can organise to consolidate their members, to agitate and campaign against their fellow citizens, and to overawe and dominate the rest with the legal weapons which the ignorant and the ill-informed have provided. As I look ahead, I am filled with foreboding; like the Roman, I seem to see 'the River Tiber foaming with much blood'.

And it is in Powell's sense of the word that integration pops up in contexts such as the 2017 UKIP manifesto, which advocated banning the niqab (the veil worn by some Muslim women to cover their face), 'because we believe that is a literal barrier to integration in our society'. Historically – and in the present day – 'integration' has all too often meant stripping immigrant communities of their culture, their religion and their identity in order to retain the supposedly pure and undiluted character of the culture that they are joining.

This context also makes it uncomfortable for me to say what I really think – which is that there's a strong link between social mobility and integration. Of course, I don't define integration in the sense of 'take-off-that-niqab-and-take-a-bite-of-this-bacon-sandwich'. For me, integration is more about the feeling one has towards society: being invested in it, willing to support the whole of that society, being prepared to sacrifice for it, having every right to criticise it, seeing yourself or people like you feature in every echelon, and seeing your children's future in the same place where you've grown up. I do not see this being incompatible with, for example, being Somali, Indian, Nigerian or Polish. It doesn't mean leaving behind those elements of your culture or religion that you feel to be important: at home I wear the Somali sarong, I used to argue in court while fasting for Ramadan, and I love

Somali comedy as much as anything on Netflix. But until you lay down some foundations and start to build, you're not going anywhere: and that means committing, on one level or another, to being British.

It would be dishonest of me to pretend that integration means that no compromises must be made with your original culture. The choice that younger Somalis have to make between speaking English as a first language and mastering the 'mother tongue' that would connect them to their families and heritage is one such example, but there are myriad others on the road to integration. It is worth remembering that becoming socially mobile in the UK often involves engaging with a society, a profession or a professional class that your parents may not necessarily approve of, or even understand. The chasm between the generations, together with the lack of understanding, means that an individual often feels, perhaps falsely, that they must choose between two incompatible ways of life, or must find the courage and confidence to reconcile their two worlds, something that is a real task and challenge for the young and inexperienced. Moving away for university, for example, is undoubtedly a big step for so many who might never have ventured far from their family. And so is attempting to build the foundations of a new life 'outside the community', rejecting proposals to work in family businesses, or pressures to marry or settle down, or evading other plans aimed at bringing individuals back into the fold after education. To turn away from all this, or even to turn away from nothing, often needs an enormous amount of courage, self-belief and determination.

But the rewards are clear. Integration, a wide range of social connections, and an openness to other ways of living are strongly associated with social mobility. A 2015 report from the Joseph Rowntree Foundation found that two of the key factors that reduced your likelihood of being poor were having a mixed ethnic friendship network, and having friends from outside your neighbourhood.[25] The decision to join a society and make a home there can be enormously freeing, removing an emotional weight that allows the individual to move forward and make progress. Dina Nayeri, though she has complicated feelings about it, writes movingly of the rush of emotional well-being that can come from accepting, and being accepted into, your new country:

> I became as American as a girl can be, moved far away, grew into my mind and body and surrounded myself with progressive, educated friends. The bad feelings disappeared. I started to love the western world and thought of myself a necessary part of it. I moved around with ease, safely flashing my American passport, smiling brightly when customs officers squinted at my place of birth. It didn't matter: I was no longer an asylum seeker.[26]

But, of course, the imperative to integrate cannot be something that sits solely on the shoulders of the immigrant. The rest of society has a duty to shape itself so that it is welcoming to those who wish to join in. It's difficult to ask people to integrate unless you can promise them opportunities: that if they work hard, they'll have a share of the riches of society, riches that are not preserved just for the few. They, and their children, should feel able to build lives in this country, with the same rights as those already here, and create futures for themselves that are free from the kind of molestation or eviction by the government that, for example, the Windrush generation, British citizens long since settled here, have been subjected to.

Because I'm involved with a number of organisations that aim to promote social mobility, I am often invited to speak about my life and journey at community centres or events. And fairly often, on some cold and dreary December evening, when I finish speaking and ask if anyone has any questions, perfectly normal young men and women ask if, following my success, I have been invited to a secret society. Initially I found it puzzling, but now I find it incredibly sad: the only explanation they can imagine for my success – a black Muslim man from a deprived background in modern Britain – is that I have pledged allegiance to some shadowy organisation. Conspiracy theories thrive among those who feel a lack of control over their own destiny: if you're able to blame an external force, there's at least something you can explain, point to, shout at. And as we've seen, immigrants and ethnic minorities often receive far from a fair chance in Britain today. The tension between older and younger generations, the hostile environment created by sections of the media, and, latterly, made explicit by the home office, enormous income inequality that sees half of the world's wealth in the hands of 1 per cent of its inhabitants,[27] and the fact that ethnic minorities are clearly blocked from elite professions and institutions have combined to create massive cultural and economic isolation in some parts of Britain, especially among the Muslim community. To many people, success is a certain path, reserved for certain people, and not accessible simply through talent and hard work. And conspiracy theories do not flourish in a vacuum; they are an expression of frustration, dashed hopes and dreams, and a climate of despair and pessimism.

* * *

Integration is necessarily a question of groups: of families, nationalities, religions, societies, cultures. But identity is a question of the individual, and, as we established at the beginning of the chapter, each of us is composed of a unique combination of different selves, and for social mobility to gain traction in your own life, you must first settle the important question of who you are. The sooner this is settled, if it can be truly settled at all, the better. And the sooner you can get on with getting on.

Afua Hirsch's book *Brit(ish)* is about identity and belonging, particularly in relation to the challenges faced by successive generations of immigrants. Hirsch was born in Norway, to a British father and Ghanaian mother, and brought up in relative wealth in Wimbledon. It was a life full of privilege, evidenced by a 'spacious house, a garden with fruit trees and swings, summer holidays walking in the Alps, a private education'. As an adult, she fell in love with a man named Sam, whose background both chimed with, and lay in stark contrast to, her own: 'He comes from Tottenham, one of the most diverse inner-city communities in Europe. Almost all of his peers have parents who are, like his Ghanaian family, first-generation immigrants from African or Caribbean countries.' Sam experienced the sorts of material deprivation growing up that Afua was insulated from by her family's wealth, but, unlike Afua, he was very sure of himself and his place in the world, something she envied. Describing herself as 'shocked' by the deprivation of his childhood, 'when it comes to identity, I tell him, he was born with the equivalent of a silver spoon'.[28]

Any social mobility journey will involve asking difficult questions, making difficult choices – and living with the results. Those results might pop up in surprising ways, and be expressed differently between different individuals: my experience is different to Afua's, which is different again to Sam's. Sam, she says, doesn't understand why she and her friends – graduates of Oxford and Cambridge with 'the best degrees' – are so unsure of themselves. But where they are rich in social and cultural capital, they feel adrift, never quite belonging anywhere. They feel like intruders in the white middle and upper classes, but their privilege alienates them from the kind of black communities that Sam comes from. Where Sam 'thinks in terms of generating wealth and opportunity, I think in terms of identity and belonging. Where he imagined gaining access to elite institutions like Oxford as a road map to making money, I lived it as a crisis of confidence.'[29] And this makes sense. While the first generation of immigrants – of which I am one – is often focused on survival and 'making it', the more established second generation, freed by the efforts of their parents from the effort of survival, have time to explore the experience they are having, and they often find it a jarring one. For when the moment arrives for the individual to step into the upper echelons of society, it can raise more questions than it answers. But while musings about belonging and identity *are* a luxury, one that is perhaps not available to someone worrying about where the next meal is coming from, neither can they be ignored. Ultimately, who you are, and where you fit in are not vague, self-indulgent questions: they are the first building blocks of the future you are building for yourself.

3

Painting the Room
Blue: Education

The roots of education are bitter, but the fruit is sweet.

Aristotle

I was fourteen when my head teacher was beaten almost unconscious in the school playground. One afternoon in 1997 at Wembley High School, the failing comprehensive I went to in North West London, my classmates and I were disturbed by a sudden commotion coming from outside. Students were running down the corridor outside, banging on each classroom door and shouting '*fight, fight, fight*'. There wasn't anything particularly unusual about this – it was a fact of life in a school where there was always a fight going on somewhere. Our teacher told us to ignore it, but we couldn't resist looking out of the window.

What we saw was – even for us – shocking. Mr Shaw, our head teacher, was being violently assaulted. One person bolted for the door, and before you knew it the sound of the teacher yelling 'sit back down' had been drowned out by the stampede that followed. The whole class rushed to the playground to see the action. By the time we made it, half the school was already there.

The playground area, now a state-of-the-art science block, was, back then, just open concrete. In the middle of it, Mr Shaw was politely asking a man to leave the premises. But each time he did, the man would punch him, or kick him to the ground like a rag doll. Mr Shaw never tried to fight back: he would regain his composure, get back up, and again politely ask the man to leave. It was probably his only option: Mr Shaw was a short and unassuming man, who always wore crumpled suits, which we often made fun of, but he was generally respected and ran the school the best he could. The man he was facing that day was almost twice his size, both in height and build. Later, we learned that the man had come to the school because his daughter had recently been permanently excluded.

The assault continued for a good fifteen minutes before any other staff members showed up. At one point, a student from the school handed the man a small umbrella, which he took and used to beat Mr Shaw over the head. By now, someone had called the police and the man began to walk towards the exit of the school, Mr Shaw still staggering behind him, urging him to leave. A police van pulled up as the assailant began walking away towards Vale Farm sports centre across the street.

The next morning there was an emergency assembly for the whole school. As we packed the hall, Mr Munro, the PE teacher, came out to speak. He talked about how brave Mr Shaw had been in order to protect all the children. Some parents had turned up, and members of staff were clearly still profoundly affected as they stood and listened. There was stunned silence and shock throughout. And then Mr Munro asked Mr Shaw to step out from behind the stage curtain to address the school. There he was, his wounds stitched up, but with cuts, bruises, barely opened eyes, and yes, wearing another crumpled suit. His shoulders were slumped and he seemed dazed.

After a few seconds, a smattering of laughter began

at the back. It became a chorus, and finally a roar that engulfed the whole hall. The small and battered man before us became even smaller, the teachers flanking him frozen with anger. I am ashamed to say that I recall laughing myself.

Mr Shaw never returned to Wembley High School. I don't know what became of him afterwards.

* * *

The failing state schools of inner-city London during the 1990s were wild places. Many schools, particularly those in Brent, where my family lived, were seriously underperforming and a shadow of what they are today. My cohort was unlucky, sandwiched as it was between a chronic lack of investment during the Thatcher era, and the unprecedented expenditure by the Blair and Brown governments, which began some time after they took office in 1997 (the Blair government stuck to Tory spending plans right up until around 2000). That the schools we attended were badly underfunded was something we were conscious of every day. When I talked to one of my former teachers during the course of my research, she recalled a building in such poor repair that at one point the ceiling of a classroom caved in. But crumbling infrastructure was only part of the problem: there was also a fundamental lack of stability when it came to both the teaching staff and the student body. Teacher turnover was high, there was little in the way of overarching authority, and as a result discipline was poor. The student body was drawn from deeply deprived communities that had their own problems, problems that didn't disappear once those children walked through the doors of the school. They weren't always the same doors, anyway: Brent Council regularly moved families in social housing around the borough, taking them in and out of the catchment areas for the schools. Fights and misbehaviour, often leading to suspensions and exclusions, were common. And there was not much inspiration available. We were rarely properly tested, encouraged or pushed, and the poverty of ambition was palpable among pupils and many of the poorly motivated, over-stretched staff. The level of disruption was such that at one point we had a resident police officer, in theory to teach us about law and order, but in practice more often a first responder. In short: we were a failing school, the school was failing us, and society was failing the school *and* us.

Schools in London are indeed very different places today, though they still deal with many of the same problems as they did during my own schooldays: poverty, disadvantage and prejudice are every bit as much a part of our society as they ever were. So is violence: a 2019 survey by NASUWT, a teacher's union, found that nearly a quarter of teachers had experienced some form of physical abuse from a pupil *each week.*[1] The fact that schools tend to reflect the problems of the communities they serve complicates the often optimistic predictions of politicians and policymakers for whom education is the 'great leveller', a magical resource that – if only access could be evened out – would raise up the talented poor to flourish alongside their better-off peers. Tony Blair famously set out the top priority of New Labour as 'education, education, education', in order to raise 'the ambitions of all our young people'[2] and the myth that education holds the key to social mobility is one that successive governments have clung too as well. But it's as much a part of our own mindsets as those of our leaders. As social mobility has stagnated, there has been a sharp increase in anxiety over education: in 2017, education was rated ahead of immigration and housing as a source of concern in polls, only outdone by terrorism, the NHS and Brexit.[3] Many parents are desperate that their children don't fall behind or miss out on opportunities – and the pressure is often either transferred to teachers and schools, or channelled (by those who have the financial resources) into tutoring, summer camps and other methods of nudging children to the front of the pack.

And it's impossible to deny that to some extent the anxiety is well justified: education does open doors. In 2015, the Social Mobility and Child Poverty Commission found that 'if the head of a British household holds A-Level qualifications, they are 20 per cent more likely to exit poverty and 25 per cent less likely to re-enter it'. Likewise, it would be ridiculous not to acknowledge that almost all elite professions require a (good) degree, which means staying in school and getting (good) A Levels. And even if you don't want to be a doctor or advertising executive, almost all jobs will require at least a C grade in maths and English at GCSE (something that in 2017 half of all students in England failed to achieve).[4] Of course, education can also be transformative in itself. In the American academic Tara Westover's bestselling memoir *Educated*, she reveals how her discovery of education allowed her to leave her complicated and dangerous family circumstances in order to forge an independent life, eventually ending up as an academic at the University of Cambridge, 'a changed person, a new self'. 'You could call this selfhood many things,' she says at the end of the book, 'Transformation. Metamorphosis. Falsity. Betrayal.' But, she continues, 'I call it an education'.[5] We eat up stories of poor children who made good through hard work and brains: when Brampton Manor, a state school in South London, announced that forty-one of its pupils had secured places at Oxford and Cambridge, it made headlines across the country. Many of the pupils were from extremely deprived backgrounds – the care system, refugees, struggling single-parent families – and they frequently identified their Oxbridge offers as a transitional moment not just for them but for their families as well.[6] We're drawn to these stories because they offer both a satisfying moral curve – effort and worth rewarded – and a sense of drama, of rags to riches.

But do these stories hold any more meaning for the ordinary British schoolchild than, for example, Cinderella or Dick Whittington? From one perspective, yes: in the last twenty years, there has been some encouraging progress. Between 2002 and 2011, the achievement gaps for the richest and poorest 20 per cent at GCSE level narrowed by 13 per cent (to 18 per cent), with London schools in particular seeing rapid improvement since the 1990s.[7] Between 2004 and 2009 the university attainment gap between the most and least deprived also narrowed by 3 per cent (to 37 per cent).[8] There are nearly twice as many people aged eighteen to twenty-four in full-time tertiary education as there were when my family arrived in the UK in 1992.[9] But these relative improvements throw into relief the huge gulf that continues to exist – and which persists far beyond university admissions. For a start, while stories about education and social mobility often focus on admission to university – and especially to Oxbridge – a more significant factor is the way in which *not* being educated abruptly curtails any chance of improving your circumstances. According to the OECD, young people in Britain are the 'most illiterate in the developed world',[10] and the number of children leaving school without basic numeracy and literacy is rising, rather than falling.[11] Lacking these basic skills affects your life in almost every way: your employment opportunities, your ability to claim your legal rights or manage your interactions with institutions and government bodies, your mental and physical health, the likelihood of being on benefits or in prison.[12] I experienced the effects of illiteracy first hand, as I saw my older relatives exploited, and struggle to get even the most basic tasks done, at sea in a society in which being poor requires endless forms, letters and paperwork.

In fact, knowing the background against which stories like Brampton Manor's unfold does lend them a slightly magical air, their achievements thrown into relief by the weight of the statistical probabilities behind them. As we have seen, children from disadvantaged backgrounds start school already behind their well-off peers, and they also make less progress while they are there, with the result that lower-ability but better-off children overtake their brighter but poorer schoolmates in early childhood.[13] A further widening of this gap occurs in secondary school, where only 36.7 per cent of disadvantaged children achieve five good GCSEs (including English and maths), compared with 64.7 per cent of other pupils.[14] Signs of progress are often illusory: for instance, compared to ten years ago, 90 per cent more nineteen-year-olds from the most deprived areas hold 'Level 3 qualifications', equivalent to an A or AS Level. But these are almost entirely non-A Level qualifications – apprenticeships, NVQs, and so on – which do not offer the same access to top universities.[15] Only 2.2 per cent of the most deprived children achieve the A Levels that the top universities demand, almost ten times fewer than the least deprived children (20.6 per cent).[16] Perhaps most notably of all, these discrepancies both cut across ability levels and have significant impacts in later life: less able pupils from wealthy families are 35 per cent more likely to be high earners as adults than are high-ability children from low-income families.[17]

In fact, one of the most remarkable things about social

mobility and education is the intractable nature of this attainment gap, the final nail in the coffin of the 'great leveller'. As previously mentioned, a cruel paradox is at work: although not being educated curtails your chance of social mobility, being educated doesn't guarantee it either. Even when young people do everything that is asked of them – stay in school, get good A Levels, beat the odds to get into a Russell Group university – they *still* lag behind better-off fellow students and are nearly 25 per cent less likely to get a 2:1 or a first. Even if their time at university is stunningly successful, it won't necessarily translate into the same benefits that students from privileged backgrounds enjoy: in *The Class Ceiling*, Friedman and Laurison note that even between graduates of the same university, with the same degree, there is a 'class pay gap', and graduates from well-off backgrounds but unimpressive degrees still did better professionally than working-class graduates with firsts.[18] Clearly, education cannot bear the weight of expectation that is placed on it.

* * *

To explain our reaction to the appearance of the bruised and traumatised Mr Shaw at assembly, I should explain what life in Brent was like in the 1990s for me and for many of my friends. To see our head teacher badly beaten was only shocking because it happened *inside* the school grounds: violence and sometimes death were common occurrences in our borough at the time, and many of us were living in extreme deprivation and in dangerous, unpredictable environments. In Brent, Stonebridge and Harlesden, and especially the infamous St Raphael's Estate close to where my family was living, major fights were commonplace. Although it was then a very different place to the Brent of today, where I still live – just a short bus ride away from what is now Wembley High Technology College – it's debatable whether things have truly improved. Drug dealing and gang violence were certainly ever present, and always an easy route to take, but, unlike today, there was not active recruitment: you could stay out of things. (This is no longer the case, and in March 2019 it was reported that Somali mothers were sending their children back to Somalia in order to protect them from grooming and abuse by 'county lines' drug gangs.)[19]

In any case, back then, there was no such thing as stability. You rarely felt like you had a future to look forward to: you took each day as it came and tried not to be too surprised. Our aspirations were limited to the two professions in which we saw young black men making money: football and drug dealing. The violence and poverty that formed the backdrop to my school years is just one example of the sort of baggage that children from poor backgrounds carry when they arrive at school, and that schools are woefully ill-equipped to compensate for. Although, since our arrival in the early nineties, the total number of children living in poverty has fluctuated – declining in the second half of the decade and the early noughties, and then undergoing a number of years of stagnation[20] – it is now on the rise again. Regardless of the relative level, the fact that children live like this at all is a shameful situation in an absurdly rich and well-resourced society. But, if you look at the way that schooling is structured in the UK, you would be forgiven for thinking that there is nothing troubling going on; at the very least, the situation in which the poorest children in our society find themselves appears to be invisible to the policymakers who decide how state schools operate.

Take the assumptions upon which our education system is based. It is presumed that each child who turns up to school will have had a good night's sleep, something to eat for breakfast, and at least one parent who will be paying attention to their progress at school. The child will spend most of the day at school able to concentrate and not pre-occupied by anxiety, and the school will be a nurturing environment, rather than a dangerous and stressful one. The child will then go home, where a nutritious dinner awaits, along with a parent or carer who will make sure that homework is done, helping if necessary, and enforce an appropriate bedtime in a quiet, peaceful room. It assumes that the child won't need to cook dinner for themselves or siblings, or help care for a parent or relative. It assumes that between the end of school that day and the next morning, the child's parents or caregivers won't be too exhausted or overwhelmed to spend some time with the child, or to have a conversation at the dinner table about their day, and that they will understand and be aligned to the school's aims. It assumes that each child feels like they matter, and that they're reminded of this every day.

Even the simplest assumption – that the child has access to a decent food supply – is often wrong. In 2018, heads of schools across the country complained of children arriv-ing at school with 'grey skin, poor teeth, poor hair and ... thinner'. Hunger was particularly acute over the weekend; according to one head teacher, at his school 'children are filling their pockets with food. In some establishments that would be called stealing. We call it survival.'[21] It is an even worse problem over the school holidays, when parents who are already struggling have to find another meal a day. It is no wonder that parents with problems like these weren't able to support their children's education outside of school: at the same time, teachers also described children arriv-ing into the education system unable to hold a pencil, sit quietly or even ask a coherent question.[22] The Department of Education's objective continues to be to create a country where everyone can still work towards 'going as far as their talents will take them'. But no one's talents will take them very far on a Monday morning, when they haven't had a proper meal since Friday lunchtime.

Or take summer holidays. For well-off children, they're the best bit of the year. For poor families, though, they are often a long drawn-out catastrophe. Where privileged children can look forward to a holiday (or two), visits to museums, zoos and galleries, summer camps or schools that cater to their abilities and interests, for disadvantaged children, the summer holidays often represent a vast swathe of nothing to do at all. For my siblings and me, the holidays were a long period of structureless boredom and idleness, with few options other than playing football or video games. The situation is hardly improved by the closures of youth facilities and libraries – since 2010, a staggering 478 libraries have closed in England, Scotland and Wales.[23] It's unsurprising, therefore, that during the school holidays, students from low-income backgrounds experience what is sometimes called the 'summer learning loss'.[24] In other words, while middle-class pupils continue to make modest gains during the summer, their less advantaged contemporaries experience a decline in reading skills, starting the new school year even further behind.

There is no end to the underlying assumptions of the British education system. That at exam times, children will be given the space, the time and the peace to prepare themselves, that whatever extra assistance required is provided at home. That children will be able to control their emotions, and will have been taught appropriate ways to behave in class. That parents will themselves be in a position to help with school work – possibly even with tutoring, if their children are struggling. That there won't be profound misunderstandings about the nature of the relationship between school and carers: the older adults in my family, accustomed to a more African, it-takes-a-village style of parenting, where lines between school and home are clearly demarcated, would have been astonished to discover that the school expected them to help with educating us.

All of these things need to be in place in order to be a true beneficiary of our education system. Some poor families and parents may be able to meet some or most of it, but most will not, as was the case with my family. Many more, especially in deprived communities, are unlikely to meet any of this description, which, for them, is secondary to daily survival. To that end, we need to find a way of redefining how our teachers teach, how our school systems are structured, and the relationship between parents and schools: they cannot work only for those who are already best placed to benefit from them.[25] What is shocking is how, before we can even start to work towards this, we are still lacking even in the most basic requirements. The children who are being failed by this system deserve better, whatever the circumstances. No one should be given up on. Living and growing up in poverty is not a choice. A human being does not set out into the world to live a humiliating life: often children who are stigmatised and excluded are doing the best they can with the cards that life dealt them by an accident of birth.

* * *

What this tells us is that, far from offering a way out of disadvantage, education in the UK has mainly worked to reinforce already existing inequalities, causing social mobility to stagnate, or even get worse. In other words, education does not happen in a vacuum, and billions of pounds poured into the education system to improve the chances of poorer children have not offset the inequalities in our society at large. But that isn't all. Not only are poorer children held back by their circumstances, but parents with greater resources will always be able to make sure their children retain a competitive edge.[26] Just as disadvantaged students are held back by hunger, stress and tiredness, and by a general disruption in their lives, advantaged students will always be able to boost their attainment through comfort, support and access to resources, including private tutoring and extracurricular activities.[27] Whatever the child's potential, in the end it is almost always possible to maximise achievement via money and resources (and, of course, sharp elbows).

In Chapter 1, we looked at how middle- and upper-class children have been groomed from an early age to thrive in institutions, have large vocabularies, articulate their needs clearly, and have positive impressions of authority figures. And the corollary is also true: although children living in poverty may not fully grasp the larger social currents that shape their circumstances, the evidence suggests that they are very aware, from an early age, of their social position and the limitations it places on them.[28] While middle-class children arrive at school having been prepared for it, and perhaps familiar with the activities they will be doing there, for children from low-income backgrounds, school can be an alienating and intimidating environment: somewhere they don't feel in control and are required to perform tasks in which they lack confidence.[29] Although middle-class parents help their children in practical ways – providing a quiet place to do homework, for instance – they also shape their attitude towards school, getting them off on the right foot. A 2005 study by the sociologist Val Gillies identified differences between middle-class parents, who tended to put forward the idea that their child was bright, exceptional and worthy of special treatment, and working-class parents, whose 'hopes that their child would shine at school had been revised by an early reality of poor marks and conflict with teachers' leading to them prioritising 'a basic education, [staying] out of trouble and [surviving] the psychological injuries of school failure'.[30] The problem is a lack of faith in the school as an institution. Similarly, studies have found that children from low-income backgrounds did not have a negative attitude towards learning but rather a lack of confidence in their own ability to thrive within the system, something that is reinforced by the bad experiences they do have.[31]

And this way of thinking is to some extent justified: if working-class children arrive at school unprepared for their new context, and potentially suspicious and uncomfortable of the whole set-up (which, as we have seen, is not really constructed with their needs in mind), then there is plenty of evidence that they are also treated more harshly while they are there. For example, when surveyed, low-income pupils complained that they were often harshly disciplined by teachers, something that wasn't mentioned by better-off students. These findings were mirrored in another study, which found that 'children from high-income backgrounds described a much richer set of experiences in school, inside and outside the curriculum, while the experience of their disadvantaged counterparts were more likely to feature things like discipline and detention'.[32] There's also some evidence that a kind of structural prejudice is at play. A 2015 study found that teachers were more likely to underestimate intelligence in disadvantaged children, and many children felt that the school did not allow them to forge strong relationships with adults in authority.[33] While middle-class parents are able to position their child's academic struggles as the result of dyslexia or a learning difficulty, and may be able to pay to see a private educational psychiatrist, poorer parents are likely to see their child labelled as 'disruptive' or 'behaviourally challenged' and are dependent on the vagaries of social services and the health system for diagnosis and treatment.[34]

Ultimately, and unsurprisingly, the end result of all this is that poor children are vastly more likely to be permanently excluded from school. Using free school meals as a measure of disadvantage, we can see that poor children were three times more likely to be excluded than children who didn't qualify.[35] Looking at the numbers, it's easy to see who's at risk: the overwhelming majority (78 per cent) of permanent exclusions are boys, and they were more likely to be excluded at a younger age than girls. A special educational need also puts you at risk: to be precise, it makes you *eight times* more likely to be permanently excluded from school. Ethnic minorities are more likely to be expelled than white children: Gypsy, Roma and Traveller children have the highest rates of exclusion, with black Caribbean pupils being the next in line.[36] As children get older, matters tend to get worse. By the time they are fourteen – right before their GCSEs – children on free school meals are four times more likely to be permanently excluded.[37] But looking at these 'risk factors' separately is misleading. It's only when we put them all together that we can see that, as one researcher calculated, 'A black Caribbean boy eligible for free school meals who also has special educational needs (SEN) is 168 times more likely to be permanently excluded than a white British girl without SEN and not eligible for FSM.'[38] This is what the statistics and studies tell us. But I know what it's like on the inside, because I've lived it. I was angry and out of control.

I fought, disrespected and disrupted the lives of my teachers and classmates until I was offered a very simple choice – find a new school, or get expelled anyway.

* * *

In the summer of 1995, when I had been in Britain for nearly two years, the band Pulp released 'Common People'. Written by Jarvis Cocker, the song satirises privileged people who 'want to live like common people./ ... want to do whatever common people do.' But, as Cocker understands, if you're not actually poor, if you always have the safety net that wealth or class confer, 'You will never understand/ How it feels to live your life/ With no meaning or control.' It's a song that always feels poignant to me: that summer was the first time I properly understood that something was wrong with my life as it was, that I was one of Cocker's Common People, with little control over how things turned out for me. I was eleven.

Ms Walden was the first primary-school teacher whose class I attended for more than a couple of months after arriving in the UK in June 1993, without either of my parents. In April I had helped to bury my father in Kariako, a suburb in Eastern Nairobi. Somalis are nomadic people, so the instability and constant movement wasn't unfamiliar, but this new and foreign land remained baffling. Ms Walden, with her soft voice and woolly jumpers, gave me a much-needed sense of normality. During the winter, my first experience of this strange new season, my lips had split from the cold, and she would apply Vaseline from a pot she kept in her desk drawer.

Ms Walden's class was full of young children whose parents had little or modest means. She had devised an ingenious system whereby everyone, including those who would otherwise struggle to pay, brought in £2 a week from the start of the school year for the end of year day-trip to France. Importantly, therefore, no one could tell whether your family found it hard to afford. By the time the summer came, you had thus raised a little over £50, the base cost per child. (You were expected to bring your own lunch and snacks – which was the moment when the difference in family income would immediately become obvious.)

I was desperate to go, and made sure that every little bit I had went towards this trip. Ms Walden had encouraged me throughout the term, but that afternoon, when she'd said 'don't forget to bring in your passport' she had seen the look of puzzlement on my face and had realised that I wouldn't be coming after all. She left the room, and I imagined her finding my passport somewhere. But when she came back she was in tears, and I walked home with a deep sense of bewilderment and anger. Anger that everything I was working towards that whole year had been lost. And bewilderment because I didn't fully understand why (poor Ms Walden hadn't really managed to explain it). I didn't speak to anyone at home or school about this incident, and a part of me was relieved that primary school ended there and that I would not have to face my classmates the following year.

It was the first time I realised what it meant to be a refugee: stateless, without a passport, without an identity, unable to move freely, in limbo and without any value. It would set the tone for the rest of my life, and, as a young man, I would focus all my energy on making sure that never again would I lack control over my own life, becoming self-sufficient to the point of selfishness. At the time we were still going through the asylum process: for years we were marooned, and, although we lived side by side with ordinary British people, we were clearly very different. But waiting for our asylum status to be resolved, I realised that day, was no neutral state of being. It was debilitating, disempowering, even if that young boy lacked the vocabulary or the precise terms with which to articulate these feelings. I had invested so much in the school trip, in being like my schoolmates, never suspecting that it was pointless. To not have a parent, or an adult, or anyone to speak to about it, also brought home a profound loneliness.

The effect of all this anger, fear, confusion, helplessness, and, what I thought of then as betrayal, made itself felt the following year. Sick of feeling like I had no ownership over my life, I became out of control myself, and angry at everyone and everything all the time. I wasn't interested in school or spending time doing anything worthwhile. It seemed supremely pointless: you go to school and it's chaos, no one is paying attention, the teacher is just shouting – and at home it's also chaos, and no one is paying any attention to *you*. In the first year of secondary school, I was highly disruptive in the classroom – when I bothered to turn up. I argued with the other kids, got involved in physical altercations, played truant and talked back. It never ended – as it sometimes did for my classmates – with the police being called, but it was serious enough for me to be suspended half a dozen times over the course of nine months. At the end of that year, my head of year made it clear that if I didn't leave of my own accord, I would be expelled on return. So I made an application to Wembley High, at the time the second-worst school in the borough. It just so happened that most of my siblings and cousins were there: because we'd been moved again during the school application process, my siblings and I had ended up at different schools. At least, I thought, if nothing else, I could be with people who understood what it was like to be me.

I was badly behaved, aggressive and not interested in taking up the opportunities offered to me. I disrupted the education of other children, preventing them from taking up opportunities themselves. But there were reasons for my behaviour: I was grieving, confused, alienated and very, very lonely. I didn't have a future – and neither had I come to terms with my past. Young black boys are still being excluded from British schools, for reasons that are nominally to do with behaviour but are, in reality, more to do with childhood poverty and, arguably, an implicit racial bias in which black students are not perceived to have the same potential as their classmates. But it's also to do with the state of the education system, a zero-sum, results-at-any-cost system, which forces schools to prioritise league tables at the expense of the children they are supposed to serve. In some state schools, this has resulted in a shameful practice, sanctioned right at the top, of selection by exclusion. If you wondered why exclusions among poor pupils spike before GCSEs, then this may well be your answer. Black boys – who are statistically more likely to underachieve at school – are victims of this in particular. Usually, something relatively minor is blown out of proportion, in order to build a spurious case against a child so as to exclude them. Conversely, children who are appallingly behaved but gifted will be kept around because it's thought that they'll go on to do well in exams, and – regardless of the effect on the other pupils – that's ultimately perfect for the statistics. This is happening in many state schools across England.[39]

Exclusions matter in the context of social mobility because, as you might suspect, they disrupt children's schooling. I was perversely lucky in that, once I got to Wembley High, my own bad behaviour was dwarfed by that of my new classmates, to the point that I no longer registered as particularly disruptive. But for many others, exclusion set them on the path to an early exit from education, woefully unprepared for the outside world. In many ways, social mobility is about delayed gratification: transforming your life means hard graft, sacrifice, and waiting what could be years for everything to pay off. Young boys, and, increasingly, girls, who are excluded from school are pushed out of an institution that could help them make sense of their lives, and are likely to find that meaning instead on the streets: in dealing drugs, in gangs that provide them with an identity and status – and in the instant gratification of making transformative amounts of money. Gang members are five times more likely to have been excluded from school; and are almost twice as likely to have some sort of emotional, social or mental health problem.[40] Social mobility is primarily a matter of fulfilment and opportunities, but it is occasionally also a matter of life and death: as the epidemic of knife and gun crime among young people continues, the same event that deprives them of the opportunity to better their lives also puts them at risk of losing it altogether.

* * *

But to talk about failing state schools and the exclusions of poor black boys from mainstream education is to address only half of the question. There are around 2,600 private schools in the UK, educating 625,000 children, or around 6.5 per cent of the total school-age population (7 per cent in England).[41] If this seems like a relatively minor proportion of school leavers, then consider what those children go on to do: they form 74 per cent of high court judges, 71 per cent of senior military officers, 51 per cent of solicitors and journalists, 61 per cent of senior doctors,[42] and 29 per cent of MPs.[43] In the creative industries things are no different: 67 per cent of British Oscar winners were privately educated, as were 42 per cent of BAFTA winners, and a (relatively egalitarian) 19 per cent of Brit Award winners. When the newly appointed prime minister Boris Johnson appointed a new cabinet in July 2019, it was announced as the 'most diverse in history'. Not in educational background: 67 per cent of its members were privately educated, and 37 per cent had attended private school *and* Oxbridge.[44] But while we're familiar with these statistics, we seem unable to really respond to them: something about them prevents us from addressing the astonishing, paralysing unfairness of the society they represent. As Alan Bennett put it:

> If, unlike the *Daily Mail*, one believes that the nation is still generous, magnanimous and above all fair it is hard not to think that we all know that to educate not according to ability but according to the social situation of the parents is both wrong and a waste. Private education is not fair. Those who provide it know it. Those who pay for it know it. Those who sacrifice in order to purchase it know it. And those who receive it know it, or should. And if their education ends without it dawning on them then that education has been a waste.[45]

'Private school', of course, covers a wide spectrum, from small religious schools to world-famous, centuries-old institutions like Eton College. But whatever the format, there's no denying that going to a private school gives you a major hand up. This is why education is such a white-hot subject in the UK: the historic sense of pride in a public school tie has in many sectors of society given way to squirming embarrassment at the privilege it reveals.

Parents argue and agonise over this; sometimes they even divorce over it, like the Labour leader Jeremy Corbyn and his second wife Claudia Bracchitta, who were rumoured to have split over her decision to send their son to a selective grammar school rather than the local comprehensive. But the benefits of private education – the magical extra something that they provide for their pupils – are not necessarily what you would expect.

For a start, it's almost never about the results. Whether private schools get better results for their pupils is arguable: although they undoubtedly produce better results at both GCSE and A Level, the exam results gap between private and state schools has narrowed significantly in the last decade.[46] It's also worth considering whether those children would have done well anyway: many private schools are highly selective academically and parents who send their children to private school are likely both to be pro-education in general and to vigorously support their children's learning outside school. Meanwhile, some state schools are producing the best results in the country,[47] while some famously academic independent schools – like Eton – are lagging well behind state schools, particularly in science and maths.[48] So why do parents shell out the astronomical sums that private education costs? Dulwich College, the alma mater of anti-elitist people's champion, Nigel Farage, is the most expensive school in Britain, setting you back £42,681 for full boarding – and that's just for one child. (The median pre-tax salary in the UK is £28,600.) The economic capital held by these parents allows them to unlock two further forms of capital, both of which are crucial to social mobility: social capital and cultural capital. In essence, social capital is connections, friendships, and networks, while cultural capital is knowledge, behaviour and skills. For example, if you're a young person who wants to get into the film industry – a notoriously difficult profession to penetrate – social capital is having a godparent who can get you some work experience as a runner on a film set. Cultural capital is what tells you how to behave when you get there: what to wear, how to speak, the sort of rich background knowledge that allows you to drop a reference to Fellini or *Citizen Kane* into conversation with someone you need to impress.

Private schools offer social and cultural capital in spades: in this case, it's both what you know *and* who you know. Private schools offer a chance to mix, bond with and learn from other privileged children, as well as the opportunity to absorb the culture of the most well-off and powerful members of society. If you're already well-off, highly educated and privileged, then your children will spend their education mixing with the children of other people like you. And if you're not, then if you can scrape the money together, you can give your children the opportunity to spend time in a different social milieu – and come out with the kinds of contacts and confidence that will smooth their future path much more than a handful of A*s at A Level.

The result of all this social and cultural capital is another thing that parents are paying for: whether you call it 'polish', 'public school charm' or any of a number of other euphemisms, its essence is *confidence*. Confidence is something that comes up again and again in relation to social mobility, so much so that it gets its own chapter later on in this book, but it is worth discussing here in direct relation to education. It's the confidence to know you belong: to ace a job interview, ask for a pay rise, to walk up to someone important at a party and make the right impression. It's the deep-down sense that you matter: the opposite of the feeling that I had as a young, angry, lonely refugee. My schools were crumbling concrete buildings built in the seventies and already falling apart from neglect: they could have been any crap comprehensive, in any forgotten part of the country. By contrast, the children who attend the country's public schools step into a grand history on their first day of school. Their new home is often a historic place, hundreds of years old, and set in beautiful buildings and grounds that echo the sorts of institutions that their alumni will go on to inhabit: the quads of Oxford and Cambridge, the Inns of Court, Parliament. They will eat and work surrounded by traces of former students who did great and wonderful things: Eton, for instance, has educated nineteen British prime ministers – and the prime minister of Thailand as well. They will have access to extraordinary facilities – sports pitches, concert halls, art and design studios, state-of-the-art computers – and opportunities to try out drama, music, debating and many other extra-curricular activities. If a talent is there, the school will find it and squeeze out every last drop: children who aren't 'naturally academic' are able to find other things at which they excel, which is perhaps part of the reason that, in recent years, the privately educated have appeared to be over-represented within the acting profession. And, of course, it's an environment optimised for the kind of learning that education policy assumes all children are capable of: in the case of boarding children, all their waking hours are carefully structured, including the 'black hole' period between 5 p.m. and 8 p.m., and their homework is carefully supervised. There is the space, the time, the resources and the environment, as well as ample opportunity, for whatever you're good at to be discovered. And there is no risk of being consigned to the dustbin of wasted talent once you've been made to believe, or convinced yourself, that you're not 'academic' or good at anything.

Given all this, it's not surprising that parents will

bankrupt themselves to get their child access to such places. Private school, after all, is an excellent investment: according to the analysis of sociologists Lee Elliot Major and Stephen Machin, privately educated professionals are paid around 41 per cent more than their state-educated but similarly qualified colleagues.[49] Yet again we come up against the bald fact that increased social mobility directly conflicts with the desires of parents to get the best possible outcome for their own children. And neither are these parents necessarily pearl-clutching snobs nor dead-eyed social climbers: I am grateful to many of those I have spoken to who have been candid about why they have made their decision. They included an Asian taxi driver from Birmingham and a white working-class postman, both breaking their backs to get their children the best start in life – which wasn't the local comprehensive. It is somehow both hugely admirable but incredibly sad. If you don't have children (like me) it is easy to be sanctimonious about private schools. But to see parents who send their children to private school simply as selfish people who don't want to play their part is to refuse to see the whole picture: holding back your own child (as you may well believe you would be doing) for the greater good is a lot to ask of anybody, and the answers lie with the larger societal structures, not the decisions of individuals. The problem, as the philosopher Kwame Anthony Appiah points out, is not that there is anything 'wrong with cherishing your children'. But when we live in a world in which parents have access to vastly unequal resources, we must confront the fact that this instinct, however natural and understandable, cannot reign unchecked without harming others.[50] With private schooling we have created – and maintained – a system that allows parents to purchase success for their children; we can hardly be horrified that they take it up.

So what's the answer? Close down all the private schools? Force Emilia and Rory down to the local comp to share their social capital with children like me and my siblings? It's a solution that many would find tempting, but hardly a practical one – if only for the fact that the relationship between the establishment and private schools is such that it would involve many of the people in charge of education policy shutting down their own alma maters. To my mind, the answer is to concentrate on raising the standards of state schools to the point where they become the obvious choice. It is not about changing the minds of the small minority of parents who can't contemplate their children attending anywhere but Eton or St Pauls, but wooing the majority of parents who choose private education because they can't bear the thought of their child losing out. It's an argument that is ripe for winning, especially as in many places in the UK parents are now having to make a choice between buying a house or affording school fees. Today, more than ever, there is a real opportunity to reach a tipping point: universities are now attaching a particular premium on the results of children who have attained excellent results in dire or difficult circumstances, and they are under increasing pressure to address the imbalance in private and state school intake. I strongly believe that in the not so distant future we can steer a significant majority of parents towards the state sector – if it is capable of meeting their requirements.

But to get there we need to invest in our school system like never before, and to plan for a future that's very different from our own school days. At the moment, this is far from happening. Despite the claims of the government to the contrary, there have been profound and biting cuts to education in the last ten years – equivalent to an 8 per cent effective decrease in school budgets,[51] and even more in sixth form education – that have left a demoralised and disintegrating education system in place. Hardly a day goes past without a news story of dedicated teachers abandoning ship due to stress, teachers having to buy their own supplies out of their wages, schools in such poor repair that they use buckets to catch leaks, and funding deficits so severe that schools are closing early because they can't afford to stay open. One mother, the MP Jess Phillips, was provoked into starting a crowdfunded protest that would deliver the children to 10 Downing Street instead, so that 'if they will not [educate our children] in our local schools they can do it in their offices'.[52]

We must ensure that teachers aren't forced from the education system through stress and overwork, creating a vicious cycle leading to larger class sizes and greater disruption,[53] and that black and ethnic minority teachers join the profession in greater numbers – and stay.[54] As was the case in the 1990s when I was growing up in London, schools in the capital are struggling to fill teacher vacancies: 'over half of London school leaders report that they face a shortage of teachers',[55] and the teacher turnover rates in London primary schools 'represent the greatest increases in the country in recent years'.[56] This is especially alarming because London's schools are facing unprecedented demand: by 2025, 737,000 primary-school children and 498,000 secondary-school children will need state school places.

It's a case of 'if we build it, they will come'. If we can raise the standard of the entire state sector, parents who otherwise remove themselves from the picture – along with their social and cultural capital – will reinvest in their locality, get involved in the local schools by being governors, and help to raise the standards and hold teachers to account. And, as is happening in many corners of London, we can get to a place where schools are genuinely socially diverse, diminishing the power of private-school social networks to dominate the social mobility story. Individually, parents may not think that they can affect enough change to transform their local state schools, but together they have more power than they realise.

* * *

It is, however, essential to recognise the fact that many of the best schools in the country are in fact state and grammar schools: so much so that even the super-snobbish society magazine *Tatler* publishes a list of the best state schools ('World-beating education that doesn't cost the earth').[57] While I was writing this book I was taken to task by a friend, from a privileged background, who pointed out that there are plenty of smart state schools whose alumni are just as, if not more, confident than the glossiest of public-school children. But the existence of these excellent state schools doesn't necessarily translate to availability for poor and underprivileged children: buying – or renting – a property in the catchment area of a brilliant school can be a sensible investment for parents who otherwise would be sending their children private. This has a knock-on effect on the local area, driving property prices up by as much as £26,000, and forcing less privileged families out of the locale and down the waiting list, perhaps to travel miles to a much worse school.[58] It's a strange negative image of my own school days, in which we were shunted from catchment area to catchment area, constantly in the process of moving school, and always to our disadvantage.

The flexing of economic muscle in the catchment areas of desirable schools is only one manifestation of the unpromising picture of a divided nation that you find when exploring the connection between social mobility and education. And the sign of this divide is not economic or social, as is often presented, it is geographical. It is no secret that – as the social mobility index reveals[59]– there is a growing gulf between booming London and the well-off South East and the rest of the country.[60] So it's not surprising to learn that, in the same way that the socio-economic status of your parents influences your future prospects, the place of your birth can also have a significant impact. In fact, geography may compound an accident of birth – *where* you're born is therefore just as important as to whom you're born. A disadvantaged child born in a social mobility 'hotspot' like Kensington and Chelsea – somewhere that offers opportunities and is thus conducive to social mobility – will perform over three times better in primary school than the same child born to a struggling family in a 'cold spot' like Arun on the West Sussex coast.[61] However, this divide doesn't run purely along north/south lines: in 2017, the worst social mobility cold spots were (in order): West Somerset (South West), Newark and Sherwood (East Midlands), Weymouth and Portland (South West), Corby (East Midlands) and Carlisle (North West). Cold spots, it would seem, are concentrated in remote rural and coastal areas such as Devon, as well as in former industrial areas, most notably in the Midlands.[62] The best performing areas, by contrast, were all in London: Westminster, Kensington and Chelsea, Tower Hamlets, Wandsworth and Hackney.

The cold-spot effect starts early, and has a significant impact on education. Highly deprived coastal and rural areas have one and a half times the proportion of unqualified secondary teachers than do inland rural areas with low levels of deprivation (7 per cent compared with 4.6 per cent).[63] As in London, the problem of teacher retention in underperforming schools – something that I had personal, painful experience of – is particularly acute in cold spots:

a secondary-school teacher in the most deprived area is 70 per cent more likely to leave compared to one in a more affluent area.[64] Perhaps as a result, only around 14 per cent of children from cold spots go to university, compared to 27 per cent in hotspots.[65]

Once out of school, young people growing up in cold spots have few prospects: as the Social Mobility Commission put it, 'these rural and coastal areas combine low educational outcomes with weak labour markets that have a greater share of low-skilled, low-paid employment than anywhere else in England'. Only a quarter of cold-spot residents have managerial and professional jobs, although over a third of people living in hotspots do.[66] Low economic productivity is also compounded by a dearth of transport in these regions, 'restricting opportunities still further'. People who have the qualifications, means, or opportunities to leave are able to do so – and therefore do not stay to start businesses, to work in schools or as doctors, or generally enrich the local area.

This geographical divide also has consequences for the prospects of social mobility for ethnic minorities, who tend to be largely concentrated in certain areas of the country. This unfavourable geographical distribution is exacerbated by the fact that ethnic minorities such as the Bangladeshi and Pakistani communities are less likely to move for work: Bangladeshi women tend to have the lowest internal migration rates of any group in the UK.[67] Similarly, 'ethnic economies', sectors that are dominated by a particular ethnic group, can lead to the development of concentrations of ethnic minorities in one area. While such economies provide 'protection and opportunity', ethnic economies play a role in the segregation of the labour market and therefore can limit social mobility, as some groups within society will not leave these low-skilled industries.[68]

At the other end of the scale is London, where nearly two-thirds of all social mobility hotspots are found. According to the Social Mobility Commission, the capital's 'formidable global economic strength' and (now) 'excellent schools' has meant that it is able to 'provide more opportunities for its residents, most notably its poorest population'. The London effect can be seen in the results it produces: whereas the average percentage of children on free school meals achieving 5 A*-C in English and maths GCSE is 36 per cent across all English regions, in London the figure is 51 per cent.[69] Similarly, while 50 per cent of disadvantaged children in Kensington and Chelsea go on to higher education, in cold spots such as Hastings, Barnsley and Eastbourne the percentage falls to just 10 per cent.[70]

However, although far ahead of other areas of the UK, London remains a city with entrenched social mobility problems, some of which aren't so very different from the ones facing rural cold spots. By the age of five, London children on 'free school meals are already almost three months behind their more affluent peers'.[71] And this educational attainment gap increases as children progress through school, being a third larger at secondary school compared with primary school.[72] Currently, 'one in ten sixteen- to twenty-four-year olds (89,000 young people) are not in education, employment or training'.[73] In some ways, London's schools are barely recognisable from the institutions I attended as a child; in others, they are all too familiar.

* * *

Much of this chapter has been about the importance of education in a negative sense: what happens when it's disrupted, abandoned or simply not there in the first place.

But it is also true that the education system is full of inspired and inspiring people whose dedication can have a transformative effect on the young students involved, regardless of their circumstances.

Halfway through my time at Wembley High School, in 1998 when I was about fourteen years old, one of my teachers – a woman called Denise Adler – took it upon herself to make an intervention. One year, just before we broke up for summer, she told my class that she would be taking us on a trip: this time I wouldn't need a passport, because it was to B&Q, the DIY and home improvement company. It was the first time I had ever set foot in the place. It had never occurred to us to improve our 'home', and, in any case, since at that point Brent Council had moved us from one squalid accommodation to another for four years running, it didn't particularly feel like we had a home to improve. Everything felt transient and unsettled, and I had no desire to set down roots for the future.

Ms Adler knew that none of us had anything to do that summer, and that we needed a project: painting our form room might give us something to focus on. The 'form class' was the starting point of your school day, where the register was taken. You'd then set off for your various classes in different parts of the building, coming back again for another registration after lunch. Form class was a point of consistency, a team that stayed the same even though its members' daily routines diverged.

I loved Ms Adler: she was full of life, always laughing, always smiling, always kind and forgiving of minor transgressions. She looked at you as though you mattered, and I think it was true: each and every student mattered to her. She was the French teacher but we also considered her a spiritual guide, a mother figure, a sheltering tree around which we all huddled. She had gone to Wembley

High School herself many years before, was still local, and understood her community, a community she loved dearly. I remember her often telling me that I had 'the best smile', even if, deep down, I often had little to smile about. I am sure she said the same to many others.

At B&Q Ms Adler asked us to pick two colours. We picked blue and white: a colour scheme simple enough for a group of young, rowdy teenagers to agree on. She paid for the paint and equipment herself and we made our way on the 245 bus to the school on East Lane in North Wembley. This was quite an expedition for me: the 40-minute bus ride was one of the first times I had left my immediate area and the places I was accustomed to. Over the course of a week, we cleaned, brushed down the walls, and applied multiple coats of paint to the walls (blue) and the ceiling and borders (white). As we shared pizza, and laughed and bantered among ourselves in the empty school, a bond grew between us. It was our room. We painted it, we showed it love, it was going to be our home away from home. It was more of a home for me than the place that I slept in at night.

I never actually got to ask Ms Adler why she did this; why she gave up her summer holiday to spend time with us when she really didn't need to. What drove her to think that, actually, these children deserve better than six weeks of utter boredom? I don't know what the answer is, but I have some ideas. I think she was aware that poor children from deprived backgrounds fall behind in the summer months, largely due to the lack of stimulation, and I think she knew that, in our case, we were at risk not just of boredom but of something much worse.

Brent, and in particular the areas where we grew up – Wembley, Stonebridge, Harlesden – was a pretty awful place in the mid-1990s. Newspapers referred to it as a place where murder was commonplace, and we felt it. There was never a long gap between shootings, usually over drugs and usually 'black on black'. When Operation Trident, a Metropolitan Police Service unit, was set up in 1998 to tackle gun crime and homicides in London's Afro-Caribbean communities, it was created mainly because of a series of shootings in the London boroughs of Lambeth, and, yes, Brent.[74] The local community, through its churches and charitable organisations, helped to set up campaigns such as 'Not Another Drop', the emblem of which was a red tear to symbolise the blood and tears shed by many of its inhabitants. It was extremely easy to fall into the wrong crowd, and even easier if you had little or nothing to do, and especially during the long and (sometimes) hot summer months. Today's challenge is slightly different; there is a pernicious new phenomenon known as 'county lines', which is the criminal exploitation by gangs and organised crime networks of young and often vulnerable children to sell drugs.[75] Children are often made to travel across counties, with the promise of instant financial reward, and they use dedicated mobile phone 'lines' to organise the supply of drugs.[76] The use of violence, weapons, intimidation and the control of victims, who are often exposed to horrifying exploitation which can include physical, mental and sexual abuse, is evidently very effective. London continues to be the urban epicentre of county lines offending; and county lines groups continue to pose a significant threat to young and exposed people, and to actively search for and identify potential new victims.[77]

To me, looking back, for that week, during which she kept us from hanging around the streets or simply being idle, Ms Adler was undertaking a critical piece of public service work. It didn't dramatically change any of our lives, but it did provide us with a level of continuity during what was an otherwise chaotic existence. She invested in us, and she also allowed us to invest in something ourselves: when school reconvened after the summer, we were full of pride at what we had achieved. For the rest of the year, the form classes were a particular highlight of the day, and you'd sometimes see one of us checking whether other kids who had been in there had left marks on the walls. If they had, we'd carefully wipe them off.

The moment that I walked back into that blue and white room, sat down, stared at the walls and quietly whispered to myself '*this is my work*', was the moment when I began to feel a part of this new society, a society that I was beginning to embrace – and felt it embracing me. It was the first feeling of genuine contribution to a society I could perhaps one day call my own. Just like that, I was hooked on this feeling. I wanted more of it. I wanted the feeling for myself, for my family, for my friends, for everyone. Forever.

This was the beginning of my own personal search for meaning, for a deeper understanding of my context, of who I was and what I was supposed to do with my life. It was the start of me developing the tools that helped me honour a difficult past, seek to find my own place in the present, and build the best possible future. The tools I could use to help so many, in my family and beyond. It was the last time I really believed in our immigrant mantra, 'we are going back'.

4

In Pursuit of Purpose: Confidence

Out of the night that covers me,
Black as the pit from pole to pole,
I thank whatever gods may be
For my unconquerable soul.
In the fell clutch of circumstance
I have not winced nor cried aloud.
Under the bludgeonings of chance
My head is bloody, but unbowed.
Beyond this place of wrath and tears
Looms but the Horror of the shade,
And yet the menace of the years
Finds and shall find me unafraid.
It matters not how strait the gate,
How charged with punishments the scroll,
I am the master of my fate,
I am the captain of my soul.

William Ernest Henley, *Invictus*

In 2010 I was at Bar School at City University in London, doing the vocational training required to become a barrister. In the British legal profession, unlike many jurisdictions around the world, lawyers are split into two types: barristers and solicitors. Solicitors are to law what general practitioners are to medicine; barristers are its surgeons. Solicitors meet the client first, identify the issue, advise, prepare legal documents and may also take matters to trial (as 'solicitor-advocates'). But if your solicitor can't resolve your problem – and especially if it looks like you'll end up in court – you'll also need a barrister, who will be instructed by your solicitor to prepare the case for the trial and then to argue it in court. Barristers handle those disputes that are serious, difficult and higher-value, and to do that, they must cut through a case to the bare essentials, and identify the winning points, quickly. They also tend to have a particular area of expertise, which they develop early in their careers: my area is predominantly planning and environment law, and I also do quite a bit of general commercial litigation.

Becoming a barrister is difficult, and there are many hurdles along the way. Some are mere formalities, but some are so challenging that most people will never clear them no matter how hard they try. At Bar School most of the students were still seeking pupillage, the twelve-month traineeship required in order to become a barrister. The competition is intense, and the difference between the candidates often minuscule. Each set of chambers (a community of self-employed barristers akin to a firm of solicitors) may have more than 400 applicants in any given year. Of that initial pool, roughly a hundred applicants will be invited to first-round interviews, of whom around twenty-five will get through. Usually only two places are up for grabs, but sometimes there's only one place – or none at all, because if a chambers doesn't find the right candidate, they may choose to not recruit that year. For comparison, even if you get to the first-round interview stage of a pupillage, you're still around five times less likely to get a place than you would be if you applied to study medicine at Cambridge.[1] Against such odds, success inevitably involves an element of luck: many able candidates will never secure pupillage, and those who do will often do so at the third or fourth attempt. And getting a pupillage is no guarantee that you'll be retained by the chambers: only after nine months will you learn your fate.

At Bar School a tiny handful of students had secured pupillage already. These lucky few were considered to be the crème de la crème, and were studied carefully by their contemporaries for clues as to the secret of their success: what did they have that the rest of us did not? What lessons could these immortals impart? One of them was Mike, who later became a good friend. As well as sharing classes, we had a similar kind of background: he came from a working-class family and had studied at Cambridge. He had secured pupillage ahead of the year at Bar School and carried himself with the confidence of someone who knew precisely what he was doing at all times. I used to bombard Mike with questions about his success: how had he managed it? How could I separate myself from the other candidates who, like me, had the bare minimum of qualifications, and compete with those at the top? And Mike used to reply, 'Hashi, you have it. Whatever it takes to make it in this profession, I am certain you have it.' But what was 'it'? Try as I might, I never got a clear answer: ironically, for such an articulate person, Mike couldn't explain what he meant. I prodded, I poked, I asked again and again what he meant, how he was able to tell, was he just being kind, could he explain it with examples? The best I could get out of him was that I was clever enough and I had the gravitas needed; everything else I would pick up in time.

Now, six years since my qualification as a barrister and now mentoring prospective candidates myself, I think I know what he meant. Because today, when I meet a group of youngsters who wish to pursue a career at the Bar, no matter where they have come from, I can usually predict who will succeed and who will fail. It's a gut instinct – and only now I'm on the inside can I see and feel what it takes to make it. This elusive quality – which I am going to define as *confidence* – comes up again and again when you begin talking to people about social mobility: from the employers who are looking for it, to the Oxbridge interviewers who are taking account of it, to the teachers who are trying to nurture it and the upwardly mobile people who are trying to find it within themselves. And I think they are right: it can make all the difference to whether or not you make it.

* * *

As much as we'd like to believe that we can objectively measure the qualities of different candidates, whether for a job or a promotion or a university place, there are certain things for which we can never find the right metric. Things like confidence are hard to explain, define or teach: they are often a case of *I know it when I see it*. It's often described as a 'soft skill', the kind of ability you need in addition to any formal qualifications. But don't let that fool you into thinking that it has any less of a direct impact on your career: how confident you are will most likely define whether you get hired in the first place, whether you're able to argue for that pay rise, whether you're considered suitable for senior positions. It is one thing to be capable, clever and talented, but the ability to inspire confidence, project competence, get others to believe in you and what you're capable of is, quite simply, crucial to success.

This is especially true when you're just starting out, as I was, in a new kind of world, one where you stick out, and may be seen as a challenge to the natural order of things; you're untested, unvouched for, a rough diamond. It's true that I was also trying to make my way in a profession where confidence is of paramount importance: the stock-in-trade of barristers is gravitas, authority and assurance, and performing often comes naturally to them. But really, confidence matters in all walks of life: from school to further education, to the workplace to parenting, to happiness. Having confidence can create a virtuous circle: feeling secure in your own achievements and worth allows you to perform well, meaning that you're met with validation from others, allowing you to imagine a more exciting future for yourself – and persuade others to help you make it happen. But the opposite is often true, meaning that the socially mobile often feel like they are caught in a negative spiral of low self-confidence, lack of faith from others, and a future that looks increasingly limited.

The Oxford English dictionary offers the following definition of confidence:

> The feeling or belief that one can have faith in or rely on someone or something.
> A feeling of self-assurance arising from an appreciation of one's own abilities or qualities.

What we can take from this is that confidence is both internal and external: confident individuals believe they are good enough *and* they believe or trust that other people and institutions will recognise this. Partly, confidence is a responsibility you must take on yourself: to believe in your strengths and talents and keep faith with them. But you also need to have a certain amount of trust in the world around you, and that it will treat you fairly. And it's much easier to do that if you feel comfortable about your place in it: no definition of confidence would be complete without acknowledging that it's entirely contextual. All of us are more at ease in some situations than in others, and few of us find ourselves behaving most naturally somewhere new or with people who aren't like us. This confidence of familiarity cuts both ways: in his book *Poverty Safari*, the rapper and activist Darren McGarvey, writes about the first time he left the extremely deprived area of Glasgow where he grew up, to attend therapy in a part of the city where 'it is not unusual to find a small, fashionable dog waiting in the retro wicker basket of an upcycled penny-farthing while its owner proceeds into a café to politely complain to a barista named Felix about being undercharged for artisan sausage.' While there, he sees a group of young people from the local school, confidently chatting among themselves, 'using the kind of words I always had in my head but felt too inhibited to speak'. But as he passes them, they go silent and turn away, a response he recognises as fear of him. He is ashamed, and feels 'harshly judged by snobs who could do with a clip around the ears as an introduction to the "real world"'.[2] His trip to the other, more well-to-do side of town has brought him into collision with a different social milieu, and with both kinds of people – poor and privileged – feeling uncomfortable as a result. It's clear how this might come into play in a job interview, for example: the interviewee feeling nervous, out of place, looked down upon, and the interviewer uncomfortable, unsure, already looking for an easier option.

Looking at all of this, it's easy to see why a 'confidence divide' has grown up to match the class divisions in economic, social and cultural capital that I've already talked about. In Britain, the kind of confidence I am talking about sits at the intersection of a number of factors: your childhood and close relationships; the availability of role models; the kind of positive reinforcement you get at school and in the wider world; and your ability to achieve, and see those achievements recognised. It's clearly simplistic to say that confidence is a preserve of the middle and upper classes, and that everyone else is unconfident, self-doubting, unable to visualise a better kind of life for themselves. Neither am I romanticising the middle-class childhood: I know plenty of people who have had a privileged upbringing, but who, when they came home for the holidays, practically had to sign a book if they wanted a hug. I know plenty of middle-class kids who buckled under the expectation that, having been gifted a good education, endless tutoring and a happy home, they would excel, end up at Oxbridge and carry all before them. And I know plenty of working-class parents who harbour passionate aspirations for their children, and are well aware of their talents.

But it's also true that in general, poor children and those from disadvantaged backgrounds are on the wrong side of all these factors. Statistically, among our fellow successful applicants for pupillages, Mike and I will have been outliers: the Bar is dominated by privately educated Oxbridge types. And this is not because they're innately superior beings, but because throughout their lives these individuals have had their intellectual abilities recognised and rewarded to the point where they have a crucial edge over people whose childhoods may have been more about survival than academic excellence. They exhibit that elusive 'it' that we're all looking for because they have a deeply rooted sense that they are good enough, and that their – often prodigious and genuine – talent and ability will be recognised. Life has been good to them so far – why would that change?

Contrast this, for example, with the experience of a

young, under-privileged, black man. In *Why I'm No Longer Talking to White People About Race*, the journalist Reni Eddo-Lodge explores how the confidence of young black men in 'the system' is undermined at every turn: at school by the lowered expectations from their teachers; by the poverty of ambition of the culture that surrounds them; by bad experiences with authority, particularly the police; by the fact that, if they get to university, they'll have to work harder to get the same grades as their white peers; by the far higher rate of rejections they'll receive when they send their CVs out; and by the extremely high unemployment rates that affect young black men. As she puts it:

> Our black man can try his hardest, but he is essentially playing a rigged game. He may be told by his parents and peers that if he works hard enough, he can overcome anything. But the evidence shows that that is not true, and that those who do are exceptional to be succeeding in an environment that is set up for them to fail.[3]

A version of this fate exists for a young black woman from Peckham, a young white man from a north-eastern 'cold spot' or a young Muslim woman of Bengali heritage, wearing a headscarf and sporting a foreign name. We are all bruised by trying to force our way through the structure of a society that isn't set up for us and it takes extraordinary levels of self-belief to arrive on the other side still believing that you have something to contribute (whereupon you're often held up as an example of how people from diverse backgrounds absolutely *are* welcome – if only they had the confidence to apply!).

* * *

Entitlement has a bad reputation. When the American politician Beto O'Rourke gave an interview to the magazine *Vanity Fair* saying that he was 'just born to be in' the 2020 presidential race, he was roundly mocked for his presumption. O'Rourke apologised for his poorly chosen words, saying that 'I don't know that anyone is born for an office or a position'. But that's not true, because the kind of confidence that allows you to aspire to the highest levels of society *is* inherited, handed down from the older generations in the form of their own success. It whispers *you're special*, just like those who came before you – and look at where they are now. It's feeling entitled to be present, entitled to be there, entitled to be heard, entitled to be recognised, entitled to be promoted, entitled to be earning the maximum salary and then some. It's harder to acquire if those who came before you were school drop-outs or – like some of my brothers – ended up in jail.

There's nothing wrong with entitlement in principle: in an ideal world, every member of society would feel that they had the right to participate in any part of it they liked, to the best of their ability. But in the world we actually live in, only a small proportion of citizens feel this way. We're back to the monopolisation of cultural capital: raised in environments and schooled in institutions that closely mirror the elite professional and social worlds that they will later find themselves in, privileged young people arrive already knowing the ropes and the right levers to pull. But if, as I did, you conspicuously lack cultural capital, it is hard to explain how alienating and disorientating your transition into a new world can feel, and how things that might be a familiar part of everyday experience for a person raised within that context can, for you, be bizarre and unexpected. In *Hillbilly Elegy*, J. D. Vance describes attending an important dinner held by a law firm he was in the process of applying for. The evening turns out to be an exhausting parade of potential pitfalls, from pronouncing the name of wine to being confronted with nine separate pieces of cutlery at dinner. As he sits down, the waitress asks if he'd like 'sparkling' water, which he assumes is a 'too pretentious' term for some kind of extra-clean water. But when he has a sip he ends up spitting it out on the tablecloth – 'It was the grossest thing I'd ever tasted' – and discovers that it's simply a fancy term for carbonated water, something he's never tasted before.[4] I have experienced this feeling of constantly getting things wrong – of never quite knowing how you're coming across – and it is exhausting. I was endlessly alert, trying to assimilate new information as soon as I came across it: the only experience I can compare it to is the way that, in football, you are trained to take a split second before you receive the ball to look around you, see where everyone is on the field, and decide what you are going to do next. I did that every day for years.

When I first began to understand privileged British society, which was after I had been to Oxford and Bar School and finally joined the Bar, I found myself often confused by what some might consider to be straightforward behaviour. Self-deprecation is a central part of the British self-image, and particularly so the further up the social scale you go; but I couldn't understand why people worked so hard to achieve great success, and deservedly so, and yet, when it came to enjoying the fruits of that labour, would cloak it in layer upon layer of self-effacement and false modesty. What everyone knew were hard tasks or difficult exams were downplayed, the enormity of some of the challenges that faced us were rarely acknowledged, success was often explained away as dumb luck or a fluke, something to not dwell upon for too long. For someone who has fought against enormous odds for a long time to get to the dreamed-of place, and who then meets a group of people for whom the appropriate form of behaviour is to never mention it again, it can be galling. It forces me to respond to a question about whether my mother is proud of my success with a flippant comment like 'Well, she's just happy I am not in jail', when what I want to say instead, is 'Absolutely, hell yeah, like any African mother she's telling the whole neighbourhood twice a day!'. Of course, I didn't expect to take a lap of honour round the office every morning, but I found being forced to pretend that it happened seamlessly profoundly discouraging.

This partly explains why social mobility doesn't simply *happen* once you get people through university and into the workplace. Social mobility is not only about having the best possible qualifications (and, as any socially mobile person will tell you, having to work twice as hard) but it is also about networks, the right people believing in you, taking a risk on you, sometimes against their instinctive 'better judgement'. It also means that in those settings you have to be able to inspire confidence, to know how to act, know how to respond, to have the confidence not to bother responding to a tactless remark or subtle provocation. But although we know that confidence is both a product of familiarity and something that is built up over time by the kind of positive reinforcement that privileged people receive in higher doses than the rest of us, the hiring patterns in elite institutions and professions often reflect a belief that confidence is an innate quality that can be identified and tested for. The problem is, they say, that applicants lack confidence: the confidence to apply, the confidence to push themselves forward, the confidence that marks them out as a future leader. But if they were to examine what they really mean, they might acknowledge that it is simply that the people they dismiss don't fit a narrow definition, one based on the behaviour of those who already dominate the profession. An example might be a willingness to take risks – to give up your job to retrain, for instance, or to hold out for a higher salary despite the possibility that you might lose the position. From one perspective, this looks like an admirable confidence in yourself and your worth, a willingness to take responsibility – a leadership quality. But looked at more closely, this more often reflects the fact that the same risk would be exponentially greater for a socially mobile person: to take the risk of losing a position doesn't look like such a worthy choice if you're supporting the rest of your family as well.

Increasingly, it is becoming obvious that rewarding only the kind of confidence that is, as Friedman and Laurison put it, an 'image *of* the privileged'[5] has become an existential threat to our society. In 2018, the journalist James Ball and former senior civil servant Andrew Greenway published a book called *The Bluffocracy*, which reveals in painful detail how we have set up our public life so that the people best placed to flourish within it are 'eloquent chancers' who are all confidence and, well, not a lot else:

> We have become a nation run by people whose knowledge extends a mile wide but an inch deep; who know how to grasp the generalities of any topic in minutes, and how never to bother themselves with the specifics. Who place their confidence in their ability to talk themselves out of trouble, rather than learning how to run things carefully.[6]

We can see the results of this in almost every area of our political system, which is dominated by 'the same sort of chap with the same sort of chat', a 'male, well-polished

... product of public school'.[7] Their bluffing talents were honed to a razor's edge in Oxford tutorials and they have, in many cases, made a careless disregard for facts and experts a positive virtue.

The trouble with having bluffers in charge of your country is fairly obvious. Through sheer confidence they are able to talk themselves into plum posts and positions of power and influence, leaving better, but less stylishly assured, workers in the dust behind them. But for a socially mobile person, they pose a particular problem. Their great advantage is confidence – they are supremely at home in the system, of which they know every twist and turn (and how to exploit it to their benefit). They are intimidating at face value, and because the system works in their favour, these shallow characters can be hard to expose and flush out. But knowledge is your weapon: learn to recognise a bluffer, and they lose a lot of their power over you. Barristers – despite the preponderance of public-school types – tend not to be bluffers. They couldn't survive in a place like the Bar where, in front of a judge or tribunal, one must deliver a solid, evidence-based argument; bluster is unlikely to help. If you want to counteract the bluffer, work on maintaining a deep, not easily shaken confidence in what you are saying and offering; prepare yourself carefully. Study your subject and opposition. Spend time thinking through every eventuality. If you're an employer or interviewer, look beyond what you're hearing and seeing: look not just at qualifications, but qualifications versus starting point. Consider setting exercises for potential employees, and give the results as much weight as you do the formal interview process. Try – however hard it might seem at the moment – to create a place where substance prevails over style and bluff.

* * *

Throughout my career I've been asked a variation of this question: 'So where does all this confidence come from?' On the surface a polite – even admiring – enquiry, it conceals a judgement and a challenge. It assumes that my confidence, the fact that I feel at home in the law courts or an Oxford College and act like it, is surprising – that confidence should be reserved for the sorts of people who are normally found there. 'Does someone like you have *the right* to feel so confident?', it subtly implies.

I usually try to reply with something like, 'Well, I didn't pay for it'. It's a joke, but a pointed one, because this question overwhelmingly comes from privileged people, who all hail from the same sort of privately educated, middle-class background, and who dominate the top tiers of almost every profession. In the summer of 2017 I shared a platform with Nick Clegg, the former British deputy prime minister, at an event hosted by the Social Mobility Foundation at the top of the BT Tower. One of the first things he said amounted to a disclaimer: he had, he acknowledged, the best education money could buy (at Westminster School) and went on to Cambridge University, in a context of a loving and stable home environment. But he was passionate about social mobility and the need to improve it, and he thought that one of the most significant ways in which to promote social mobility was to instil in children a belief in themselves and their place in society. I agreed with him: but I also wondered how we'd even start on such an ambitious task. When it came to my turn, I joked that, at the kind of school Nick Clegg had attended, confidence was something that was rammed down your throat in a way that could only be compared to the process of making foie gras. Instilling this confidence can sometimes be cruel, but the quality of the product it produces is worth the wait. But, as we all know, it's very expensive.

The ability of private schools to inculcate soft skills in their students – and how that might in fact be their real point, as far as parents are concerned – was covered in the previous chapter, so I will limit myself here to the following observations. Parents will tell you that it is the confidence that these private schools provide, more than anything else, that is the goal. These parents want their children to feel at ease in most surroundings and believe that they belong at a prestigious company, or university – that that institution might, in fact, be lucky to have them. Confidence like this will help them grow up to project competence, intelligence, gravitas, insight and creativity through crisp and clear self-expression. They will speak as though they are there to be heard; will walk into a room and believe they belong.

At the school I went to, teachers were more likely to encourage you to lower your sights in line with your surroundings. Dreaming of a different life and destiny was discouraged, and – coupled with the unstable environments pupils like me often experienced at home and in the neighbourhoods where we grew up – any hope for a better life was snuffed out before it was able to take root. Confidence takes root in childhood, which is when the expectations for your life – astronaut, academic, ballet dancer, scientist – are often set. The impact of what has been called 'the soft bigotry of low expectations', the idea that certain sectors of society are simply not built for success, that what's good enough for your parents is good enough for you, can be crippling. All too often, the schooling of working-class children is overshadowed by the idea that certain things and places are not for them, and it would be better for them not to face the dislocation and disappointment that comes with aspiration to them. From my own experience of speaking with teachers and parents, I know that this rarely stems from a deliberate attempt to limit the ambitions of working-class children: rather, those in authority seek to set 'realistic' goals and achievements, and in the process project their own doubts on to the child, undermining their confidence.

Having what is in effect a two-tier education system – what the historian David Kynaston has called 'educational apartheid' – also means two different streams of teachers. Each year, when the Oxbridge interviews roll around, a furore is raised over the resulting intake: too many pupils from private schools, not enough pupils from ethnic minorities, too few working-class students and so on. These ratios are indeed damning: between 2010 and 2015 Oxford offered more places to applicants from one school, Eton, than to children on free school meals from across the whole country.[8] But at least some of the problem is that both students and teachers lack the confidence to apply – if not in the sense of valuing their own talents then in the sense of expecting Oxbridge to recognise them. When the journalist Sathnam Sanghera, who went to Cambridge University 'desperate to escape the poverty of my childhood', returned to assess their admissions procedure, he found that while children at the top of the social scale 'expect [to be admitted] ... at the bottom, they are increasingly wondering whether it's even worth bothering to hope'. Among the group of young people he accompanied, comments like 'They don't really accept people from the north, do they? They prefer private schools' were common, as was similar ambivalence from teachers, who spoke about poor children feeling it was 'not for them' and having no sense of what Oxbridge interviewers were really looking for.[9]

Contrast this with the expectations of teachers at a private school, selective grammar, or high-achieving state school in a well-off area. They automatically think in terms of Russell Group universities for their pupils, and those expectations are backed up by mainly (if not exclusively) positive experiences of what happens to their pupils when they engage with elite institutions. The significantly lower level of staff turnover means that such teachers are likely to have been around long enough to have built up experience of preparing students for admission. Remember, also, the importance of context: it is much easier to take the plunge and apply to Oxford or Durham or UCL if your school has a track record of having sent a dozen students just like you in the preceding years, and the school's confidence in their approach – and you – is high.

I should say, here, that I don't want to fall into the trap of fixating on Oxford and Cambridge, as if the answer to improving social mobility is to get every child from a failing school into those institutions. Success doesn't equate solely to going to Oxbridge, and those universities have a long way to go before they are truly welcoming places to working-class and ethnic minority (or both) students. (It is worth noting, however, that in 2019 Oxford announced a foundation-year programme designed to help state applicants from difficult and lower-socio-economic backgrounds to acclimatise to the university – a welcome development.) But Oxbridge – and the other Russell Group universities – are important in this story: you only have to look at the dominance of Oxbridge in public life (all but four post-war British prime ministers have been educated there)[10] to see that their graduates wield disproportionate influence in public life. It's a sign, yet again, that Britain is a closed shop at the top – and mostly comfortable with that.

* * *

Some of you might be thinking, 'isn't all this obvious?' Well, that's the point. For many others reading these pages it is not obvious at all; and even if it is, they do not have the luxury of acting on it. It certainly was not obvious to me growing up, and many people like me: we tended to take our value at others' estimation. For us, the fact that our school saw the best-case scenario as scraping through with a handful of GCSEs, that our families' main preoccupation was with putting food on the table, that no one had the space or time to take the long view about what shape our lives might take ... that was just normal.

But we can do better by poor children. At least once a month, I'm invited to attend the morning assembly at a school somewhere in the country. In the course of the year, I speak in front of hundreds of children and teachers about my own story. I tell the children to work hard and believe in themselves, and that they deserve to be successful – that if I made it, they can too. Afterwards, I try to stick around for a few minutes to hear what teachers and students have to say. It's usually a variation on two themes: a young person with a complaint along the lines of, 'I want to pursue my dream of doing medicine or law, but my teacher, whose helping me with the university applications, keeps telling me that it's not for me. What do I do?'; or a teacher who is tearing their hair out because the gifted children in their care lack the self-confidence to achieve more and to see themselves in the kind of places they deserve to be.

It puts me in a difficult position. In the first case, if I don't know the child, it's hard to judge whether the teacher is subjecting them to the 'soft bigotry of low expectations', or is simply trying to avoid them wasting time and emotional energy pursuing a future they aren't equipped for.

The most I can offer is some words of encouragement, and a suggestion that they *really* research their goal – before making their own decision. But to the teachers, I can say: being a teacher is one of the hardest, most exposing jobs there is. So what gave you the confidence to stand in front of thirty children and do it every day? Who was reassuring you when you were their age, encouraging you to believe in yourself? What were you seeing, hearing, experiencing that was reinforcing that confidence? Now compare that to the kid you're talking about – what's the difference?

Unlike many of the things that limit a child's potential, confidence can blossom at any stage: never underestimate how much confidence can be inspired in a child by a single person's sustained belief, even if that child is being undermined elsewhere. Make them believe that you have something invested in them; that if they won't do it for themselves, they can do it for *you*: remind them of the teachers who believe and invest in them; the parents making sacrifices for their success. You might not feel like you're getting through. In my case, though I never acted on my uncle Ibrahim's often repeated advice that I was capable and should apply myself more, underneath it gave me an enormous amount of confidence to know that he believed in me, even if I was doing my best to make him think the opposite. Providing consistent and steadfast support is paramount; for there will be moments when a young person will surprise themselves and may then believe that what they have done is a fluke. They will need reminding that their success is the result of hard work and determination, and that they can make it happen again. That they have control, or, at least, more control than they realise – that they are the captains of their soul.

* * *

The trouble with all this is that it takes time, investment, close attention: something that is hard to expect of teachers who have large classes, vast numbers of targets, and endless exams for which to prepare their students. There are no easy answers, nor shortcuts. Teachers in some state schools, particularly in deprived communities, will not always have the benefit of teaching a classroom full of students from stable homes, and must make up for that deficiency in *addition* to their own duties. Some of these children, as was my own experience, carry burdens that are too much for any child. Some may have care duties, or health problems, or assist with household responsibilities, such as looking after younger siblings. As I write, there are hundreds of thousands of children across England caring for an adult, or, as my siblings and I did, parenting younger family members.[11]

That your family situation can shape your confidence growing up is self-evident. If you recall the research of the sociologist Annette Lareau discussed in Chapter 1, you'll recall that wealthier parents were more likely to talk things through with their children. They reasoned with them, expected them to talk back, to negotiate, to question adults in positions of authority.[12] In contrast, poorer parents found interacting with authority intimidating and preferred to stay in the background.[13] It's easy to see how this might translate to feeling at ease in an Oxford tutorial or a job interview later in life, but imagine how these general findings could be compounded by cultural differences. If you grew up in a culture where 'respecting your elders' means never challenging them, and those elders are themselves intimidated and at sea in the world around you, then you're getting a double dose of lack of confidence and lack of control. Imagine a parent attending a parents' evening, full of a desire to help their child. But they speak very little English, are reliant on the child's interpretation skills, and are unable to fully grasp the latest grading system or targets, or know how to build relationships with the teachers, all the while juggling their other commitments and responsibilities. In this manner, all the ways in which a poor child's self-esteem can be undermined – the lack of role models, parenting that prioritises passivity over entitlement, and the tyranny of low expectations – begin to intersect and interact.

However, I am going to choose just one example of how family circumstances can be determinative, one that's very personal to me. The absence of my father was and remains a huge part of my identity, who I am and how I see the world. It is a reference point that defines what kind of man I want to be, the kind of father I hope to become, and the kind of leadership I wish to show to my family as a whole. Father figures for young black boys growing up in the Brent of the 1990s were quite a scarce commodity, and in many similar areas of London this remains the case today. Most of my closest black friends in school were either estranged from their fathers, or had never met them, or their fathers were dead, like my own. In general, being raised by a single mother, and often looked after by a grandmother, was a pretty common experience.

Each family is different, and each missing father has their own story. For the Somali community, it was often because the men had died during the civil war. For others, it was because their fathers were in prison, estranged, or for one reason or another never made an effort to play a role in the lives of their children. I felt relatively lucky, because, as my grandmother, my uncle and, later, my mother would often tell us, had our father not died he would not only have been there for us, he would have given us the best life possible. We were the children of a strong and decisive man who would have done anything for his family. When I interviewed relatives as I researched this book, this counter-factual narrative came up a great deal. Everyone told me that our father would have regretted that we sought asylum – he would have preferred to make the best life for us in Kenya. This cannot be proven, of course, and if his previous actions are anything to go by this rosy, reassuring supposition remains, to my mind, an optimistic hypothesis. But at least my siblings and I were able to say: I am wanted; my father would have done anything for me, he would have been present, and my life would have been better but for this bad luck; but at least we were loved.

It wasn't something that those of my friends whose fathers were alive and well but who *chose* to be absent could comfort themselves with. I saw first-hand how many of my friends struggled with this profound rejection, became numb and immune to the way that their mothers would speak ill of their fathers, and failed to find a male role model who they could rely on. It's not surprising that many young men are so vulnerable to gangs and gang violence – dangerous and violent though that life is, they offer a twisted sense of belonging for those in search of a family, as well as substitute father figures (who, in reality, only seek to exploit).[14]

When I say that, for a young black male growing up in, for example, inner-city London, perhaps the one thing you need above all else is a strong male role model, I don't mean to take away from the role played by mothers. My siblings and I were, after all, raised entirely by women, and they were powerful examples of courage, resilience and pride. They loved us, laughed with us, and did not hesitate to tell us off when we stepped out of line: but they were also fighting an uphill battle without reinforcements. The evidence suggests that, once other factors are taken into account, coming from a single-parent family has little effect on your ultimate happiness or success.[15] But there is a strong correlation between single parenthood and poverty: a report by the charity Gingerbread in 2018 found that a third of single-parent families where the parent was working were living in poverty, the highest level in twenty years. And the 'single parent' referred to is almost always a mother – over 90 per cent of single parents are women.[16] So, not only are young children raised by their mothers already more likely to be subject to all the confidence-sapping effects of poverty, but they are also competing for their remaining parent's attention.

But, as the MP David Lammy, who grew up as one of five children raised by his mother in Tottenham, has pointed out in an article dissecting the aftermath of the London riots, the lack of confidence felt by young black men without fathers is not just about growing up in poverty. While grateful for the support given to parents like his mother by left-wing parties, he recounts his mounting irritation with 'those same liberals who fought so hard for [help for] single mothers [and who] now give the impression that fatherlessness does not matter at all. They insist that it is the quality of parenting that matters, that the loss of a father matters only if it means a loss of income.' But it's much harder to maintain a 'high quality of parenting' on your own: 'it becomes twice as hard to set boundaries with half the number of parents.'[17] The chain of events that follows the absence of a father stifles confidence: financial difficulties, a mother shouldering a burden made for two, feelings of abandonment, less individual attention, and more stress and conflict in your life as a whole. And, as we saw earlier in this chapter, young black men face their own particular set of challenges in trusting the world to recognise their value: a missing father is often not just a missing parent, but the absence of the one person who could help explain and guide you through those treacherous waters.

I was – again – lucky, in that, although my father wasn't there to help me, I had my father's younger brother, my uncle Ibrahim. Ibrahim was someone my brothers and I could look up to: a successful, highly educated, happily married black man. For two years, before my GCSEs – perhaps the most stable period in the ten years after we left Kenya – I lived with Ibrahim , his wife Aunty Zahra and their four children. Aunty Zahra was an enormous source of strength and stability at this crucial time. While I was there, he told me that, in the end, he was the brother of my father and that, despite his best efforts, he could never be my father. It was something that I needed to hear, and I understood that it wasn't a rejection: he was gently reminding me that I would never be able to find a replacement for my father, and that I needed to find a way to live in peace with that knowledge. It was a turning point for me, bringing something that had previously been a vague and amorphous sadness in my life into sharp focus – and triggering a desire to seek a new kind of meaning, which would ultimately take me back to Kenya, where my story started.

Everyone's story is different, and in telling my own I neither want to suggest that it is easy to flourish in the absence of a father, nor that not having a father dooms you to the kind of difficulties that I, my brothers and my friends all experienced. For the journalist Stephen Bush, his missing father was compensated for by 'investment in schools, museums and fantastic teachers, and the world's best mother', meaning that 'while a number of people – the taxpayer, society, my mum – have a legitimate grievance against my father, I don't, not really. It worked out OK.' When he ran into his father at Blackfriars tube station, he simply walked away, feeling 'I had nothing I really wanted to say to him.'[18] That enviable self-possession is not an option for everyone, but what I will say is this: either way, you have to settle the issue for yourself. Whether it means finding your father for the first time, re-establishing a relationship, or learning to live with their absence (as both I and Stephen had to do in our different ways), you have to do it to be able to move on with your life. On this, I am with the mother of comedian Trevor Noah. Noah, who is mixed-race, was brought up in apartheid South Africa, and born at a time when interracial relationships were still a crime. His father wasn't around during his childhood, and when he was twenty-four, over his own protests, his mother told him:

> Too many men grow up without their fathers, so they spend their lives with a false impression of who their father is and what a father should be. You need to find your father. You need to show him what you've become. You need to finish that story. [19]

* * *

If you are socially mobile, then sooner or later you will find yourself in an entirely new world about which you know nothing. Gaining the inner strength that comes from having confronted trauma, and being able to fortify it against the insecurity that makes you feel as though you do not deserve to be there, is essential. The issue isn't always, as you might suspect, about feeling out of place in your new world, or suffering from imposter syndrome or the attempts of others to undermine you. It might be, as it was in my case, just as much a question of having to face down family or friends who consider you to have 'abandoned' your roots; or it might involve trying to hold on to a sense of self when you find yourself caught between your old and your new world. I have had to spend a lot of time away from family and old friends over a number of years: working, studying, trying, failing, failing again, concentrating on my next steps, delaying gratification, making sacrifices, finding ways to answer endless questions about when I would finally be 'this lawyer', all to build a different and more prosperous future, not just for me but for my family as well. This has required a great deal of confidence and discipline; something which, to some of those closest to me, has translated as self-centredness, aloofness, abandonment of my origins, a focus on the future to the exclusion of all else, an implicit judgement on the past. To hear all this was hurtful, and, at a time when I was trying to forge an uncertain new future, to be told that I would have to leave, for good, the world I did know was terrifying.

I have no patience with the idea that, by speaking in a certain way, by dressing differently from how you did before, by having a new group of friends, enjoying new things, or seeing the world differently, you are betraying your past. I have not, however, faced this from people who *actually* know me; the accusation comes from those who really do not know me at all. But it is a challenge that anyone who wishes to transform their lives and become socially mobile will face. It takes resilience, resolve and plenty of self-confidence to meet it head on. To my mind, the entire concept of abandoning your roots is part of a series of ridiculous preconceptions that seek to keep people in their 'rightful place'. There are those *within* the system who sustain its dominance by suggesting that success is down to breeding or background; and those from *without* who hold each other back by buying into this flawed narrative. The sum of *all* your parts make up the whole; one does not invalidate the other, one is not superior to the next. Learning to be comfortable in your new life will be impossible unless you find a way to bring together these different ways of seeing the world, and the value systems they contain: to take the resilience and adaptability of your refugee family, and marry it to the structure and self-discipline of your professional life, and the self-belief and pride that might come from overcoming an obstacle or growing as a person.

Although I don't believe that you have to choose between your two worlds, you do, by the nature of what you're trying to accomplish, have to go it alone. There will be moments when it will be impossible to put into words what you're feeling, what you're going through, when you instinctively know that no one will *properly* understand, and yet you need to muster up the confidence to stay the course, and keep believing that around the corner lies the new landscape. When you've never really known your father and you encounter colleagues whose fathers are senior figures in the profession, when you go home and your grandmother can't understand what you're doing, when there is nobody who can fully appreciate your efforts and what you're achieving – that all undermines your confidence. It has always been impossible to explain to my family what I have achieved – to this day. But you can, strange as it may seem, harness this sense of vertigo, the dizzying sense of the ground shifting beneath your feet, for good. In his book *The Social Animal, A Story of How Success Happens*, the political and cultural commentator David Brooks explores the source of ambition and achievement. In one section, he notes how ultra-driven people are often plagued by a deep sense of existential danger, and that historians have long noticed that an astonishing percentage of the most prominent writers, musicians, artists, and leaders had a parent die or abandon them while they were between the ages of nine and fifteen.[20] Though I'm hardly claiming to be a significant leader, I do relate to this. At the age of nine I lost my father and moved to a foreign country without my mother – and I do feel in some way haunted by the knowledge that life is precarious.

Of course, plenty of people achieve success without experiencing crushing tragedy, and many who *have* suffered in this way never recover. Trauma is no assurance of resilience, nor is it worth suffering through for the benefits it might bring. If I had a choice to make at the age of nine between having both my parents and staying in Kenya or what actually happened, I would choose the former, every time. But I do think that a factor in my ability to transcend the dire circumstances of my childhood is an underlying conviction that, unless you scramble to secure a safe place in the world, everything could be destroyed by a sudden blow.[21] This feeling, uncomfortable though it is, has also provided a level of clarity that has served me well in steadying my confidence at the worst of times. I found the resilience needed to push on into uncharted waters in the idea that life just couldn't get any worse – and in time that feeling of precariousness gave way to unprecedented freedom and drive. Anything I did, anything I tried, would surely be an improvement – and perhaps even a pleasant surprise – so why not push my boundaries as far as I could, far beyond what I would ever have imagined for myself, and certainly more than was ever imagined for me? Even as I write this, the idea of me writing this book seems quite surreal. But why not?

It might seem a surprising effect of an existential crisis, but the momentum it granted to some extent insulated me from the enormity of the odds I faced. While I was researching my radio documentary, one of my mentors, a QC practising in a chambers in Lincoln's Inn Fields, commented that I came across as blithely unfazed by the challenges that face even the most able candidates trying to break into the Bar, and which were enormously complicated by my 'non-traditional' starting point. The truth is, I only remember thinking that if I do not at least give it a shot, I could never forgive myself. That's the real answer of where the confidence came from: an ignorance of the odds and a fearlessness about failure.

* * *

Confidence is as fragile as it is hard to build up – especially in already vulnerable children and young adults, many of whom may find it difficult to build the kind of long-lasting friendships and relationships that help build and support self-esteem. Many will find it a life-long struggle to be comfortable, not only in their own skin but especially in comparison to others. I was very lucky to have grown up at a time when there was no Snapchat, Facebook, Twitter, Instagram or indeed any of the social media platforms that place enormous pressure on youngsters today to present a successful, well-off, 'best life' façade to the world. Years of investment in your personal development can be undone by a family tragedy, a crushing heartbreak or an awful and life-changing workplace event – if you have been racially abused or sexually harassed, or overlooked for a promotion you felt you deserved, for example. This is why it is critical to build coping mechanisms and resilience alongside confidence, along with a strong support network of people who can challenge you, hold you to account, build you up, help you to grow and allow you to help them grow in return.

When I meet young people – when, for example, I speak at a school, award ceremony or an event for youngsters, who are full of hope, but often overwhelmed by the lack of control over their lives – I always try to repeat my mantra: *it's all about how you react.* In the spectrum of your life, no one but you will remember that job rejection, or the horrible thing someone might have inadvertently said, that nasty encounter involving racist abuse, the way the end of a relationship plunged you into a depression. Those times will be hard, but you won't be defined by them in others' eyes. Instead, the focus and perspective with which you face these events can become a source from which you draw strength.

It can be faith, it can be friends, it can be therapy, it can be your own personal way of finding solace. Whatever it is, you need to find it long before you meet any of these moments, if you can. My strong recommendation to young people is to get some therapy in their late twenties, should they have the opportunity to do so. NHS waiting lists are long, it's not cheap to do it privately, and a certain social stigma persists, but I believe it is vital. Do not be afraid to ask for help: don't go through life seeking treatment for every physical bump or bruise, and yet refusing to contemplate the same kind of help for your mental health. Throughout the disappointments in my life (and there have been plenty) it is the ability, which I only developed in my early twenties, to ask for help, to be able to zoom out and take the long view rather than obsess over why something happened, and what others' motives were, that has made the greatest difference to my happiness.

It can be hard to let go of bitterness that may have been festering over many years – but like a parasite it will eat you from the inside if you let it. Of course, you're entitled to be angry, or feel frustrated or helpless; this is entirely normal. But dwelling on what you can't control is a waste of time and a waste of hope. Instead, focus on what you *can* change: how hard you work, looking after yourself and seeking help where you can, and the kinds of people you surround yourself with.

* * *

At the end of my A Levels in the summer of 2002, the rest-lessness that had been building inside me over the chaotic preceding decade reached a peak. In the ten years after our arrival, I do not think I lived in one house for more than a couple of years at most. We had constantly moved around – from an uncle's to an aunt's, to my grandmother's, back to my mother's and then on again. My family was full of conflict and confusion. I spent my free time playing endless games of football and I had some fairly mediocre A Levels that had somehow got me a place at the University of Hertfordshire. But none of my older siblings had gone on to further education, and I wasn't convinced that it was the answer for me either. A life on the streets in Brent was easily available and, while I never seriously considered it, I do remember thinking I would probably be good at it. These guys getting caught on the street corners were making such elementary mistakes, I used to think.

Clearly, something had to change. But how? I did not have the confidence at that moment to imagine what it might look like – nor did I understand where and how to begin. All I knew was that I was profoundly unhappy with the present. What I know now, looking back, is that it is important to realise, as early as possible, that we all have our particular advantages and disadvantages. No matter what your starting point, however weak and unfair it may seem, there is almost *always* something to build on. It could be a particular talent waiting to be developed, it could be a strongly knit family unit, it could be a strong sense of self. You just have to find what that is and, the sooner you do so, the more time you will have to turn things around.

The starting point for me came the following year, when I became a naturalised British citizen. For the first time in my life, I could travel anywhere I wanted, at any moment, for as long as I pleased. My status was no longer precarious, no longer unclear, I was no longer simply a refugee in limbo. A citizen of the United Kingdom of Great Britain and Northern Ireland. I read every word on the document carefully, unsure about what it all meant. But I clearly understood that Her Majesty's Secretary of State 'requests *and* requires' that as the hereby named individual, I was to be allowed to 'pass freely without let or hindrance'. I was to be afforded 'such assistance and protection' as I needed. I had a new country, on paper at least. Whether I belonged to it, though, remained an open question.

At the time, I was trying to make sense of myself and my place in Britain, something that bothered me no end. My family were clearly not going back to where we had come from, but, at the same time, whatever it said on that passport, this country did not feel like it had a place for people like me. I felt that the answer didn't lie in London or Britain. My profound frustrations were affecting me in a serious way: disrupting family relations; reducing my ability to concentrate on anything; stopping me from properly testing my capabilities, or understanding what this all meant. I was overtaken by a powerful urge to go back to Kenya, to the place we had left, and where my father was buried. It was a call I had to answer. So, in August 2003, I boarded a plane bound for Nairobi. During the flight – and in the months leading up to it – I was incredibly anxious about the trip. Nairobi was the place where I had stood over my father's body while it was washed and prepared for burial, and again as it was draped in white sheets and lowered to the ground unencumbered by any coffin, in the Islamic tradition for burial. It was an agonising time for us all: to this day, my grandmother does not even refer to Kenya as a country: instead, she calls it the place where her eldest son is buried. I didn't know what I would find, but I knew I must go.

I was met by a distant uncle and his wife at the airport, which was much as I remembered it: the Soviet-style blocks of concrete, the tunnels from cabin to airport lounge, the same colours from a decade before. My uncle had left for Germany a few years before the war had broken out and had returned in the mid-1990s to set up a business in Nairobi. Together with his Somali-German wife he began selling second-hand electronics imported from China and Japan, and then mobile phones, just as the popularity of mobile banking began to boom in Kenya. Working hard, and combining the Somali entrepreneurial spirit with German discipline and efficiency, meant that they became very wealthy. Their children attended the private German school in Nairobi, and they lived the kind of life reserved for Kenya's wealthy expat elite. We drove from the airport, chatting in Somali, and an hour later, as I was driven through the massive gates that sheltered their home, I asked, 'Is this Eastleigh?'

I'd assumed that they would live near the semi-slum that had been our home when we had lived in Nairobi. But laughter rang out in the car, and my uncle and aunt were quick to explain that their expensive neighbourhood in Westlands was a long way from Eastleigh. That first night I slept little, desperate to explore this country with which I had such a strong connection and yet knew so little about. I kept on looking out of the window, which was simple glass protected by thick bars, for protection against what the locals dub 'Nairobbery'. I wondered, had my father lived, is this where I would have grown up?

The next morning I met my cousin Guled. Although we're roughly the same age, we hadn't met before – and had led very different lives. But we connected instantly, chatting away, and feeling like we'd known each other for years. A few hours later his friends came, keen to meet the son of Mohamed Hashi Omar, once a famous local whose life was taken away too soon. I met Jesko, a German Chilean who had been living in Kenya for ten years, and was fluent in German, Spanish, English and a little Kiswahili; and Amanuel, born to a Swiss father and an Ethiopian mother, who had attended the German school with my cousins. He too was fluent in German, Swiss German in particular, and had a little French, Amharic and of course English. And then there was Peter, who was of Indian descent but had been adopted by a white American German mother and a Sikh Kenyan father. These were dynamic young men, who were personable and well travelled, carrying multiple passports and leading privileged lives in Africa. I was in awe of them – but I also felt sick at the idea of what could have been, remembering the humiliating reality of the past decade in Britain. My uncle told me that he and my father had big plans together, which were interrupted by my father's death. He told me that I would have grown up in Kenya living in an even bigger house than the one his children resided in. The following night, I went to sleep sobbing with rage into my pillow.

All of this came together for me in a moment of revelation. I remember thinking, what have I done with my life thus far? Why do I not speak more languages like them? Why am I not as well travelled as them? I saw these young men, who had the best that life could give them, make the best of their talents in a way – I had always thought – that was never meant to happen for me. But it was not too late. Now could be a new start, I reasoned. On returning to Britain, something had fundamentally changed in my mind: it was as though a mist had lifted before my eyes. I realised three things.

First, I was not 'going back' anywhere. I had happy memories of the nine years I had spent in Kenya. But it ended when my father was buried. When I went back to Nairobi, I went to collect what I had left behind ten years before: my thoughts, my consciousness, my confidence. The clock would start from zero now. Secondly, I had survived the worst thing that life could throw at me – the death of my father. It had become the single, most central event, one that dominated my perspective on everything else. But I had survived it. Nothing – no job rejection, no break-up, no other tragedy – would ever be as bad. I could put that on the list under resilience demonstrated, survival displayed, experience acquired. I came back unafraid to fail, and determined to make the most of what I did have. I could try to learn a new language and catch up with these guys who speak three just for fun. I had a lot of catching up to do. Thirdly, I felt an opening up of my horizons. While many, including some in my family, claim today to not be surprised to see me where I am now, it would be mad to suggest that anyone saw it coming. It would have been a totally implausible prediction. But the absence of expectation was a liberating force: it meant that I could try my hand at anything and see if it works, and if it fails, it didn't matter because no one was even expecting me to try.

At this point in my life I had never met a barrister, let alone knew what it took to become one. The idea of a career in journalism or broadcasting was ludicrous: I had never even written an article for a school newspaper. But, in the end, I did start my undergraduate degree in law and French at the University of Hertfordshire. I spent nine months in France as an Erasmus Scholar, avoided all the Anglophones, and became fluent in French. Returning to Britain armed with a new language and a fresh appreciation for my world, and my place in it, was a profoundly life-enriching experience. I tried my luck at Oxford for postgraduate studies, and was accepted with a full scholarship. Then, again on a full scholarship, I started Bar School in London, and secured pupillage first time at one of the top sets of chambers in the country. No one I knew could guide me through all this, but the only burden of expectation placed on my skinny shoulders was the one I had placed on myself. But the strides I was making felt natural, as though I was meant to be there, and I recalled how, all those years ago, Ibrahim had told me that I was capable of good things if only I could be bothered to apply myself. I recalled all the teachers who, just by their looks of encouragement, had told me that I deserved better. I hadn't listened at the time but this confidence in me was there, waiting to be triggered; and suddenly I was fulfilling the purpose and potential I was always told I had.

5

What Is and What Could Be: Imagination

Plan new achievements, and set about achieving them.
Failure and disappointment simply don't matter; go ahead
with your dreaming, let your enthusiasm run away with you.
You were made to rise and soar, and come down to earth with
a bump, and rise and soar again. If you accomplish nothing
else, you'll have kept the rot and the rust away. Let me warn
you: it's the practical people who stay rooted on the earth,
who make the money. But it's the dreamers who touch the
stars. Which is the success you plan? Are you to 'play safe'
for the rest of your life, or are you to adventure? You must
make a choice, and make it early; and having made it, you
must abide by it.

Alfred Wainwright, *A Pennine Journey*, 1938

One early afternoon, I thought I would walk down and surprise my young cousin as he was leaving school – maybe take him for an early dinner before sending him home with some pocket money. Adam, who is fourteen, is a shy, clever boy with a quiet kind of confidence; the youngest of ten boys and one girl, he has had to grow up quickly and is mature for his age. He's a sharp dresser and a gifted mathematician: he can solve a Rubik's cube in less than three minutes, always trying to catch up with his elder brothers who are even faster than he is. And – even if you sometimes need to coax *precisely* what he wants to say out of him – he's a clear and measured thinker.

I met Adam at the gates; apparently he had plans to go to the local chicken shop with his friends, so I said I'd walk him there and then leave when they ordered their food. When we got there, we found a big group, chatting and bantering about their day as they tried to decide on their orders. A friend standing close to him whispered, '*Is this your brother?*' I can see Adam anticipating what's to come; I've done the same thing to his brothers in different settings. I spot a wry smile and wince as he replies, 'Cousin'.

It's my opening, so I say, 'So, Adam, how many of your friends know that your cousin is a barrister – or that your mother is a businesswoman? Or how about your uncle the engineer and your brother, the accountant?' One of his friends pipes up, 'what's a barrister?' and Adam starts explaining about wigs and gowns in his soft quiet voice. I feel like I'm being cruel for putting him on the spot in this way – but it's not as if he has not seen it coming. I let the moment linger for a little while longer. Now, almost the whole chicken shop is listening; I give it another minute and then put him out of his misery. I make a few jokes about how much cleverer he is than me; how he has much bigger plans than being a mere barrister. That, given he was the youngest child in his family, the best was saved for last, how he had the benefit of learning from all of our mistakes. It's possible that he finds this if anything even more embarrassing, but I want to underline – in front of his friends, no less – not only that he has relatives striving to do well, and is close to people doing good and important things, but that he's someone his family have expectations of, that we want the best for him – and that nothing less should suffice.

The guy at the counter shouts a few orders that need

to be collected, one of which is Adam's. The small crowd breaks up as he makes his way to the counter. I follow him and offer to pay, but he's already done it – granny gave him some money that morning. I give him a bit more anyway, say goodbye to the group and leave; whispering in his ear as we hug, '*I expect big things from you*'.

I don't, of course, hang about in fast-food restaurants embarrassing my younger relatives just for the fun of it. Adam and his friends are at a critical point in their lives: a moment when ambitions may become fixed, expectations are raised or lowered, and doubt and insecurity – if not carefully guarded against – can start to shape your entire worldview. Young people like my cousins very rarely see someone who looks like them, who talks like them, from their background, in any position of power or prestige, and it's easy for them to internalise the feeling that some things are simply not for them. When I next saw Adam, I asked what his friends had made of our encounter. With suppressed laughter he said that they all 'thought that you spoke like a white man ... they couldn't believe that we were related'. I wasn't surprised at all: the idea that an accent like mine, which would generally be categorised as 'received pronunciation', is reserved for the privileged, white and middle-class few, is very common among the community I grew up in.

I want Adam and his friends to know that there's no path that isn't open to them; no way of being that is reserved for people who aren't like them. I want to fulfil the role that Ibrahim and so many others performed for me: the person who sees the person they could be, who believes in the best version of themselves. I want them to grow up into confident, inspired young men and women who see this poisonous narrative for what it is: a lie that has been allowed to flourish by a massive absence of imagination in our society.

* * *

The social mobility 'leap', particularly within one generation, is like trying to sprint up a mountain in a hurricane, without a compass and with absolutely no training. As you make your way up, the gravity of low expectations pulls you down from below, and a stiff wind of engrained prejudice forces you down from above. Among the poor and underprivileged communities where I grew up, imagining a better future often seemed simply impossible: we were, as I have said, mainly focused on staying alive and out of trouble. Our ambitions were shaped by our circumstances, and our imaginations by the kind of material we had to work with: we didn't have much sense of what sort of things we *could* do, beyond what we saw in our own families. As a result there was a profound, deadening lack of aspiration surrounding us – from the teachers at school to our parents, friends and acquaintances.

But when I did leave, and found myself among the better-off, I encountered a corresponding inability to see beyond the existing stereotypes, to reimagine what a chairman of the board, or a senior partner, or a promising new trainee might look like. I was tickled, shortly after my visit to the chicken shop with Adam, to run into a colleague who had listened to my radio documentary. Clearly, he hadn't known anything about my background before, and couldn't resist asking me how my story could be true, given that 'you sound as though you're from the Home Counties'. It's the same assumption, delivered from the opposite direction: a black, Muslim immigrant from a deprived part of inner-city London has no business sounding like you do.

Throughout my career I've come across similar attitudes. The people who hold them aren't necessarily hostile – in fact, often they are interested, admiring and supportive.

But the *fact* of their surprise, and the comfort they feel in expressing it, hints at deeply entrenched attitudes that block progress for the upwardly mobile. They experience me as an anomaly: something to be interrogated, inspected and explained. It's the mirror image of an unquestioning acceptance that a certain kind of person – middle-class, well-spoken, highly educated, perhaps white – is the 'basic model' candidate for elite professions. It is, to say the least, undermining. It highlights (if you weren't already aware of it) that you're seen differently by your colleagues: at best as a sort of curiosity, and at worst as someone who 'just doesn't fit in'. It is especially cruel that, once you have conquered your own self-doubt and the poverty of ambition that might have surrounded you growing up, the battle continues unabated. Even if, on paper, you've become an insider, in reality you often remain an outsider.

And over a long period of time it's exhausting. One cold and snowy February morning I spoke about my journey and the importance of imagination to a crowd of senior executives at a very glitzy event at Lords Cricket Ground. I told them that they had a responsibility to think outside of the box, to avoid the easy option of recruiting in their own image, and to take real risks if they are to make a real difference in order for society to reach a more inclusive future. The only black face in the crowd – a tall, elegant man in a grey suit – approached me in the lunch break. He was somewhere in his fifties, with a firm handshake; and he was visibly emotional. He began mid-sentence, 'I am tired. I am so proud of you, but I was as hopeful as you once.' His voice crackling now, 'I'm just tired now.' He told me that over the years, as he rose through the ranks in many organisations, he found his status being constantly questioned, directly and indirectly. He said that he had always believed there would come a time, as he continued to do better and better, when this would end. It never did.

* * *

The social conditioning that shapes our worldview starts in childhood. As we've seen, the early years of an individual's life are crucial to their chances of later social mobility, and what they see around them during that time appears to shape their ability to imagine a different future for themselves. The phrase 'the worst poverty is the poverty of aspiration' was first used by the Labour politician Ernest Bevin in the 1940s, and ever since the idea of 'aspiration' has reverberated through the social mobility debate. It's the idea that social mobility is partly hamstrung by a lack of desire on the part of some people to improve their circumstances: in 2018, the Labour MP Angela Rayner, herself from a deprived background, drew both criticism and praise for saying that 'we are not telling [white working-class boys] that they need to learn and they need to aspire. They are under the impression that they don't need to push themselves ... I think we need to do much more about the culture of the white working class in this country.'[1] And it is – I think – true that social mobility is partly driven by passion, enthusiasm, ambition, desire: you have to *want* to make it, if you're going to get there. Certainly, nothing happened in my own life until I returned from Kenya with the idea that things could be better. But how do we raise children and young people to dream bigger, be more ambitious – and, just as importantly, what will they find if they do?

In 2018, the charity Education and Employment surveyed primary-school-age children across the world about their career ambitions.[2] Although, as the charity pointed out, policymakers in England rarely think about the employment ambitions of young children, they found that these aspirations already reflected the children's circumstances. Gender stereotyping was well established: boys were more likely to want to be scientists, soldiers and engineers, whereas girls opted for roles like nurse and teacher. And, unsurprisingly, socio-economic status played a role, with children at schools with a high number of pupils on free school meals more likely to see themselves as mechanics rather than engineers, hairdressers rather than vets. Children at more deprived schools appeared to barely consider themselves at all for creative professions such as acting, music or writing books. (And, while being a vet or a film producer is not inherently better than being a hairdresser, ambitions should be set by talent and interest, not by socio-economic status.)

Perhaps we shouldn't place too much weight on this. After all, as anyone who has spent time with young children knows, their likes and dislikes change on an almost daily basis. Who's to say that those choosing hairdresser and mechanic today aren't thinking of themselves as a surgeon or an MP by the time they're doing their GCSEs (or visa versa)? After all, the most popular choice across all groups was sportsperson, and, unless we are harbouring a generation of elite athletes, most of those children will end up doing something else. But there's evidence that these patterns do persist: research by a different charity found that fourteen-year-olds made very similar choices to four-year-olds.[3] Aside from the worrying fact that very young children seem to already have absorbed the idea that some jobs are reserved for a certain kind of person, it was clear that their aspirations were shaped by what they saw around them: the most influential figure in their choice was a family member, and they are likely to be hitting their GCSEs in circumstances similar to those of their early childhood.

It's easy to think that the answer to this is raise the aspirations of the children: that is, after all, why I make a point of reminding Adam that people like him do interesting things, run businesses, have careers in academia, speak any way they want to. The impact of seeing someone who speaks like you, looks like you, acts like you doing something – teaching, appearing on television, on the board of your company – can never be underestimated. But while role models can help inspire children, can help concretise a dream and turn it into a set ambition, those people by definition are likely to be outliers: to have beaten the odds. MPs like Rayner are an inspiring presence in our politics. But, as she said herself, her success doesn't mean that anyone can make it: 'My mates, who are struggling now, are no different to me. My brother and sister are smarter than me. But I'm the most successful because I've been given opportunities that they never had.'[4] There's little point in tinkering about with children's ambitions and self-perception if they are never given the chance to act on them.

It's possible to compare the situations of young people in the workplace today with their earlier aspirations through data released by the Office for National Statistics.[5] In 2011 and 2012 – when our cohort was somewhere between the ages of sixteen and twenty-one – they were pretty ambitious for themselves: the most popular jobs were those in the creative industries (writing, acting, film production), teaching, the health profession, the police or fire service, and nursing or midwifery. Respondents also thought that they'd be earning a pretty decent wage: 50 per cent thought they'd be earning £35,000 when they were thirty if they'd been to university, or £25,000 if they hadn't.

Those young people are now somewhere between twenty-two and twenty-nine. The most common job in which they were employed, and this remained the case for this age group in 2017, was cashier or sales assistant, followed by caring. The only job that was also in their original top five ambitions, teaching, came in third, at 4.5 per cent. The average salary for a thirty-year-old in 2017 was £23,700. Partly, this can be explained by the historical context. Those who were twenty-one in 2011 started their careers in the immediate aftermath of the credit crunch; their generation – millennials – are the first to do worse than their parents in a hundred years.[6] It's a lot to ask of a young person from a deprived background to take on a prevailing economic and employment climate like this armed only with their aspirations, but it's something we continue to do: as opportunities to make a success of your life have declined, we keep repeating that we're a meritocracy, that success is there for the deserving – if only they'd aspire to it.

* * *

So if you are a young person from a background like mine, seeking to become socially mobile, what's the answer? Give up and wait for society to match the dreams you have for yourself? At the heart of what's happened for me, and for people like me, is the ability to imagine a better place for oneself. But that doesn't mean the kind of imagination that consists of closing your eyes and praying very hard; it doesn't mean a wilful refusal to accept the nature of reality. But it doesn't mean limiting your ambitions either. Instead, it's the kind of imagination that sits alongside a clear perception of the challenges – and sees a way through them, as well as grit and resilience that allows you to keep going when things get tough. Your imagination is like a muscle: if you work it enough, and in the right way, it'll give you the strength to push through barriers and climb up ladders.

The Belgian footballer Romelu Lukaku grew up in poverty. One day he came home to find his mother mixing milk with water to make it last longer; 'I knew we were struggling. But when she was mixing in water with the milk, I realized it was *over*, you know what I mean? This was our life.' It was an epiphany for him: 'I made a promise to myself that day. It was like somebody snapped their fingers and woke me up. I knew exactly what I had to do, and what I was *going* to do.' After that, 'every game I ever played was a Final. When I played in the park, it was a Final. When I played during break in kindergarten, it was a Final. ... I used to try to tear the cover off the ball every time I shot it.'[7] The grit and resilience that allowed Lukaku to deal with the daily humiliations that come with living life at the margins of society – believing, hoping, dreaming and striving towards a better future for yourself, for your family and for a more dignified present – propelled him towards the unlikely future as a famous and wealthy footballer that he had imagined for himself. Of course, it could have been very different; we'll never know about the other boys in Antwerp who made themselves that promise and didn't go on to tear up the pitch for Manchester United. But I do know one thing: if he hadn't gritted his teeth and pushed forward with the determination he did, it would *never* have happened.

For me, as I traced my own very different route upwards, I had to call on many of the same resources. I had to check the map again and see whether there was a different way, a quicker path – but, like Lukaku, the direction of travel was never in doubt. Like him, I was able to step outside what I was used to and see my world as inadequate; and that I owed it to myself, to my family, to the legacy of my father to realise something more. It also allowed me to be flexible: to see myself differently as I changed and grew and learned, and to be at peace with that change. Deep down, I wanted badly to improve, for not only my *life* to be better but to be better myself: better educated, happier, more fulfilled, in control of my own destiny. I was able to see myself in a world about which I knew nothing, and have the courage, the discipline, the determination and the resilience to pursue it.

This isn't 'the power of positive thinking'. I'm not telling you to visualise your success, that 'if you can dream it you can do it'. This is not about triumphing through sheer force of will. I am a positive person, an optimist, but I am also a realist: I know that what you want and what's possible are often very different things. What matters more is really understanding your options, and pursuing whichever path you choose with the conviction that Lukaku talks about. As someone overcoming poverty, there will be a lot of things outside your control, so it's all about identifying the things that you *can* control – and what you can do with them. Chief among these is your outlook. The Stanford University psychologist Dr Carol Dweck has written extensively about two 'mindsets': the fixed mindset and the growth mindset. Either you take your personality and intelligence to be immovable or fixed, or you see it as constantly changing, evolving and developing throughout your life in a way that helps you achieve what you've set out to.[8] For instance, do you see yourself as someone overwhelmed by the challenges ahead, or do you see another opportunity to test what you're made of? Is effort without reward wasted, or is it a chance to hone your skills, to lay down foundations for something that may pay off, not in a week or a month but next year or the year after that? Are you someone who looks at criticism as yet another opportunity to grow and learn, or do you seek out the reasons to ignore each negative feedback? Are you the type of person who is inspired by the success of others or only threatened and undermined by it?

I don't want to give the impression that my journey has been a series of triumphs. In fact, much of what I've tried has failed: there have been plenty of false starts, plenty of missteps, plenty of cases I've lost, plenty of job interviews I've bombed. For each success, I'd estimate that I've been knocked back six times. And that is okay: failure is a normal part of life. Dweck's work, which has been hugely influential to me, is not about being exceptional. It is not about being born with talent. It's about grafting, day in, day out, learning, trying, failing, trying again – and the idea that there's always room for improvement.[9] Improvement obviously isn't the same as transformation: there's no growth mindset on earth powerful enough to convert me into a prima ballerina or fighter ace. But it did give me the opportunity to take my talents and point them in the direction of something I *could* do: be a barrister. And it gave me the strength to keep going when things got tough: as Dweck says in her book *Mindset*, 'the passion for stretching yourself and sticking to it, even (or especially) when it's not going well, is the hallmark of the growth mindset. This is the mindset that allows people to thrive during some of the most challenging times in their lives.' In fact, failure can even be a crucial part of success: elsewhere in the book, Dweck points out that a particular skill developed by 'exceptional people' is the ability to convert a setback into a success. It's something I try to consciously acknowledge myself: the setbacks in my life have led directly to many improbable successes, including the fact that I am writing this book.[10]

Think of our socially mobile person, sprinting up their mountain. The people at the top may have been born with all the equipment they need: kitted out with crampons and ice axes, and with a map of the best path to the top already supplied. There's nothing you can do about that. But you can prepare yourself: with as much information as possible; with the conviction that you deserve to be there; and with the kind of mindset that will allow you to survive the knocks you'll sustain on the way up.

* * *

But while a growth mindset is a major advantage, social mobility does not operate in a vacuum. No one can make it entirely on their own. A crucial part of the puzzle will always be the people on the other side of the equation: those who already inhabit the elite spaces, and who choose who gets through, and who doesn't.

I was lucky, at various points in my career, to have the support and guidance of a number of brilliant and imaginative mentors, who saw my potential early on, and guided me through the treacherous waters that could have sunk me at the beginning of my journey. One of these was a woman called Fenella Morris, who began her career as a barrister as someone who, in her own words, was 'from a state school, not rich, not privileged and not very self-confident'. Despite this, she was extremely successful: she's now a QC, which is as senior as you can get as a barrister, and in 2018 she was invited to become a bencher at Middle Temple, honouring her distinguished career at the Bar. She invited me to the ceremony at Middle Temple Hall, where she gave a short and deeply moving speech. As I sat absorbing it, next to her two proud sons, I was overwhelmed by the feeling that, while we like to talk about how much progress we've made, in many ways we have really not moved at all. Fenella recounted a very familiar-sounding anecdote about her starting point:

> On my first trip to Middle Temple, I met someone I knew from university. We hadn't been particularly friendly because he seemed so different from me – he had gone to a top public school and his father was a High Court Judge. Just the sight of him made me imagine a long string of Judgey ancestors floating like spectres behind him. Anyway, he was kind enough to say hello and asked me what I was doing in Middle Temple. I told him.
>
> And he said – and I remember it so clearly although it is thirty years later – 'it's really good that people like you are coming to the Bar'. That sentence contains a host of meanings. Whatever 'people like you' might signify, I thought it meant that he thought that I was not like him – the sort of person who did become a barrister.

Fenella also described three important points in her career at which a senior man had pushed her to apply for something that 'I didn't think was for me'. In other words, someone else was able to imagine a future for her that she couldn't see for herself, and that made all the difference. But although Fenella gave tribute to the effect these men had had on her career, it was the throwaway comment of her colleague, which planted 'the thought that I was not quite the right sort of person to be a barrister – to convince a judge, to inspire a client, to persuade an opponent' which 'haunted' her and had to a certain extent shaped her belief in her talents. Imagination, dreams, vision, ambitions ... whatever you call them, they are fragile things, and comments that may seem minor and inconsequential to the people who make them can have a devastating effect.

What I admire most about the Bar is not the pomp and ceremony, the arcane rituals, the toasting to the Queen and the royal family, not the wigs or the gowns or the port. It's that it concentrates, within a square mile, some of the sharpest intellects and the cleverest people I am ever likely to meet. People who are quick to react or assimilate information, curious, gifted with a sharp and flexible intelligence. But, as in any walk of life, the Bar is also full of people with their own preconceptions, prejudices, and unconscious biases, and worldviews coloured by their own backstories. In other words, just as they are gifted in one sense, they're also collectively flawed. There's a well-known riddle that goes like this: a man and his son are both badly injured in a car crash. They are taken to hospital, where a surgeon prepares to operate on them. But the surgeon, on arrival in theatre, takes one look at the young boy and says: 'I can't operate on him – he's my son!' The answer, of course, is that the surgeon is the boy's mother. But the 'brain-teasing' nature of the puzzle stems from the strength of our conditioning: when called on to visualise 'a surgeon' many of us default to the cultural 'standard', in other words, a man.

I've experienced many examples of this, but one in particular sticks in the mind. Because my debating partner Henry and I had won the Lincoln's Inn mooting competition – a mock legal debate, and the closest you can get as a pupil to real-life courtroom experience – we were sat at the 'top table' for the formal dinner that trainee barristers must attend in order to be accepted as members of the Bar. These dinners, which take place in a Hogwarts-like environment, are an actual requirement. They are a way of ensuring that you mix with your future colleagues, learning the etiquette and behaviour of the profession that's likely to dominate your daily existence in the future. If you have attended a public school or an Oxbridge college, the setting will be instantly familiar, dining in gowns, grace in Latin, and toasting to the Queen. After I sat down, one of the barristers next to me, who had watched the mooting competition earlier in the evening, leant over to say: 'So, tell me, what fine school taught you to moot in that outstanding way?'

Of course, you might say that he was simply trying to be nice – to put a younger colleague at his ease with a compliment and a question about his background. But I didn't have much to tell him: the Wembley High that I attended wasn't a fine school, and any debating skills I had picked up were more likely to have come from having to talk myself out of being stabbed. I said as much to him, and his reaction was one of bewilderment; I was aware of him searching my face for a hint that I might be making a joke. The rest of the dinner was awkward. Henry, I noticed, wasn't asked the same question. I knew then, and I know now, that we'd won the competition through skill, determination, hard work, quick thinking (and, of course, luck). The schools that we went to were irrelevant. But it ended with a reminder that, to some members of the profession I was joining, my background was everything. My questioner was simply unable to imagine a world in which someone who debated like me, who sat at the top table with him, had come from anywhere else.

Our inability, as employers, to look beyond the obvious holds back socially mobile people. We've seen in the previous chapter that hiring and promoting often hinges on vague concepts of 'fit', 'polish', 'partner material': in other words, 'an image of the privileged'. They are all references to a shared image of the same kind of person: confident, at ease with clients, sharing the right kind of opinions and the same kind of cultural shibboleths, wearing the right kind of clothes. But this simply isn't good enough: if any of us are genuinely serious about improving diversity or access to our own professions, we have to look beyond the easy, the tried-and-tested. In many ways, I owe my position not only to my own aspiration but to the imagination shown by other people. While I was researching my BBC documentary, I came across a letter from one of my mentors – a senior barrister named Graham Eklund QC – to my producer. While I was at Bar School, I had sent Graham my CV, which he had apparently found 'underwhelming': 'His GCSEs were not good – Cs & Bs. But I realised that his educational achievements got better the older he got. And, of course, he didn't even speak English until he was 9.' Graham found it interesting that I 'even mentioned' my GCSEs – 'many would have brushed over them. Was that because he did not understand CV rules or was it that he was very proud – in the [circumstances] – of those grades? [I] don't know. But it was a CV someone like me had rarely seen!'

There was an easy option here: to see the CV as simply not good enough, tragically out of sync with its owner's ambitions. I was lucky that my CV landed with someone like Graham, who showed more imagination in interpreting what it might mean than many would have done. Graham was able to put the poor GCSEs and unpolished CV in context and see that here was someone who could, in fact, make a good barrister: whose achievements, measured against their starting point, weren't out of line with their competitors. Graham went on to support me throughout my training, offering wise advice and an often invaluable ability to not only see things from my perspective but to recognise the gaps in his own knowledge. But, in my experience, the Grahams are few and far between: more often, we seem unable to separate our image of what successful, promotable people look like from the kind of people who already do that job.

* * *

As a socially mobile person, being able to picture your-self in this country as an equal and productive member of society, dignified in your place, full of purpose and ambition, requires a robust interrogation of your identity. But young people today find themselves more than ever caught between two competing – but, as we will see, oddly aligned – narratives that seek to define their identities for them. Take, for instance, British Muslims. Of all the groups in our society, Muslims are least well represented in top professions, politics and in public life. They are disproportion-ately more likely to be affected by poverty, unemployment and the general lack of opportunities.[11] In most cases, they suffer from the 'full house of discrimination', in terms of both ethnicity and religion. Many live under the constant threat of Islamophobia, verbal abuse or physical attack – a state of constant wariness that one woman described as a form of post-traumatic stress disorder, with the difference being that the trauma is being lived here and now. It's the result of a multitude of factors, from the legacy of colonialism to the influence of the right-wing press, but whatever the cause, it has put enormous pressure on these communities (for Muslims are not a homogeneous group) to define their own identities in opposition to the external forces that seek to define them. In some cases, this has led communities to become inward-looking, seeking solace in their faith as they perceive themselves to be under attack (the appeal of radical Islam is often that it offers alienated Muslims the appearance of community, acceptance and dignity).[12] Young, second-generation European Muslims, who are caught between two cultures – that of their parents, which they don't always share, and that of their country, which doesn't fully accept them – are faced with the challenge of both making their way in the world and finding an identity they can live with and be proud of. For them, the business of getting on is charged and politicised as well as racialised.

We have seen how the question of imagination is two-fold: it is about how someone sees themselves, and how the rest of the world sees them. Feeling like an outsider can be deeply alienating; and for someone who looks visibly different, the opportunities to blend in, to simply get on with the job without distractions, are few and far between. The part of your identity that marks you as different can come to dominate all others. For women who wear the hijab – as some of my sisters, my nieces, and my mother do – this one element of their identity, that of the Muslim woman, can easily become dominant and magnified to the point that it takes over everything else. Very little room or capacity is left to explore or express anything of their other identities: female, black, African, a Londoner, a student, a mother, a professional. Whenever some horrendous attack takes place in London, Paris or Brussels, almost always carried out by men, it is always the Muslim women who wear a visible symbol of their religion who pay the most immediate price. They are the ones who get attacked or abused on public transport, while in the background senior politicians play a tune of dog-whistle Islamophobia.

Many other people from marginalised groups find themselves similarly forced into a particular box; their identity defined by others, and not in a way that benefits them. Muslim women may find themselves stereotyped as passive, oppressed, unworldly; young black men as aggressive, uncooperative, even criminal; poor white men as crude, lazy, feckless. As a result, as Francis Fukuyama points out in *Identity*, marginalised groups have been faced with a choice: demanding that society treat its members in the same way as everyone else, or asserting a separate identity and demanding respect for that identity as *different* from mainstream society.[13] It is not surprising that, in response, a movement has started that has attempted to push back against the weight of expectation, to bring people experiencing similar kinds of oppression together to seek solidarity and support in numbers. I am talking, of course, about what has been termed identity politics: the impetus for people who share a particular trait – gender, race, sexuality, religion – to band together politically in order to exert pressure in their common interests.

The notion that someone's identity – something almost infinitely nuanced and unique to themselves – can be determined by characteristics such as race, gender or religion baffles me. These things are important, of course: 'Oliver Smith-Jones', who's white, middle-class and living in North Oxford, will have a very different experience of the world from 'Fatima Begum', living in a deprived community in a social mobility cold-spot like Blackpool. And identity politics has undoubtedly accomplished great and important things: from the suffragettes to Black Lives Matter and the campaigns to legalise gay marriage, movements based on identity have changed the global conversation and pushed the rights of oppressed groups to the forefront of government policy. It has given people from all walks of life a vocabulary to talk about difficult subjects, and an insight into the lives and experiences of others. All of this is deeply admirable.

But I cannot ignore the suspicion that at heart, both identity politics and the kind of structural lack of imagination that keeps people like me from progressing have something in common: they both encourage people to see themselves in terms of a single, disadvantageous aspect of their rich and varied individuality. Identity politics insists that I must see myself as a black Muslim immigrant – and that my identity will therefore always be in conflict with the world in which I now find myself. Like my colleague who instinctively rejected the idea that a black man from Wembley might speak just like him, it says to me: you'll never really belong here. These people will never really accept you.

All too often, the way in which politics is presented to minority or marginalised groups is as an endless competition between special interests: everyone screaming for attention within a hierarchy of misery and grievance, as if there's only a certain amount of oxygen available. While we are distracted by the endless quest to determine a spurious pecking order of victimhood, urged to turn from the travails of the white working class to the plight of immigrants to the challenges faced by LGBTQI people, real battle lines are drawn along class lines: societal inequality, lack of any real opportunity for those who most need it, access to a decent education, freedom from want and violence, and the opportunity to realise your full potential. These things are compounded by race, ethnic identity, gender or religion, but they do not give birth to it. This fundamental misunderstanding can cripple an individual's outlook and their mindset, their ability to imagine a better future for themselves.

The truth is that we're all in this together. Fatima Begum has more in common with her white neighbours, who send their children to the same failing schools and contend with the same depleted job market and lack of opportunities, than those neighbours do with Oliver in his comfortable Oxford suburb. Growing up, my siblings and I had more in common with white working-class kids growing up in Stoke or Dagenham than we ever did with a black Etonian. Intersectionality is a concept that's deeply engrained in identity politics but the *kinds* of intersections we're encouraged to make are closely policed, and often do not include class, poverty or access to opportunities. In the process, the divisions between different identities are elided. For example, as a Muslim, I may pray in the same mosque as a Bengali professional, and we can share our experiences of discrimination – what it's like having a surname that immediately marks you out as 'foreign', for instance. In theory, we belong to the 'Umma' – the global Muslim community in solidarity with each other, everywhere – and yet I know that if I wanted to marry his daughter, it's very possible that I'd revert pretty quickly to being just a black man. Yet the type of identity politics that's most prevalent in Britain today assumes some monolithic Muslim world, crushing together wildly different groups, with different interests, and facing very different challenges.

If my own journey has taught me anything, it's that communication is key. The siloing of identities – and the underlying message that different groups must always be in conflict – hardly helps this. Even when I was writing this book, I found my editor reflexively self-editing, prefacing feedback with caveats such as, 'well, bearing in mind that I'm a privileged, middle-class, white woman, my thoughts are ...'. It's not that there's anything wrong with being aware of your own privilege, and accounting for how it might shape your worldview, but it also means that, on one level, she wasn't responding with *what she really thought*; her feedback had gone through layers of editing before reaching me. Of course, this process can be benign – raising people's awareness of the impact of micro-aggressions, for instance – but it still places a barrier between the people who have privilege in our society and the people who don't. When you're moving up, you face a disorientating information blackout, and the current climate has led to a stifling of debate, and the unhealthy censoring of thought processes, preventing the free flow of information that people like me desperately need to learn about the situations that confront us.

Of course, people in privileged positions should be conscious of the power and advantage that this confers on them – shame on them if they aren't – and those who aren't in privileged positions should be conscious of the odds against them, and of their right to demand something different. But ultimately, what we need is for people to see the similarities between them, to form meaningful relationships and dialogue. Instead, we have division and suspicion, caution and shame, pointless minority networks and diversity boards set up by businesses, rather than active, organic networks of people sharing information.[14]

* * *

Success is, to a great extent, an act of redefining what is familiar – and in the process transforming it. It is, in a way, an act of imagination. But of course, there are limits to what imagination can achieve: it cannot overcome a basic lack of ability, or opportunity, or create space where there is none. In the society we live in, social mobility is likely to be relative, rather than absolute, which means that for some to move up, others must move down. There isn't space for everyone at the top, and so the most we can realistically achieve in terms of diversity in elite professional or social circles is for some of the current occupants to move out in favour of new incomers. That's a start, but it doesn't feel like a solution.

To me, one of the fundamental ways in which we can use imagination to reshape social mobility in the UK is to rethink what we mean by success; and to redefine aspiration, and change how aspiration is rewarded. My relationship with my own 'success' is complicated. I am lucky to have many of the outward markers of social mobility. I am a higher-rate taxpayer, a home-owner, and a member of an esteemed and ancient profession, and, as previously mentioned, I have two degrees, one of them from Oxford. But to my mind, social mobility is not a destination: there was never any point where I felt like I had 'arrived'. My success does not consist of those achievements; they are things that have happened because I was able to change my life, to learn about the world, grow as a person, to make up for the time I spent lost in grief, endlessly playing football. That has been my success, and if it had ended differently – as it very well might have – I would still have counted it a success. Success is a life-long journey to discover what we are good at, to improve on it, and to find ways of doing less of what we do not enjoy, or identify early on what may not come so naturally to us. There are people just like me, who worked as hard, addressed their traumas and past as I did, who challenged the expectations of others, but who don't have any of the things that I have. It might be because the cards didn't fall in their favour (in which case it seems unfair to blame them for it) but just as often it's because their vocation carried them in a different direction.

Success isn't a zero-sum game, but we live in a world that tells us it is: that money is a measure of value, that a nurse is less successful than a lawyer, that a valuable person fits into a certain kind of mould. It's important, of course, to have a metric in order to judge progress: millennials are much less likely to own property than their parents; and the number of lawyers who attended private school is disproportionately large in relation to the percentage of the population who are privately educated – such information gives us a way of framing the problem of social mobility. And it's important that children with the talent and desire to become barristers, pilots, authors, accountants or actors are taught to aspire to those professions. Access to a good education is crucial in allowing children to discover what they are interested in, and good at. But to make social mobility about attaining a particular portfolio of jobs, possessions and status is to misunderstand, in my view, what human progress is about. But, if we are to see success in terms of happiness, fulfilment and genuine contribution to society then we need systematic change.

Among the relatively low and stagnant levels of social mobility in European nations, a handful of countries stands out: Sweden, Norway, Denmark and Finland. In Britain, for example, 50 per cent of your income is determined by the income of your parents; in Denmark, Norway and Finland, the figure is 20 per cent.[15] Although they have risen somewhat in recent years, the Nordic countries also enjoy low levels of poverty and income inequality, as well as a generous welfare state, which is funded through high levels of taxation. The relationship between income inequality and low social mobility is clear: as Lee Elliot Major and Stephen Machin put it, 'extreme inequality of incomes at one point in time leads to greater inequality of opportunity over time which in turn leads to widening gaps between rich and poor.'[16] In other words, having significantly greater resources allows the rich to gain control of opportunities for advancement, either for themselves or for their children. Even among developed countries, Britain has a very high level of income inequality: it comes fourth in Europe, behind Luxembourg, Estonia and Greece.[17] The top earners in Britain get 40 per cent of the total income for the country; the bottom only 8 per cent. Britain also has, as we know, very low levels of social mobility.

Could we learn something from the 'Nordic model'? Reducing income inequality, after all, takes some of the pressure off the precarious middle classes, by reducing the financial penalty for downward social mobility. Higher taxes mean better social housing, better schools, more childcare, more libraries, more access to public services, all of which can make a crucial difference to the socially mobile – and higher wages for jobs that are socially important but poorly remunerated, like those in nursing, the caring professions, teaching, and the emergency services. A more equal society is one that can give its citizens space to find their own definition of success: instead of a narrow winner-takes-all mentality we could find something that rewards – and sees as a genuine end in itself – jobs that support others, strengthen our society from within, where compassion and generosity are as valuable qualifications as intelligence and drive. For some, happiness will always be linked with material possessions: flashy cars, higher salaries and exotic holidays. For some, it will be about power and status. But for others, it will be about a happy family, love, belonging; or about making a difference, creating change. We could build a society that values all these outcomes equally – but we will need to use our imaginations.

6

Filling In The Blanks: Mentoring

Mentor, because badass miracle worker isn't an official job title.

Inscription on the side of a mug from a mentee, July 2018

You cannot hope to build a better world without improving the individuals. To that end, each of us must work for our improvement and, at the same time, share a general responsibility for all humanity, our particular duty being to aid those to whom we think we can be most useful.

Marie Curie

In the summer of 1998, I had just been reunited with my mother and Abdi, my youngest brother, who had arrived in the UK less than a year before, having stayed in Nairobi when we left. We had spent four years apart and I was getting to know them all over again. For the first time, my siblings and I were all living together in Britain, in a hostel off Kilburn High Road in North West London with the misleadingly fancy name of 'Priory Mansions'. Although it was run by a kind, chain-smoking, middle-aged house-keeper (and a Sudanese man, also a chain smoker, who did the night shifts) it was a horrible place: dirty, crowded, infested with bedbugs and cockroaches. We slept three to a room, with the beds crammed side to side; a slight improvement on the arrangement of the preceding years, which had been five or six to a room. That summer, the only escape we had was to play football practically day and night. It was also the summer of the World Cup in France, with which we were similarly obsessed. Even then, I was deeply invested in England and its success, but – inevitably – we didn't make it far, crashing out on penalties against Argentina in the quarter-finals after an infamous incident in which David Beckham was sent off for kicking at the Argentinian player Diego Simeone.

On the evening of 8 July 1998, we gathered to watch the semi-final between France and Croatia. I had no particular interest in France, apart from the fact that they seemed to be doing well. I knew little if anything about French history or culture, I had never been to France, I didn't speak any French. But what happened in this game changed French football forever – and left an indelible mark on my memory. I'm telling this story because to me it illustrates everything you need to know about mentoring, something that is critical to social mobility. Mentoring provides from the outside what is missing from the inside; inside your family, inside your friendships, inside your neighbourhoods, inside your school or universities, inside your particular professional circles. And to me, the story of the 1998 World Cup semi-final tells you everything you need to know about helping someone, or seeking help yourself: whether it is understanding where you stand, making a plan, moving on to the next level, or overcoming an obstacle.

Back in Paris, half-time had just finished. No goals had been scored. As the players emerge through the tunnel, one of the Croatian players has his arm over the shoulder of a French player. It's a French national from Guadeloupe,

Lilian Thuram, and the arm belongs to the Croat Mario Stanić; both play for the Italian club Parma. They know each other well, and as they leave the tunnel, Stanić whispers into Thuram's ear 'this game is for us'.

To start with, it looks like he's right: within a minute, the Croatian striker Davor Suker manages to get a goal past the French goalkeeper. But suddenly, Thuram – a right back, not a midfielder and certainly not a striker – is halfway up the pitch. He takes the ball from the Croatian captain Zvonimir Boban, passes it to the French striker Djorkaeff, who's just a little too far from goal. The striker makes a split-second decision to pass to the shadow in the French blue jersey just visible in the corner of his right eye. He passes, and realises he's sent it back to his teammate, Thuram (later he would say, 'if I knew it was him, I would have just taken a shot myself, he doesn't know how to score.'). The ball reaches Thuram just before the goalkeeper is about to block him, and, just like that, he scores. There was complete disbelief from the commentators, supporters and (as it turned out) from his teammates. Back on the sofa in Kilburn, we were losing our minds.

That's enough on its own to get into the record books. But twenty-three minutes later, Thuram is once again running up the pitch with a great deal of determination. He fumbles, but then manages to get behind the ball and sends a curling shot into the bottom right-hand corner of the goal. Here's the even more remarkable thing: he shot it with his left foot. A man who, as his teammate Emmanuel Petit, pointed out afterwards, could barely score with his right foot, let alone his left. The game ended with France winning 2–1 – and into the first World Cup final in their entire history.

There's one more extraordinary fact in this whole amazing story. Lilian Thuram is the most-capped player in

French history. Born in Guadeloupe, French West Indies, his family relocated to mainland France when he was nine years old. They suffered the effects of profound racism when he was growing up. In his whole career, he only ever scored twice: in the second half of the semi-final against Croatia. Impressive, you might be thinking: but what does this have to do with mentoring? Mentoring is what Lilian Thuram – unflashy but inspirational – did for his nation 142 times. He was the consummate professional, turning up at every game, doing his best time and time again, thereby raising the spirits of the whole team. Mentoring means giving the task at hand your full attention, playing for the team while knowing that you won't be the star of the show (and that you might *never* find out what effect your contribution has had); being there, day in, day out, when it matters and when it doesn't seem to matter (but it probably does).

Above all else, it is about scoring the right goals – even if you have to use your weaker foot – when it matters the most. It is impossible to know when that moment will come, but you must be ready for it when it does. Your equivalent of Thuram's two goals – in whatever form it takes – could be the slight nudge that someone needs to get them to the next stage of their lives, or it might be getting them on to the pitch for *their* 'World Cup final'. Mentoring is hard, it is relentless, it's not something that can only be done for a few months or a few years. You have to be ready for the long haul, ready for sweat and tears and drama. It's a task for which you won't receive a trophy, but at the end of it, if you get it right, lies a huge reward: the chance to help someone else, to pass on the privileges you have received, and to make a contribution to levelling the playing field.

* * *

But what exactly is mentoring? According to Collins dictionary, 'a person's mentor is someone who gives them help and advice over a period of time, especially help and advice related to their job'. This is the definition we're most familiar with: a mentee, often someone on the cusp of entry to the workplace or beginning their career, finds someone, probably older and definitely more experienced, who can tell them how to navigate the world they want to enter. But mentoring can take many other forms, be haphazard or regimented, fluid or clearly delineated: your mentor could be a teacher, a university tutor, a colleague, a friend, an elder sibling, someone you're matched with as part of a scheme, or someone you meet quite randomly. At the heart of it all, though, are enduring relationships, and the basic principles of reliability and consistency.

That's what mentoring is *as a relationship* – but what does it actually do in practice? At heart, mentoring is about the third part of the three components of success in our society: economic capital, cultural capital and social capital. In a general sense, social capital is who you know: your relationships with other people, and access to wider social networks. For people with a lot of social capital, this can be a huge advantage; when we talk about the 'old boys' network', for instance, we're talking about how going to private or public school gives you access to a valuable social network that concentrates jobs and information for its members. Indeed, this kind of mentoring, based on access to social capital, is built into many middle-class and upper-middle-class experiences of the working world. It's the godmother who works in the industry you want to enter and who takes you out to lunch once a month, the family friend who'll 'take an interest' in your progress and give you a little push in the right direction every so often. It's the alumni networks that grow out of top universities, which often actively work to connect old members with new graduates: of course, the more prestigious the institution, the more likely that your fellow alumni are occupying significant positions of power and influence. These mentors can provide invaluable help, passing on not only opportunities in the form of work experience or internships, but also the kind of insight that helps a new arrival avoid the sorts of faux-pas that people like me might make for no other reason than ignorance.

I have talked before about the role of ignorance – on both sides of the social divide – in social mobility. It remains the case that one of the greatest barriers to progress is a lack of knowledge, and that is something that mentorship can address. The great French sociologist Pierre Bourdieu coined the term 'habitus' to describe a sort of fundamental understanding of the norms of any particular social context. Habitus is something that's developed over time, something that gives you an instinctive grasp over what to do or say in a particular situation: using a football metaphor, Bourdieu described it as a 'feel for the game'. Habitus is so intuitive that when you have it you hardly register it, which makes it hard to understand that other people may have absolutely no idea that, for example, it's a requirement to turn up on time for a job interview. One of my favourite examples of the essential difficulty of learning habitus comes from *Watching the English* (which, as you might expect, brims over with such examples). The father of the author, Kate Fox, is speaking to some Anglophile Italian friends who are keen to master English understatement. They're describing a truly awful meal they had: bad food, poor service, disgusting restaurant. At the end, the author's father says mildly, 'So, you wouldn't recommend it, then?' They're astounded: 'How do you *do* that? How do you *know* to do that? How do you know *when* to do that?'. The answer comes: 'I can't explain. We just do it. It just comes naturally.'[1]

But, of course, it doesn't. Acceptable behaviour is something we learn by watching others, and then internalise to the point that, like Kate Fox's father, 'we just do it'. Entering a world where the habitus is very different from the one you grew up with means making a lot of mistakes, and losing time and ground while you make up for them – or finding someone who can guide you through them. A Social Mobility Commission report[2] into elitism in the finance sector found that applicants from lower socio-economic backgrounds were being frozen out of companies because they didn't know about the strict, but unspoken, laws that govern dress and behaviour. An example might be the 'never brown in town' rule, which forbids the wearing of brown shoes with a business suit (according to one City worker interviewed by *The Guardian*, this 'makes you look a bit of a spiv', or, in other words, common).[3] It might sound silly – surely nobody cares about things like this? – but the report concluded that in fact they do, and that 'cultural competence' plays a large role in whether employees thrive in the workplace or not. When I first arrived at the Bar, I was surprised to find people casually calling each other by their surnames, something which at the time sounded weird and a bit rude to me. Today, I still find this public-school habit grating, but for a slightly different reason: although I doubt it's intended as such, it's a reminder that within the profession there is an old boy's network to whom this acts as a subtle form of bonding, not available to an outsider. You can't really learn the rules or become 'culturally competent' at something like this: either it's a sign that you are 'someone like us', that you share a background and a mindset, or it simply sounds strange. Again, these things may seem unimportant, but they build up, and can create a profound sense of dislocation for the socially mobile.

Of course, social capital also works in more straightforward ways: introductions, work experience, connections, a general aura of appealing familiarity that forges friendships across professional levels. Many people arrive into elite professions armed not only with cultural competence but also with a network of connections already in place. Once you're plugged in, you're part of the matrix and can reach out and make your own connections – but it can be very hard to penetrate from the outside. As one interviewee for the Social Mobility Commission report put it, 'other people, they already had those networks ... I was in despair, am I doing something wrong? Like, how am I not able to strike up these conversations? And it was only towards the end I realised that actually it's because these guys have a head start.' What I'm describing might not sound like an entirely bad thing: yet it is another way for the powerful to concentrate privilege and information among people like themselves. There are other words for this kind of mentorship, two of which are nepotism and favouritism. And there is no doubt that the unofficial network that connects privileged young people to older figures in their field is very effective. Friedman and Laurison note that while the success of candidates from well-off backgrounds is often ascribed to confidence and a willingness to take risks, on further questioning it would often be clear that a senior person had been involved, encouraging those candidates to apply, or ushering them through the process. But if these networks are applied differently, the result can be transformative: the power of mentoring is that it has the capacity to break these vertical transmissions between the privileged by allowing people like me to access the unofficial channels of knowledge, expertise, advice and general guidance. By its very nature, mentorship is informal, emotional, personal, vague – which makes it a surprisingly effective way to address the loose, unacknowledged, informal networks of privilege that have such a powerful shaping effect on our professions. A close reading of most social mobility stories makes it clear that mentorship often plays a crucial role: both J. D. Vance and Tara Westover's books feature powerful mentors who intervene in order to help the struggling or directionless author. Vance describes the impact of his Yale law professor, Amy Chua, in helping close 'the information gap' as 'like I had learned to see'.[4] Similarly, Westover's eponymous 'education' is shaped and propelled by various figures, from her brother Tyler to a senior professor at Cambridge, who saw her talent even when she couldn't.

During my career in the legal profession, there have been multiple mentors who have helped me. To this day I seek out guidance from more senior colleagues as my career enters a new chapter with which I am unfamiliar, sound out people who might see something I don't, who might sense something which I am incapable of seeing because of my lack of experience. My two most important professional mentors are Elizabeth Rantzen, formerly a chief executive of a barristers' chambers, and Graham Eklund QC, who we met in the previous chapter. Neither Elizabeth nor I sought out a mentor relationship: it was in many ways pure accident that we ended up in one. We got to know each other; I met her family and she met mine. I told her about my difficulties in getting work experience in the legal profession; she put me in touch with Graham and others. Elizabeth was supremely well connected – something that I certainly was not. Suddenly, I found myself with access to the same kinds of networks that some of my more privileged peers had, and was finally able to call up senior people in the industry and say, 'Elizabeth suggested we meet.' Of course, I was enormously lucky to encounter Elizabeth when I did, just as I was lucky again when my CV landed on Graham's desk. Many equally deserving people will never meet the mentors who could help them, and, in any case, relying on luck and serendipitous encounters is clearly no solution to an entrenched problem like social mobility. But the fact remains that I have not come across anything that was as effective in breaking down the barriers of advantage between my peers and me, and if we could find a way to make this kind of mentorship more widely available, it would redistribute social capital in a way that could be transformative. It also, of course, works both ways: mentors learn from their mentees in ways that enrich their own experience and worldview. It might be the perspective of someone from a younger generation, who sees things differently, but it might equally be an understanding of your own blind spots and prejudices, an experience like Vance's of suddenly 'learning to see'.

* * *

These days, I am both a mentee and a mentor; in fact, some of my mentees are now in the position to be mentors themselves. A mentor, as I have said, can be almost anyone, and the number of roles you have to fulfil can be many: role model, friend, careers adviser, shoulder to cry on, therapist, life coach. It's often thought of in terms of professional advice, but in truth it's often about much bigger things: in other words, mentorship is not just about how to work, but how to live. For J. D. Vance,

My professor gave me permission to be me. It's hard to put a dollar value on that advice. It's the kind of thing that continues to pay dividends. But make no mistake: The advice had tangible economic value. Social capital isn't manifest only in someone connecting you to a friend or passing a resume on to an old boss. It is also, or perhaps primarily, a measure of how much we learn through our friends, colleagues and mentors.[5]

My own relationships with Elizabeth and Graham created a kind of empathetic ecosystem that allowed me to shape my own vision, in my own time, to provide the space for me to imagine what life I could have, markedly different from the one I'd once led. It boosted my confidence in far-reaching ways to know that people who had such long and distinguished careers and experience in the profession believed that I could make it. I believed in them believing in me, and so was able to believe in myself.

Likewise, when I asked my mentees to tell me what they thought mentorship should be about, and what they got out of our relationship, I wasn't surprised that their answers spanned the very practical and work-focused ('career advice', 'goal setting') to the much more holistic and personal ('I think we have become friends now', 'help[ed me] identify a sense of self', 'helped me address personal obstacles'). One mentee talked about how our relationship had run parallel to a journey of personal self-discovery, during which she had addressed buried trauma surrounding her relationship with her father; for another, it was simply 'the benefit of checking in with an experienced professional in a more relaxed ... manner'. For still others, the value lay simply in seeing someone in a senior position who was like them and understood their background: mentorship can sometimes be as straightforward as offering someone the opportunity to 'see what they can be'. There's no set method or gold standard: mentorship can be a life-long, enormously supportive and personally invested relationship, or it might be no more than making yourself available to someone for six months, until they are ready to stand on their own two feet.

At the most personal end of what mentorship can be lies Friendship Works, a mentoring service in East London, which aims to connect young people from the most vulnerable groups in our society with a volunteer mentor who will be a reliable, supportive presence in their lives. Friendship Works explicitly sets no specific goals (they don't aim, for instance, to get a mentee back into mainstream education or the workplace, though that might happen in time), and it's a patient, deliberate, time-consuming process. The mentees I spoke to talked about the number of adults who've come into and out of their lives; and how for them the most important thing was that their mentor 'never gave up' on them. This was sometimes quite literal; mentors often experienced mentees deliberately testing the relationship, breaking agreements, refusing to see them, being difficult to engage with – all to see whether the mentor would really stick around. Up to this point the mentee's experience had often been that the reliable adults in their lives were care workers, or people who were, in some form or other, 'just doing their job'. This was often the first time they had an opportunity to connect with someone who was not being paid to be in their lives; to be spending time with someone who appreciated them for who they were.

Mentorship programmes like Friendship Works are not about social mobility. Rather, they are about learning how to live and be happy: how to build confidence and self-esteem, trust other people, focus on self-development, and understand the world and your place in it. Giving the mentees – whose lives may until then have felt almost entirely outside their control – a sense of agency can itself be transformative. One mentor pointed out that if you approach the mentee on the basis of 'I'm here to help', you've already returned them to the position of being a passive recipient of aid and the match between you is unlikely to work. According to the charity, the results of all this may not become obvious until a year after the first meeting, and a successful outcome may mean no more than maintaining contact. But the effects for the mentee can be significant, and are created by the simplest things that many of us take for granted: the notion, for example, that someone both values *your* time and wants to spend their time with you; that they're not obliged to do so, and are not being remunerated; and that you are a person who somebody cares about.

* * *

So, what makes a good mentor? The best of my own mentors offered me, as well as their consistent presence in my life, four things. First was access to people, things and information that I couldn't find myself, whether that was a trip to the theatre, an introduction, or a detailed breakdown of the psychological landscape of the profession. The second was a safe space in which there were no stupid questions: I could always (and still do) call them up with my latest crazy plan, and come away with a 'yes', a 'yes but', or a 'no, not yet'. Thirdly, they were honest: honest about my strengths and my weaknesses, and also about the challenges I faced. But lastly, and perhaps most importantly, they imagined for me a future that I couldn't quite see myself. Plans don't spring into your mind fully formed; they are shaped by what you know to be possible. As I spent more time at the Bar, I could see how so many of my ambitious, brilliant colleagues – who seemed to have such a clear idea of where they were going – were acting out something that had already been planned for them, following in the steps of a parent or some other role model in whom they could see themselves reflected.

Plugging the information gap can take many forms: from the simple and practical (dress codes, presentation skills, CV drafting) to the more nuanced and conceptual (human nature and psychology, reading a room, working out where you stand – and not just figuratively – in a particular group). But I think that constructing a proper plan – and establishing the difference between having a *goal* and having a *plan* – is one of the most important. All of my mentees are ambitious and driven: I wouldn't have met them in the first place if they weren't. But they are also subject to the same basic messaging from society that we all receive; that status and wealth are everything. They set their sights high, as they should, but I see my role as partly to remind them that life is also about fulfilment and happiness – and that they're unlikely to really thrive if their goal isn't a reflection of their talents and needs. I might, for instance, suggest to a clever and ambitious mentee who nonetheless struggles with organisation and self-discipline that being self-employed (as all barristers are) is unlikely to work for her: she's best placed to succeed with the structure that a nine-to-five office job would offer her. Of course, a mentor should not be making the plan for the mentee, or taking the big decisions for them: it's about giving them a compass, a few basic directions – and a reminder to watch out for quicksands, cliffs and other hazards.

Mentoring is often not about getting someone all the way: it's about getting them to the same starting line as everyone else. It's as if the path to success is a scale from one to ten, with the socially mobile starting at zero, and everyone else beginning at five. Your job is about those *first* five steps; after that, they should be able to look after themselves. An essential part of this is honesty: sometimes the unconditional support a mentee needs will take the form of tough love. Again, when comparing notes with friends and colleagues who come from middle-class backgrounds, I was always astonished by how structured their childhoods had been, how the discipline and order that is such a crucial part of professional life had been imposed on them from such a young age that it was second nature. Even something as simple as regular bedtimes and meal times provides the basis of an ability to impose order on your life, something that many people have never had the opportunity to develop.

In my experience, mentees need boundaries, and you'll do them no favours by making allowances for behaviour that others won't tolerate. By way of example, I had a young man turn up to my chambers for shadowing. He was four minutes late, and hadn't brought a pen or piece of paper. It might seem like a small thing, but at the Bar nothing is more important than being prepared and you'll never make it if you don't have your shit together. So I sent him home straight away. The next day – and for the rest of the week – he turned up to chambers before I did. We had a conversation about it and, by the end of the week, we could even laugh about it; and I'm confident that, shocking though it was at the time, this is what he needed at that particular moment. British politeness has its place, but sometimes it's the direct (and sometimes brutal) approach I picked up from my African grandmother that serves me best.

As well as fostering self-reliance and discipline, honest

mentoring also means not shying away from difficult topics. Skirting around subjects like race, prejudice and privilege because you lack the confidence to address them leaves a gap in your mentee's understanding of their situation (if they haven't grasped it immediately, which they may have), and this does them no favours. It is so important that the deeply problematic issues are not avoided: a young, working-class Muslim woman facing a panel of interviewees who do not look like her already feels different before she's taken her seat. To have someone raise these issues in a safe environment, to verbalise what she might already be feeling, to say that it's okay to feel it and here's how to deal with it – this is the *least* a mentor can offer a mentee. Failure to address these things head-on, being too squeamish to offer advice about whether they are really suited to the path they are trying to follow, or to point out an adjustable issue like poor grammar – these are all betrayals.

Mentees who come from what are sometimes described as 'non-traditional' backgrounds need to know the reality of what faces them and to be aware of an important fact: the myth of meritocracy hurts the most disadvantaged.[6] A recent study in America[7] found that 'marginalised young people who grew up believing in the "American Dream"', that ideal of success based on hard work and perseverance, show a *decline* in self-esteem and an increase in risky behaviours during their middle-school years'.[8] In social psychology there is a theory called 'system justification' – the idea that we are more likely to defend, believe in, promote and rationalise the status quo when it works for us, and thus to see the 'overarching social, economic and political order as legitimate, fair and ultimately good'.[9] According to the author of the study, Professor Erin Godfrey of New York University, 'if you're in an advantaged position in society, believing the system is fair and that everyone could get ahead if they just worked hard enough doesn't create any conflict for you ... you can feel good about how you made it.'[10] However, for those who are 'marginalised by the system – economically, racially and ethnically – believing that the system is fair puts them in conflict with themselves': who else is there to blame for things not working out? Like America, Britain likes to present itself as a land of (at least potential) opportunity, and of hard grafters who, in the Conservative MP Norman Tebbit's famous image, get on their bikes and look for work. Don't let your mentees take the strain of trying to reconcile that image with reality.

* * *

I've been criticised for my approach to mentoring, on the basis that all I am doing is making the case for the status quo. By encouraging mentees to adapt to the system as it is, the argument goes, I am cementing institutional bias in perpetuity. While I might be able to help a few minority individuals like myself, my approach leaves the overall structure intact – and perhaps even reinforces it. These are valid points, and I have never said that my way is the only way. But I think that if you are going to help young people improve their circumstances, you need to help them understand and adapt to the world they're in – not the ideal world we all wish we lived in. Change will come when people with diverse understandings and experiences of the world are truly represented at high levels in society – but it ain't gonna happen if they're falling at the first hurdle.

A mentor who's telling a mentee from a disadvantaged background that they shouldn't compromise and should instead 'be themselves' isn't pretending that the system is fair – far from it. But they are fostering an equally dangerous idea: that you can go up against the system and win, that you can somehow do it entirely on your terms, and push your way through without sustaining significant damage. As I hope I have shown, that's not the way our society works. The people who give this advice are well-meaning and caring individuals, usually middle-class folk, who want to help but who lack real insight into the lives of those who aren't like them. These are usually people who've never had to face the kind of anxieties that those who are attempting to enter a new environment have to face; have never experienced what it is like to apply for a job when you have a foreign name; or, as a woman of colour, entered a workplace dominated by men educated at public school; or been the only person in the office with a non-RP accent. Such people, perhaps named John or Jane, fail to understand that 'just being yourself' is a privilege enjoyed by those who *already fit in*, and not one afforded to a Nadiya or a Kayden from a deprived part of Newcastle.

If you're a mentee receiving this advice, especially if, like me, you're a minority, or from a disadvantaged white, working-class background, or someone who simply could not afford to eat slogans like 'fuck the system', then pause and ask yourself whether, from where you're sitting, this is advice that you can live with. Has it worked for you before? If you think you should reject it, it doesn't mean that you're accepting the system as it is currently constituted. You don't have to take it all on your own shoulders, you don't have to be a sacrificial lamb at the altar of authenticity: to draw a simplistic line between 'being true to yourself' and compromise that allows for success is to allow too much talent to fall between the cracks.

* * *

Naturally, I'm not suggesting that everyone has to look, speak, and act identically. *Of course*, workplaces must take the lead on adapting their cultures to be welcoming and supportive, and adjust their dress codes so that, for example, they are accepting of dreadlocks or braids, hairstyles that are culturally significant among black communities but often perceived by majority-white businesses as 'not professional attire'. But the reality is that everyone adapts to their context. John and Jane don't dress the same way on holiday as they would in the office, or talk the same way in an email to their boss as they do on a private Whats-App group for a hen party. Most middle-class people, in my experience, have an instinctive understanding of where the lines are drawn, which emerges from their reflexive grasp of the habitus of elite environments. But many of those from non-privileged backgrounds, like me, will never have had the opportunity to be in certain settings and to observe how others adapt in order to maximise their chances of success, and they need all the help they can get so that they can understand that context, appreciate its nuances and adapt accordingly. Advising a young person on work experience might, for example, include teaching them the right moments at which to speak in a formal meeting; the core skills of making good notes and thinking carefully about questions to ask later; and having coherent answers ready to questions from people interested in their future plans. Following these pointers should help make a work experience placement worthwhile, and will also send out a message that this is a serious young person with potential. This advice might seem obvious, and to some, all of this will come naturally. But it didn't to me, and I would prefer to assume that the young person I am helping does *not* know, and tell them, than to assume that they do, and let them make an avoidable mistake.

It's about opening up opportunities right now – so that those young people aren't hamstrung by a lack of understanding that prevents them from not only changing their own lives but from changing the workplaces they will one day run.

* * *

One of my mentees, Kevin, described a bad mentor as being like fast food: it's quick, cheap, offers instant gratification and temporarily fills the gap inside. But it's not good for you: the damage it causes is invisible and won't be obvious straight away. You'll get stuck with temporary solutions without careful guidance for the long term. In contrast, a good mentor has a plan: they look beyond the immediate problem. They're here for the long haul. But how, if you're a mentee, do you tell the difference between the two? And if you're a mentor, how do you make sure that you're not falling into the trap of offering quick fixes and easy wins? I have attempted here to lay out some general rules for mentees and mentors.

* * *

Great mentors cajole, develop, chastise as appropriate and nudge, and expose their mentees to the right type of experience and advice at the crucial time. They work to identify gaps and to plug them, strengthen weaknesses and develop strengths, boost skills, and show how to learn more – and more quickly. They turn up for all the 146 football matches, in the rain and the heat, never quite knowing when they'll need to step in and help their mentees score the right goals. In the time-poor and fast-paced environment we now inhabit, the mentor must also offer themselves as a sounding board for some personal things – hopes, fears, aspirations – and must know when to focus on nothing but their mentee, so that, at the end of an hour together, that person leaves feeling that they are valued. For me and for people like me, a huge part of the mentoring relationship is centred around filling in the blanks, trying to plug the information gap. So when I mentor, I try to sharpen my ability to identify what my mentees might be missing. As they tend to be from BAME or lower socio-economic backgrounds, I'm in a good position to do so: they are coming up against the same sort of information gaps that I did. But you don't have to share someone's background or have the kind of insight that comes from having walked in their shoes: instead, the crucial factor is that your mentee feels that you are engaged and invested, willing to see things from their perspective and understand their worldview. Like Lilian Thuram, show up consistently, and go into the relationship for the right reasons. When I was training to become a barrister, Lincoln's Inn partnered me with another barrister who was also a member of the Inn. They were supposed to help me understand the system, apply for scholarships, and be a sounding board for any questions I might have. But, despite emailing them countless times, I never heard back. I know many other people had similar experiences; and it's partly because mentoring at the Bar is often undertaken as a box-ticking exercise in order to garnish the mentor's CV. It didn't crush me, but it was very disappointing. It takes a great deal for a young person to muster the courage to write, to enquire, to seek out help and guidance. To fail to engage with them, for whatever reason, not only undermines their confidence, it deprives them of the opportunity to learn from a mentor who *would* have engaged.

At the other end of the scale is the mentor who is *too* involved, who seeks out a mentoring relationship because they feel a gap in their own lives or want to shape another human being in their own image. If you're not prepared to be part of somebody else's vision, to step back and let them make decisions you don't agree with, and to pick up the pieces afterwards (or admit you were wrong if it comes off) then you won't make a good mentor. The limits of mentoring are hard to define, and require constant monitoring: when do you cross the line from offering help and advice to interfering in someone's life? A mentor's role can often shift, in emphasis and importance: at different stages you might be a parental figure, role model, elder sibling, another friend. Initially you need to have a great deal of contact, to build that trusting relationship, but from the beginning it's critical to be clear about the limitations of what's possible. Mentors are not miracle workers. This is the mentee's journey, and you can't make the running for them. Sometimes, the best thing you can do is to step back: there are some who, no matter how much guidance you provide, are just not ready to receive or understand it at that moment in their lives. They are not mentally ready for the next leap, and so instead you have to withdraw, and think about how best to help them, in that moment, to visualise the next steps to get them where you think they ought to be.

* * *

For the mentee, I offer the following. First, seek out your mentor, and don't be afraid to ask for help. You may come across a mentor where you least expect them: at a library, at a reception, a university open day, a charity event or the local boxing club (if your local one still has funding). But to give yourself the best chance, you need to widen your network, to put yourself in as many places that would allow for such encounters to happen. Look for events that are intended to put prospective applicants in touch with people already inside the profession or institution, turn up and follow through on any leads you get. Think in terms of finding someone you can learn from and who you might want to emulate, and be prepared to accept help in the spirit in which it's offered – and to see clearly the limitations of the worldview from which it might emerge.

If you don't come across someone in the normal course of events, you'll find a good number of organisations that offer mentorship of various kinds, often specifically tailored to individual circumstances, such as mental health difficulties, entrepreneurship, or prison release. Most large companies, institutions and industries offer some kind of structured mentorship scheme, whether organised internally, related to a charity, or (as in the case of the legal profession) through a professional body. But wherever you're looking, accept that not everyone you approach will want to mentor you – they might not even reply to your email. That's okay, and it's not a judgement on you: there are plenty of other people out there who will.

Once you've established the relationship, listen carefully to your mentor's advice, but it's you who has to make the final decision: if you think it's bad advice, don't take it (and a good mentor will be around to help sort things out regardless). Think carefully about the big picture as well as the small one: ask for help not only in crafting a CV, but in deciding whether the job is the right one for you. Things you can learn from professional mentors include how to chair a meeting, how to write a pitch letter or convincing CV, how to deal with conflict at work. But it can also be as simple as learning to place the same value on yourself as your mentor does, and this is where schemes like

Friendship Works cross over with mentorship in work-places and institutions. Perhaps one of the saddest things I've noticed during my mentoring of young people over the years is how so many, from the most deprived communities, just do not understand why anyone would want to help. Some are just baffled that an 'important' person should want to help them get on, understand their next steps, improve their future, and so on. It's a battle to convince them that it is genuinely altruistic and that there is no ulterior motive. Let other people play on your team, and expect – even demand – the help and support that other people around you already have.

* * *

So much of social mobility is about large and intractable problems: government funding, cultural differences, inequality, class conflict. It can be easy to feel overwhelmed by the sheer scale of the problem. But mentoring is a simple, cheap, practical thing that we can all do – and which makes a truly transformative difference to social mobility. It changed the course of my own career and life, and taught me to see myself differently, and I hope that I have been able to pass on those advantages to the young people I now mentor. Mentoring should be seen not just as a way of burnishing a CV, or a 'nice-if-I-had-the-time' gesture, but as a fundamental and normal part of all working lives; and equally, no young person should enter the workplace believing that they have to do it all themselves. The number of mentorship programmes available shows a growing realisation of the kind of role they can play, and, whichever end of the spectrum you're on, you can start today: start asking for help, signing up for programmes and seeking guidance; or ask that young person in the office out for coffee and talk about how they're finding things, point out a scholar-ship, help them with their application, or ask them what their plans are for next year, or the year after that, and think about what they might *not* know. It won't always work, and that's fine – but the first step is reaching out and making contact. The social mobility journey is a solitary one to begin with, but it need not always be undertaken alone, and nor does it need to be completed without help.

7

What Does it Sound Like? Language

Even the closest shall cause each other pain. For there is
nothing closer than the tongue and the teeth, and yet one
sometimes bites the other unintentionally.

Somali word play

In the summer of 2002, when I was eighteen, I was homeless for a year. I had left school, and, since I was no longer in
full-time education, I had become eligible to pay council
tax: something we didn't have a hope of affording. As a
result, I ended up at Centrepoint in Soho, the hostel for
young homeless people. At the time, the system was this:
you had a bed for the first nine nights, but you had to use
that time to secure your next hostel, which meant spending your early mornings ringing around anywhere that
might have a spare bed, trying to persuade them that they
should give it to you. Your next hostel would allow you to
stay for two weeks, which you had to spend securing the
next hostel, which would be for six months, and so on.
The stakes were high: if you couldn't secure somewhere,
you'd be faced with the choice of a night on the streets, or
returning to the situation that you'd left behind.

Maybe, to you, this doesn't sound very difficult – it's only
making a few phone calls, after all. But it was immediately

clear to me that many of the young people I shared Centrepoint with were struggling. Their stories varied – one person had been thrown out by a parent who believed they were possessed, another was escaping a violent home, someone else was fleeing a forced marriage – but the themes remained the same: poverty, violence, danger and trauma. Phoning the hostels meant finding the numbers, calling round, not being put off, telling a persuasive story about why it should be you who gets the bed, and insisting, calling back, arguing your corner, winning people round. Many of these young people lacked the confidence to make the calls in the first place, or to insist that they should be considered, or they couldn't explain why they needed the bed in a way that made sense to the busy people on the other end of the phone. Despite the fact that they were so vulnerable, they weren't getting anywhere.

So, once I had sorted out my own accommodation, I started calling on behalf of other people. I sat down with them, talked with them, worked out what to say about their particular situation, and then hit the phones. It gave me pride and purpose to help others like me. It was the first time I'd ever done something like this, but somehow, it worked: everyone got a bed. And I learned a valuable lesson about the importance of language, the often random advantages that dictate who gets listened to and who gets ignored – and the power of knowing how to use your voice effectively.

Although it might not be the first thing that comes to mind when you think about the subject, I believe passion-ately that language skills are critical to social mobility. It is easy, as I've said, to see social mobility in terms of numbers: funding, budgets, quotas, percentages and income gaps. But that's only half the story, and while the other half is less easy to define or quantify, it's just as important. The effective use of language comes into this category: you can have the skills or raw talent, you can be the most deserving, the most qualified, but if you can't articulate what you want to yourself or to others, if you can't connect with people and persuade them to offer you the things that you need, if you can't argue your way on to that very first rung of the ladder, the bed for the night, it's not going to count for much.

* * *

Partly, this conviction comes from my own experience: it is very hard to explain to anyone who does not speak it the true power, nuance, versatility and range of the Somali language. The language of my ancestors, one of two languages I was exposed to as soon as I could speak, is meant to be spoken (it was only written down in 1972),[1] and is at its best in reciting poetry.[2] It is also extraordinarily hard to learn: the Foreign Services Institute, run by the US State Department, ranks it at Category 2 for difficulty, but I would argue that it deserves a place in Category 3, with Arabic, Chinese and Korean.[3] It has – just for a start – all the guttural sounds of Arabic, irregular plurals like German, and completely unfamiliar prepositions, as well as being a tonal language like Mandarin (though Somali has only a high and a low tone).

In spite of all this, Somalis love to talk, and delight in conversation, debate, poetry, aphorisms; as my friend Safia Aidid put it in a recent article, 'language is the essence of Somali society ... they talk in the nomadic countryside as they set up camp or water their camels; they talk when they encounter one another on journeys, at trading posts, at wells; they talk in huts and in houses, while resting away from the sun during its most intense hours' and anywhere else they find themselves.[4] This is just as true among Somalis in the diaspora (although admittedly it's an art form that remains firmly in the domain of the older generation, and those being raised by grandmothers). The Somali language is above all a language of persuasion: it's rare that you'll have a conversation with a Somali without feeling like they're attempting to really *convince* you of something. Making the simplest point requires a carefully crafted story, right for the moment, and above all memorable.

This bleeds into the everyday, making language an integral part of family life. When my siblings and I fought as children, my grandmother would never simply tell us to shut up and behave. Instead, she'd ask us to look at our right hands. Our father, her son, left behind five children, did he not, comes the question. Just observe those fingers, she'd add; is any finger equal to or the same as the other? Each has a differently sized and shaped nail, creases, purpose, length, form, etc. – but ultimately all make up the right hand (not the left!) – correct? Each has a specific role, whether you're holding a pen, performing a handshake, holding the keys, while in a different combination you may dial a call. No single finger is 'better' than the other, she adds. And then comes the message, unexpectedly; so when will you grow up and accept that you're all one but different; the same blood but different people?

I would wonder to myself; if we were six or four children, would the five fingers analogy have worked? How else would she have made the same point? Has she used it before? This is the essence of the Somali language; a language that relied for centuries on the oral tradition and on memory, on stories, poetry, alliteration and imagery. Quick retorts are critical, too: I would joke with her, holding up her hand, 'Okay, does that make me the skinny and tall middle finger; and Ali the thumb because he's fat?' Her eyes squinting, she clenches her fist and replies, 'this hand becomes a fist that can also land a blow to your face...' And on it goes.

Growing up speaking Somali has given me a profound sense of the importance of language. But it was also a message imparted through our experience of the world: learning languages was simply something my family did – partly to survive in the various places we found ourselves, but also for the sheer pleasure of it. My father didn't have to learn the different languages of the lands he criss-crossed in his long-haul truck. But he did, because he knew that there's no better way to communicate with someone than in their own tongue; as he used to say, a few words said to someone in their own language is worth far more than whole sentences in a foreign language.

If my father's languages formed a geography of the places he'd been, mine map my own history. I grew up bilingual in Somali and Swahili (with a smattering of English, mainly picked up from the movies). When we moved to England, I found myself suddenly struggling, attending school in a language I didn't speak. When I did learn English, it was a form known as 'Multicultural London English', the language of black inner-city London in the 1990s, a society full of rich immigrant experience, influenced by Jamaican patois and grime music, marinated in the cultures of the South Asian Muslims and the African and Caribbean cultures of my corner of Brent, North West London. When I did an Erasmus year as part of my degree and learned French, it was a marker of the opportunities that were opening up in front of me. And, as luck would have it,[5] I find myself today making a career out of speaking persuasively in the archaic and formalised language of the law courts. I still speak all these languages.

On any given day, I might begin with a visit to my grand-mother, where I listen intently as she waxes lyrical in Somali proverbs, head into court for a hearing ('My Lord, I am loath to interrupt my learned friend mid-flow but would he care to continue reading the rest of the passage ...'), go to the BBC for a meeting ('Before we touch base, let's make sure we've engaged the key stakeholders'), and then meet my young cousin back in Wembley ('Yo fam, wha' you saying do'?).

But the biggest role that language has played in my life has been in helping me get to this point in the first place. Language pops up everywhere in relation to social mobility, from hiring practices to university entrance to mental health and identity. I've seen for myself the many ways in which languages impact on success and happiness. As a recent immigrant, not speaking the language disrupted my education, isolated me and undermined my confidence. I watched as Somali adults struggled to learn English at all, or, like my grandmother, made a conscious decision to concentrate on continuing to speak to us in Somali, rather than make any real effort to learn English. (Her reasoning was that at least if we spoke Somali we could continue the legacy of our history, while English, for her, would not be useful, given that she 'wouldn't be around for long'.) I have seen how this made life difficult for the adults in our lives, stopping them from being able to effectively communi-cate, especially when it came to dealing with authority figures and government departments. I saw how the ambi-tions of my friends and siblings were shaped and limited by the fact that they never heard anyone in authority speak like them. And I saw how, by changing how *I* communi-cated, I could change the way that people responded to me. Being able to identify what you need at a critical point in your life, or what kind of ambition will shape your future, means little if you can't inspire confidence in others to help you, to guide you, to believe in your vision, and to want to be part of your story.

* * *

Fluency, articulacy, a wide vocabulary, the ability to communicate – these are all important skills, regardless of who you are and what you're doing. But they don't belong to any particular group of people or way of speaking, though, as we will see, there is an association between language development and socio-economic status. However, it is also abundantly clear that in modern Britain language is not a neutral thing: instead, it is part of a dense network of perception and interpretation, and what you sound like is determined not only by what sounds leave your mouth, but also by the mindset and preconceptions of the person listening to you. All too often, this means that speech is divided into categories of right or wrong, which are based on prejudice but have a very real effect nonetheless: your accent, your choice of words, your register can all put you on the wrong side of a rigid interpretation of what a clever person, a professional person, or an important person sounds like.

Before I get on to the fraught nature of the relationship between language and class, one very important thing should be noted: language skills are not shared out equally in our society. In Chapter 1, I mentioned the 'language gap',[6] which is present in young children and is one of the reasons that children from privileged backgrounds are eighteen months ahead of their poorer peers even before they start school. But poor children aren't just doing badly relative to better-off children: in deprived areas of the country 50 per cent of children and young people might have what are loosely grouped under the term 'Special Communication Language Needs',[7] an umbrella term that covers everything from a poor vocabulary to stuttering to basic issues of understanding, such as not knowing what a question is.[8] Poor language skills in childhood are closely linked with difficulties in adulthood: 60 per cent of young offenders struggle with it, and having a limited vocabulary as a child doubles your likelihood of being unemployed in adulthood.[9] It's not hard to understand why: problems with language undermine a child's ability to learn for obvious reasons, but not being able to express yourself is itself intensely frustrating, leading to behavioural problems that affect not just children's education but their relationships and happiness.[10]

But even children who don't have a SCLN are let down in language terms. Schools spend a vast amount of time developing reading and writing skills, but far less is devoted to the equally important skill of verbal communication. We are well aware of the devastating effect that illiteracy has on life opportunities, but the fact that many children leave school without any proficiency in spoken language, or oracy, seems not to trouble us. Perhaps because the idea that there's a 'right way to speak' is so loaded, spoken language remains a forgotten corner of the curriculum, with serious consequences for children from poor backgrounds. By contrast, private schools (and well-resourced state schools and grammars) take oracy extremely seriously, nourishing it through drama, debating, and other forms of public speaking that boost confidence and improve articulacy. In their systematic demolishing of the private school system, *Engines of Privilege*, Francis Green and David Kynaston point out that the number of theatres in London private schools is fifty-nine: significantly more than in the West End.[11]

Precisely why poor children struggle with oracy is a complicated question. Children who – like my siblings and I – are recent immigrants or refugees face particular problems: language barriers, the disturbance of their family and education, and perhaps the legacy of traumatic things they have seen or experienced. Problems with language can emerge from surprising, devastating directions. When Shukri, Hamdi, Ali and I were finally reunited with my mother, after a separation of several years, we'd forgotten most of our Swahili and Somali, and she didn't speak any English. Suddenly, we not only had to get to know our mother again – we had to do it across a significant language barrier. Something that should have been a joyful reunion, a step on the path to stability and order, became instead destabilising and alienating. For other young children, having to suddenly learn a new language can disrupt their attempts to master their first language, leading to a lack of total fluency in both, and there's also the problem of engaging with a state apparatus that doesn't understand *you*. If teachers or health workers don't share a child's first language,[12] it's hard for them to pick up any existing problems, while well-meaning attempts to help a community can founder on basic misunderstandings: my old relatives were puzzled to receive health pamphlets from the NHS printed in Somali, a language they all spoke but which very few in that generation were able to read.

But the much larger group is children born in England and speaking English as their first language, and they are also the victims of a lack of knowledge. According to a ten-year follow-up to the Bercow Report into speech disorders among young people, 'more than half of young children in school are not having their needs identified' because of a lack of training and understanding among those who should be picking it up. Whether or not you're able to access help and support is a postcode lottery, meaning that children are at the mercy of the kind of geographical disadvantage we discussed in the education chapter. Swingeing cuts to the number of health visitors means that early signs of language delay aren't necessarily picked up till later, and parents may face long waits to access help if they don't have the resources to go private.[13]

That's diagnosis and treatment. But children's language development is also shaped by their home lives. According to the Marmot report, 'parental involvement in their child's reading has been found to be the most important determinant of language and emergent literacy', with children doing best when experiencing both 'high levels of parental warmth' and 'high levels of supervision'. Middle-class parents don't have a monopoly on warmth – but, as we saw from Annette Lareau's research in Chapter 1, they have both the resources and the motivation to closely supervise their children's development. In her study, middle-class parents involved their children in discussion and encouraged them to share their own experiences and opinions, giving them a positive experience of speaking and being listened to. This creates a virtuous circle: speak well, get the right response from others, feel more confident, speak more and express yourself with an even wider range of vocabulary. As children from more privileged backgrounds grow up in a highly communicative environment, so does their confidence in their ability to speak and, critically, their expectation that they will be heard, rooted as it is in countless moments of encouragement and correction. In my own family, for all that we prized verbal pyrotechnics, we just didn't have this kind of relationship with language, or with each other. There was warmth, but it didn't – it couldn't – express itself in that way: there were simply too many of us, and too much to do. There was compassion and friendship and solidarity, but there was also shouting, competition for the scant resources of adult attention, and being left to our own devices. Where some of my friends and colleagues grew up in homes that cultivated children's books, songs and rhymes, conversations and ideas, and reading aloud, I don't remember a single occasion of anyone ever reading to us, and we certainly had no books in the house. What books would we have in a house that we were going to leave in a month? And how could anyone read to us when they could barely read themselves?

Reading can easily seem like an indulgence, or a middle-class parenting preoccupation of doubtful relevance to the real world. But it's not: it's a vital resource, as I discovered when I began, finally, to read for myself – as opposed to because I had to at school – in my late teens. It's about the benefits of cultural capital in one sense, of knowing the plot of *Macbeth* or what 'Dickensian' means, but also because books teach you about the world, and how to find yourself in it; about how to resolve problems and overcome obstacles; and that other people feel the same as you do. A lot of the answers to the problems encountered by the socially mobile can be found in books, but to be able to find something you have to know that it's there (and you have to be able to get the books in the first place, something becoming increasingly difficult as the local library becomes a critically endangered species).

* * *

When it comes to adult life and employment, the entry points for the socially mobile are marked by barriers that have as much to do with language as with qualifications: whether that be university interviews, job interviews, networking opportunities, or the many small tests or challenges that emerge from a collective cultural mindset that relies on articulacy as a measure of intelligence and value. Almost all workplaces favour the articulate: whether you're an artist, a social activist, a solicitor or a senior brand manager, self-employed, working for a large institution like the BBC or civil service, a large corporate company or a small private one, you'll find yourself at some point attending meetings where you have to command the attention of a number of people simultaneously, pitching to clients or potential employers, establishing good relationships with senior figures in your industry and, of course, networking. Notoriously hard to master, professional networking is often presented as about confidence and extroversion, but it's also about language: it's the art of selling yourself to people who you've just met, quickly, and with the right balance of inside knowledge, cunning and charm. It is fundamentally about *speaking the language* of the person you are talking to: often, because that's the way our society is, that person will be middle class. And this is where we get to a crucial point: people from working-class backgrounds or the lower rungs of the socio-economic ladder are by no means less fluent or articulate than those at the top. The musical genres of rap and grime, for example, which emerged from working-class black neighbourhoods in America and London, are almost entirely based on command of language and hyper-articulacy. But not all ways of speaking are created equal in British society, and as a result, young people from deprived backgrounds are subject to linguistic double jeopardy: first, when they're developing their language skills, and then again when they try to improve their circumstances through education or entering elite careers.

In his play *Pygmalion*, later filmed as *My Fair Lady* with

Audrey Hepburn as Eliza Doolittle, George Bernard Shaw wrote that 'It is impossible for an Englishman to open his mouth without making some other Englishman hate or despise him.' It remains true that, in modern Britain, accents remain 'the last form of acceptable prejudice'.[14] We've come some way since the days of national broadcasters speaking in a barely intelligible and strangled version of received pronunciation (and you can listen to archival material from BBC Radio or Pathé News to hear how far), but we're still a long way off real 'accent diversity'.[15] This is reflected in the regular surveys that attempt to rank people's accents. Often presenting themselves as a bit of fun – people from Devon are trustworthy,[16] Glaswegian accents are sexy[17] – in practice they reflect knee-jerk prejudices that, as one researcher put it, 'trigger social categorisation in quick, automatic and sometimes unconscious ways'.[18] It goes without saying that prejudice against accents says more about existing class prejudices than it does about individual Brummies, or Scousers or Glaswegians. It's no coincidence that received pronunciation – the generic 'posh' accent found across southern England and on the BBC, and which dominates elite professions, despite being spoken by only 3 per cent of the population – is perceived as 'powerful' and 'trustworthy'.[19] But for people whose accents aren't generally 'acceptable', these associations can have profoundly negative consequences. Birmingham accents, for instance, which regularly come bottom of the list, are perceived as 'less attractive' and 'less intelligent',[20] or, as Birmingham Yardley MP Jess Phillips, puts it 'as a tool to have a go at you ... They'll say you sound thick and you're common and you don't speak properly.'[21]

Neither are these matters of personal taste: they leak into our professional lives as well. A recent study found that '28 per cent of British employees thought they had been discriminated against because of their accent' – and they were right: a staggering 80 per cent of employers admitted accent discrimination.[22] In 2019, trainee teachers reported being told to soften their accents around the children they taught – even when they came from the same area.[23] Likewise, in a trend that repositions *Pygmalion* as social commentary, elocution (branded as 'accent softening') classes are on the rise, something that even a voice coach who taught those classes described as 'a Band-Aid on a class system that isn't working'.[24]

Such is the association between class divisions and accents in Britain that it is impossible to comment on the subject without taking a position of some sort. The way you speak is one of the most intensely personal things about you: it reflects the unique combination of circumstances that shaped you, and is a profound point of connection with the place and people you grew up around. It's unsurprising, then, that people often feel that the pressure to change their accent – whether direct or indirect – is an attempt to erase their identity. Even small changes can feel like a loss of self: as the author Kit de Waal put it, 'Your Brummie accent might have the corners shaved off in certain company. Are you still working class? Or have you hopped over the tracks?'[25] Others might take a different tack. I notice my young cousins – devoted speakers of Multicultural London English – pursuing careers that require science and maths qualifications, and barely considering the kind of professions where they'd be judged on whether their voices sound acceptably 'client facing'.

I understand all this, and yet, as a first-generation immigrant who learned English as a third language, part of my response to the way the British agonise over their accents is best described as puzzlement. But I have to admit that, even if I view it with the perspective of an outsider, I'm also a participant. I work in a profession that can only be described as being at the heart of the establishment, and where you rarely hear an accent that would be categorised as anything other than pure RP. I have never had voice coaching, training or elocution lessons, but my own accent has undoubtedly changed, and continues to change depending on where I am and who I am speaking to. I still live in the same neighbourhoods I grew up in, but my voice is one that wouldn't be out of place broadcasting on BBC Radio 4; it's the voice that a mentor described as sounding like 'someone who had been to Eton'; it's the voice that a colleague in chambers once remarked as being 'from the Home Counties'; and it does not give away the fact that English is not my first language. To me, though, it doesn't reflect compromises made and identity distorted: it's hard to imagine how my 'original' accent could be some profound expression of my inner self, given that it was formed by the quirk of fate that landed us in Wembley and not, say, Minnesota or Malmö. Instead, it shows the changes my life has undergone. With each stage, another chapter was written. I started to move in new kinds of circles, join new communities, and the world which was slowly becoming mine changed me.

All this is a part of the man I am, and none of my modes of speaking is – at least from my perspective – better than the other. I don't think that 'speaking well' automatically equates to speaking with an RP accent, or that the kind of slang you might hear at an Oxford College or on the streets of Chelsea is necessarily better or more expressive than the slang that my cousins and their friends use in North West London. But the rule that I have applied elsewhere plays a role here too; I have to deal with the world as it is, rather than as it should be. As a result, I am an accent pragmatist: if the world changed tomorrow and everyone on the BBC and the high court bench was speaking with a Brummie accent – I'd learn. I am constantly travelling the country, meeting all sorts of people from different types of socio-economic backgrounds, different expectations and prejudices; in village halls, courtrooms, dingy meeting rooms and formal dinners. I have to work out the best way to win over a potential witness, to present a client's case, to inspire confidence in people and show them what I am capable of, to explain to them, through words and actions, that I am the right man for the job, to prove why I was hired in the first place. To win. Using language and my voice effectively helps me do that, and the same applies to anyone reading this book who wants to begin their own social mobility story. Consider what will help you most, reflect on what you see in your future, identify where your personal red lines are – and ignore the rest.

* * *

The way we perceive certain accents is partly down to the kind of direct prejudice that Britain is seeped in. But it is compounded by the fact that we are naturally drawn to people who we perceive to be like us, something that is known as homophily or affinity bias. This process begins very early: babies have a preference for people who speak the language they heard most of while they were *in utero*, and by the time they are a few months old, they show a strong bias in favour of both native language *and* accent.[26] Scientists call this a 'social preference', and it continues into later life: when we want to describe having something in common with someone or being in agreement, we often reach for a linguistic metaphor like 'speaking the same language' or 'singing from the same hymn sheet'. Most people are familiar with the experience of slightly changing their accent or the way they speak just in order to get on better with someone. When the Ghanaian-British professor of philosophy Kwame Anthony Appiah found himself adjusting his accent in an American direction when telling New York taxi drivers where he wanted to go, he saw it as a natural instinct to make himself easier to understand to people who were often, like him, immigrants in America.[27] But, of course, it doesn't stop there. In interviews and at work, it's well recognised that gatekeepers who guard the social mobility checkpoints prefer candidates who seem like them, even if they don't consciously realise it: a high value is placed on someone who *already* speaks and expresses themselves like a lawyer, or a doctor or a teacher, or, in other words, who sounds like the interviewer. Now, you may not think that this affects *you*. You may think you're the most open-minded individual when it comes to judging others, that you base everything on objective observations about character and qualifications. If so, then you're not only sadly mistaken, you're part of the problem, especially if you're in a powerful position in, say, recruitment. Even though I'm more alert to the pitfalls than most, I often find myself drawn to people during interviews at my chambers who seem, quite apart from their qualifications, 'like one of us'. I have found that I preferred people who I could imagine in a meeting with my colleagues, people I instinctively felt were saying the right things, who could be confident performers before a court or in front of clients. Thinking someone is like you, often means choosing someone who just sounds like you.

This combination – of direct prejudice and unconscious bias – confronts the socially mobile person with a choice: learn to speak the language of the world you want to join or speak the way you've always spoken and take the consequences. Of course, language skills are still important – an articulate, communicative, expressive candidate should still make an impression. But when you're up against the perception that you need to 'fit in' and 'speak the same language' the answer lies (for some people) in code-switching. This is something all of us do fairly naturally, and it is fundamental to my own life. Essentially, if you view different areas of life as having their own distinct linguistic registers – a more formal, slang-free register for professional meetings, a boisterous, sweary register for a football match – then code-switching is the term for the change between them. A shared 'language' eases communication within a group, whether in the formal environment of a courtroom or the villa in *Love Island*. That might seem simplistic – surely no one needs to be told this? – but again, it's not obvious to everyone, and even if it is, working out the code of a group that you've previously had no contact with can be very difficult, as can working out what is and isn't 'allowed'. When I think about code-switching I think about how, during my childhood, my mother, my aunt and the other older relatives would struggle to get the simplest thing done for them at the housing office. The disdain they would be treated with as a result is etched into my memory. Even now, I'll take the phone from my mother, struggling to have a charge removed from her phone bill, and hear the problem melt away in front of my voice – the voice, tone and vocabulary of someone who 'sounds like they grew up in the Home Counties'. Is it fair? No. But it is *effective.*

In fact, the sheer effectiveness of code-switching can create complicated feelings in the socially mobile: as you change your choice of words, dialect, and tone, it also changes you. As the writer Lynsey Hanley put it in her book *Respectable*: 'Putting on a posh voice when you think it would be useful doesn't change you at your core, whereas learning the formal code of middle-class speech brings about permanent change, [partly] because it *works* – it gets things done, it makes people regard you differently no matter how you regard yourself.'[28] I have constant battles with my young cousins, who are confirmed speakers of Multicultural London English, about the importance of code-switching. To them, there's nothing wrong with the way they speak – it's a form of language that has evolved around them, and feels natural. And, of course, they are right, and I understand the reluctance to adopt a way of speaking that feels foreign and perhaps uncomfortable, even just in the workplace. Code-switching is difficult, tiring and involves tolerating a fair amount of cognitive dissonance – it's not an easy route to take. It is, of course, not fair that our society requires it of people who simply want to improve their circumstances. But neither is it fair to pretend to young people that they don't need to do it to get ahead. It was code-switching to which David Lammy, the MP for Tottenham, referred, when he told a group of sixth-formers in London uncompromisingly: 'Innit or "izzit" is not going to get you a job. Don't let any idiot tell you you'll get a job by saying "innit" and "izzit" because you won't. [Don't listen to] damn foolish liberals saying it's fine.'[29]

In *The Class Ceiling*, the research carried out by Sam Friedman and Daniel Laurison suggested that this is good advice: as one senior partner at a tax firm they talked to put it:

> Language and articulation is a huge differentiator and it's probably one of the few things that makes me go ... When I hear people using inaccurate grammar or things like that, it's a very obvious identifier of something, a regional dialect that hasn't been tempered[30]

I've quoted this in full because there's something interesting about it. For someone who clearly finds articulacy very important, the speaker is struggling to explain exactly what he's talking about. 'A very obvious identifier of something' – of what? I would suggest that, although he feels uncomfortable acknowledging it publicly, it's to do with employability, 'fit', 'polish' or something similar. This is the consequence of not changing your accent or your code, of forgoing the opportunity to use the tools of the world you find yourself in so that you might better help your own progress. My young cousins do not set off every morning into a neutral world in which people are only interested in what they have to say rather than the *way* they are saying it, no matter how awkward we might find it to admit. And, given that being a young black man with a Muslim name in Britain is far from a neutral existence, why should those young men compound the issue by sticking rigidly to just one linguistic register? The answer lies, it seems to me, in encouraging range and flexibility in a way that reflects both our current landscape, with its shibboleths and prejudices, and the more open and tolerant place it could become. Young people should be given the opportunity to 'speak the language' of elite institutions, which they may never have encountered, but we should also jettison the damaging idea that there is one, single, 'right' form of the language. Exposing young people, as early as possible, to unfamiliar contexts, voices and accents, to people and environments who are very different to those of their upbringing, gives them the opportunity and the tools to decide for themselves. And, of course, if you have *never* been exposed to a particular setting, such as the Bar, you need to adapt perhaps more consciously to that new situation than others do. What is wrong with that?

As we saw in the previous chapter, young people who are

attempting to change their circumstances are often exposed to the idea that they need to remain 'true to themselves' and that any change is 'selling out' or somehow inauthentic. My objection is twofold. Firstly, young black boys, for example, face enough discrimination without deliberately giving up one of the few things that is within their control: the opportunity to use language to shape their own narrative. Evolve or die; if nothing else my family's journey has been a reminder of this. The best teachers, social workers, the most supportive parents and mentors (of whom there are many) understand that it's not about who you are now – it's about who you could be. But the idea that the 'true self' of a young person from a disadvantaged background is fixed is also profoundly patronising – and not all that different from the kind of prejudice that leads my colleague to suggest that I couldn't sound the way I do and come from anywhere but the Home Counties. At heart, it's the assumption that people who come from a certain kind of background must never change or develop: that our expectations for how they act or speak must never be challenged. If you're French or Irish and settle in Britain, over time your accent might soften or you might consciously change it in order to be better understood – and no one will come and take away your passport. But if your journey is across class boundaries, and you change the way you talk, to a lot of people that means you're waving goodbye to *really* belonging anywhere. That new accent isn't really yours, because we know you didn't always speak that way – and you're not a real working-class person either, because what working-class person speaks like you? You're a fake, you've been trained, you're not *authentic*. In other words, you're trapped in one place, forever the person you were at what might have been the worst point in your life. These are the walls that, as Appiah puts it 'hedge us in; walls we played no part in designing, walls without doors and windows, walls that block our vision and obstruct our way, walls that will not let in fresh and enlivening air.'[31] This is using language *against* people who wish to better their lives, to seek more opportunities for themselves, who are shamed into a corner, forced into a box that's marked 'this is you, do not attempt to escape'. It's yet another example of the failure of imagination that at every single level holds back the socially mobile.

* * *

Despite the fact that language is demonstrably a fluid and ever-changing thing, pearl-clutching among the self-appointed guardians of 'proper English' about the way young people speak is nothing new. The tight connections between language, accent and identity are vigorously policed at all levels of society, and often reveal prejudices that are as much to do with race as class. In recent decades, this anxiety has attached itself to Multicultural London/ Urban English (MLE), or 'Jafaican'[32] (spoken where I grew up, as mentioned earlier), and this has led to criticism of young people of all ethnicities for, essentially, 'sounding black'. This is what the historian David Starkey meant when he made his infamous comments after the London riots, that 'the whites have become black', and were speaking like it, using 'this language which is wholly false ... this Jamaican patois that has been intruded in England and that is why so many of us have this sense of literally a foreign country'.[33] For Starkey, there were clearly two kinds of speech, one acceptable and one not, and they mapped easily on to racial categories. 'Listen to David Lammy, an archetypal successful black man. If ... you are listening to him on radio you would think he was white.'[34] This, presumably, was meant to be a compliment.

Starkey's statements provoked more than 700 complaints to the BBC and condemnation from both sides of the political spectrum.[35] But similar ideas – that ways of speaking belong to particular ethnicities, that 'sounding black' is not the same as sounding 'successful' – continue to bubble up throughout the debate. There certainly is a sense in which a middle-class person who adopts the accent of a lower socio-economic group will be perceived as inauthentic: witness the mockery of politicians such as Tony Blair and George Osborne for speaking in 'mockney'. The middle-class journalists and parents who write semi-humorous articles in tabloids despairing of their 'nicely bought up' children speaking 'patois', similarly often adopt a teasing tone in order to disguise, as a defence of 'proper English', their anxieties about their offspring's potential downward mobility. But if the worst thing that can happen to you is being teased, you're already on the right side of the equation: being laughed at for faking an accent to sound cool is not the same as the unconscious bias and suspicion that lies beneath statements like 'but you sound white!' or 'you can't be from Newcastle!'. The policing of these categories – and the tacit understanding that some ways of speaking can be authentically spoken only by particular groups – comes from all sides: internally from the cultures themselves, from self-appointed protectors of white culture such as Starkey, and from well-meaning liberals who assume that 'be true to yourself!' is advice that works for everyone. Some have suggested that counselling young people from ethnic minorities to change the way they speak or present themselves means advising them to conform to a form of *'whiteness'* – whatever that means. But RP doesn't belong to white people, and neither does being articulate and effective in your deployment of language. Young people have the right to speak however they wish, without boundaries or being told they must represent and 'stay true to' the culture they happen to be born into.

* * *

Language and forms of expression are at the heart of the social mobility story in Britain. But the person speaking is only half the equation: the other half is the person listening. For a socially mobile person, that means knowing your interlocutor, finding the right words and the right way to express a thought or idea, about being aware of nuances in terms of what the other person brings to the table. What prejudices do *they* carry when they hear you speak, and how best do you neutralise those prejudices and still get your point across, ensuring that you're communicating effectively? It's a careful balancing act requiring tact, empathy and the ability to hold many different versions of the same reality in play simultaneously. But crack it, and you've unlocked the key to success, to informing, influencing, inspiring and motivating others on your behalf. And it can make the difference between getting your foot in the door and having it shut in your face.

If you're the listener, your task is different – and not necessarily easier. The socially mobile person has, of necessity, to focus on the world as it is: working out the rules and how they can be bent or adapted to provide new opportunities. But yours is the task of changing that world; of freeing yourself from your preconceptions, your baked-in ideas about what constitutes intelligence or professionalism. We must challenge not only ourselves, but one another, to be guided not by prejudice, but to judge people on what they're saying and not on how they are saying it. New studies suggest that as we mix more as a society, both through social media and because we are an increasingly well-educated population, 'the old ties between accent and social class are fast coming loose'. As a result, what to do about language is becoming 'a matter of conscious choice'.[36] We need to be more imaginative, more acutely self-aware when we are making those instantaneous judgements about others, and look beyond the voice to what the person in front of you at interview – or the colleague you work alongside, or the person pitching an idea – is actually saying.

But in order to get to this point, we have to start early. Oracy is a life skill that can make a massive difference to someone's social mobility prospects. It can help young disaffected boys to find the right words to express what they're feeling. It can give children the confidence to believe that what they have to say is worth listening to, that their words, their ideas, their thinking matters. In March 2018 I spoke to a gathering of 750 teachers at the inaugural Great Oracy Exhibition, recounting the story of my origins, and the evolution of my own oracy and accent. The exhibition – the first of its kind nationally, if not internationally – was the brainchild of Voice 21, an oracy programme and charity set up at School 21 in Stratford, East London, which was founded by Peter Hyman, the former chief speech-writer and strategist to Tony Blair. School 21 has always championed the importance of spoken language, and Peter and a large cohort of dedicated and driven individuals have, ever since, been pioneering a simple idea: to make oracy one of the main areas of focus for schools and teachers, right up there with writing, reading and numeracy. The exhibition was an inspiring sight. Sixth-formers held panel discussions with a Channel 4 reporter; Year 5 students travelled from Manchester to share their performance poetry depicting the strength of their community in the aftermath of the Manchester bombings; and Year 6s fervently challenged society's apathy towards single-use plastics. Teachers, too, were immersed in participatory assemblies, vocal warm-ups, debates and discussions. Everywhere I looked, each voice was valued and every idea heard.

There is a real movement afoot, led by teachers who want to prioritise the art and science of speaking as the driving force behind a new type of education; through engaged learning, debate rhetoric and collaboration.[37] The aim of this pursuit of a more fully rounded education is to induct these youngsters into important academic disciplines while at the same time giving them a voice and a purpose; the ability to take on the world. There is some way to go: a report commissioned by Voice 21, The State of Speaking in our Schools, polled over 900 teachers and found that while the majority think oracy is as important, if not more so, than traditional areas such as literacy and numeracy, only a minority of schools are consistently providing meaningful opportunities for students to develop these skills. More-over, teachers feel ill-equipped to effectively teach their students oracy, concerned by time pressures, competing priorities and a lack of support from senior leadership. The kind of environments we need to nurture would set high expectations for students as orators, and would expose them to a wide variety of contexts for discussion across a range of subjects. And it can happen: I have seen students as young as eight being supported to deliver compelling speeches on racism, political activism, the refugee crisis and animal rights. In some European countries, such as France, it is compulsory for students to regularly present to whole classrooms, in order to build confidence in explain-ing ideas. We need to make more time for this in our cur-riculum. This is the only way we are going to close Britain's language gap, which, as we know, can be so determinative of someone's life chances.

Teaching and learning in this model are a dialogic process, where ideas and opinions are crafted verbally, with structures and feedback to enable both students and teacher to reflect on the quality of talk in the classroom. Again, I'm aware that the space and time to create these opportunities requires ample resources, leadership and consistency over a significant period of time. But recognising the remarkable impact that oracy can have, in unlocking student potential and transforming teaching more broadly, may yet encourage leaders in education to push this idea through. Increasingly, these voices are being heard, not least in Parliament, where in May 2018 an all-party parliamentary group on oracy was launched by Emma Hardy MP, setting the foundations for a wider enquiry into the state of oracy education in schools nationally.[38]

I believe that, once we get to a place where young people are trained, prepped, pushed and encouraged to be articulate, where they can deploy a wide vocabulary with a clarity of thought, and are armed with new and exciting ideas, *then* we might be in a position to reshape the current linguistic landscape in favour of social, cultural and ethnic diversity. Perhaps then we will have found a way of neutralising prejudices instead of playing right into them. Perhaps we will have conquered another corner of the social mobility story and moved one step closer to a more equal society.

8

Be Useful to Yourself
First: Employment

If you can make one heap of all your winnings
And risk it on one turn of pitch-and-toss,
And lose, and start again at your beginnings
And never breathe a word about your loss;
If you can force your heart and nerve and sinew
To serve your turn long after they are gone,
And so hold on when there is nothing in you
Except the Will which says to them: 'Hold on!'
If you can talk with crowds and keep your virtue,
Or walk with Kings – nor lose the common touch,
If neither foes nor loving friends can hurt you,
If all men count with you, but none too much;
If you can fill the unforgiving minute
With sixty seconds' worth of distance run,
Yours is the Earth and everything that's in it,
And – which is more – you'll be a Man, my son!

Rudyard Kipling, *If*

Employment. It's often seen as the final destination in the social mobility story: the point that everything else, from early-years support to education to careful cultivation of social and cultural capital leads up to and enables. There's a reason that immigrant parents the world over boast about their daughter the doctor or their son the lawyer: entry into those professions is a concrete sign that your family has made it, that it has all been worth it. The door is open – and beyond lies security, respect, belonging.

But is it – is it ever? – as simple as that? To a certain extent, yes: it's hard to deny that it is employment that often makes the difference between a story of success and one of failure. Your career is, after all, a much larger portion of your life than your childhood or education, and is arguably the legacy of your social mobility journey. It's not just about money, although that is part of it (and unless you've been poor you'll never really know how transformative having money is). It's also about status and influence: in modern Britain, being a professional allows you to demand people's respect and attention. I'm aware that – besides personal fulfilment – my own job gives me a platform that I wouldn't otherwise have. I very much doubt that anyone would be reading this book if I was just some bloke from Wembley, still working in Sainsbury's, even if many of the experiences and insights contained within would be the same. The agonising about diversity within the 'elite professions' is a tacit admission of this: even if the issue is often described in terms of enrichment, of 'fresh perspectives' and 'avoiding groupthink', it is also about basic fairness. The barriers to entry into professions such as law, publishing and banking cut socially mobile people off from more than just the ability to forge a career in that area: it pulls up the drawbridge to the opportunity to live a different kind of life, in a different kind of world. And it also, very often, prevents those people from having a practical opportunity to shape the society they live in: to make the laws we live by, produce the films, books and TV that we watch, to design the cities we live in and decide what gets sold in our shops.

But say that you do find yourself, against the odds,

entering the kind of profession that comes with a high salary and some social cachet. The chances are that you won't find yourself doing any victory laps. As we've seen throughout this book, Britain's top professions are dominated by the privately educated. Opportunity hoarding by the economically and socially privileged is rife, and not only takes the form of access to good schools, networks and contacts, informal work experience and unpaid internships, but also a continuing moving of the goalposts: as young people enter higher education in ever greater numbers, the minimum qualification for some sectors has become a postgraduate, rather than undergraduate, degree. Higher education does not appear to be the leveller it was hoped to be, and private schooling not only provides better access to top universities, but also confers an advantage in the labour market, even among identically qualified graduates. Socially mobile people who join these professions can also expect to earn less, due to the 'class pay gap' or 'private school premium': a recent study on differences in earnings by socio-economic background for graduates who (like me) left university in 2006–7 found that, three-and-a-half years after graduation, those who attended private schools earn around 16 per cent more per year on average, even allowing for differences in degree subject, university attended, and degree classification. One explanation might be that private school alumni are more likely to choose high-earning professions like law or banking, perhaps to maintain the lifestyles they had while growing up. But the results show that earnings differences persist even within occupations, with graduates who attended private schools earning 6 per cent more than their state school co-workers. This class pay gap will, of course, disproportionately affect groups that already have their own pay gaps, such as women and people from ethnic minority backgrounds, with, predictably, women from ethnic minority backgrounds subject to the greatest loss of income.

Understandably, much of the focus on employment and social mobility has been on initial access; in other words, who gets hired. And yet it is never enough to just get people through the door: it's also a question of maintenance and retention. It's true that in recent years, and of course from a completely dire starting point, there's been a marked change in the recruitment and visibility of people from diverse backgrounds, of working-class people, of women, of LGBTQI people, and of people who are all or some of those things, in the workplace. It's an encouraging start. But what happens to those people a year, or five years, after they first walk into the office? A recent report on my own profession, looking at the link between socio-economic background and early career progression, found that, while the initial intake of trainees is more diverse than it used to be, 'the focus has been primarily on who gets in, rather than who stays on, who gets ahead, and how'.[1] Interestingly, they found that those from lower socio-economic backgrounds are *more* likely to be the highest performers in their firms: among trainees from state schools, 14 per cent receive the highest review ratings compared to 8 per cent of trainees from private schools. Similarly, among trainees who were the first in their family to go to university, '14 per cent received high performance review ratings, compared to 10 per cent of non-first-generation graduates'.[2] And yet, despite this, 'those from lower socio-economic backgrounds appear, on average, *less* likely to progress in their early career'. State-school educated trainees are less likely to be retained compared to their peers from wealthier, more resourced backgrounds. On the one hand, this demolishes the notion that in order to recruit more diversely employers must compromise on quality: it's evidence that individuals who traditionally may not have entered these professions are outperforming their more advantaged peers. It's proof, perhaps, that social mobility, and the churn of talent and increased competition it creates, is good for our society. But on the other hand, it is clear that the promises held out to the socially mobile – the door is open, come on in – are being broken. We in law, and almost certainly in many other professions, are clearly wasting the benefits of social mobility, and at great cost to those whose hard work and talent isn't being rewarded.

In recent years, as diversity of all kinds has found its way on to the agenda, and indeed risen to the top, plenty of companies and organisations have committed themselves to realising a more diverse workforce – their websites tell us so. We may question some of their methods, and possibly even their intentions, but the direction of travel undoubtedly appears to have changed. Across the political spectrum, politicians continue to talk about 'fairness', 'meritocracy', 'opportunities for all', and often promises of change are backed by legislation intended to limit discrimination and promote fairness. So, how do we square this clear desire to make progress with the fact that most high-profile professions are dominated by the privately educated and the middle-class? Or the fact that the experience of many people who come from lower socio-economic and/ or ethnic minority backgrounds are often dominated by small, daily humiliations and micro-aggressions, the stressful experience of transgressing invisible boundaries? A recent survey in Britain of 1,000 people from ethnic minority backgrounds found that '43 per cent had been overlooked for a work promotion in a way that felt unfair in the last five years – more than twice the proportion of white people (18 per cent) who reported the same experience'.[3] Fifty-seven per cent of minorities responded that 'they felt they had to work hard to succeed in Britain because of their ethnicity, and 40 per cent thought they earned less or had worse employment prospects for the same reason'.

These problems are complicated, and relate to the various factors that we've already discussed: the role of confidence, social and cultural capital, the availability of role models, the impact of entrenched yet vague ideas about 'fit' and 'polish', and the exhausting toll of learning and code-switching on a daily basis. But it's likely that a great part of the problem relates to *bias*.

* * *

In 1999, a case came before the House of Lords, which was then the highest court in the land – the precursor to the now famous Supreme Court. The question it sought to answer was one that is integral to this chapter: do we always *know* that we're prejudiced against someone? The case of *Nagarajan vs Swiggs and Others* was bought by Mr Nagarajan, an Indian immigrant who had worked for London Transport for several years, when he was refused a position as a travel information assistant. He alleged that he was refused the job because he had previously brought proceedings against his employer; the potential employer simply stated that they had rejected him as a candidate on the basis of objective assessment, and especially in the light of his performance at a second interview. So what was the truth?

When *Nagarajan vs Swiggs and Others* arrived at the House of Lords, the two law lords called on to decide disagreed on two major points: to what extent our subconscious affects our motivations, intentions and ability to reason; and the extent to which courts can intervene in the domain of people's thoughts and emotions. To

Lord Browne-Wilkinson, though a supporter of the Race Relations Act, 'A matter which is not consciously taken into account by the defendant cannot in my judgement be a ground on which he acted, or one of the reasons for acting.' In other words, we cannot try to second-guess what's in someone's subconscious; we have to be led by what's present, what's explicit. But to Lord Nicholls of Birkenhead:

> All human beings have preconceptions, beliefs, attitudes and prejudices on many subjects. It is part of our make-up. Moreover, we do not always recognise our own prejudices. Many people are unable, or unwilling, to admit even to themselves that actions of theirs may be racially motivated. An employer may genuinely believe that the reason why he rejected an applicant had nothing to do with the applicant's race. After careful and thorough investigation of a claim members of an employment tribunal may decide that the proper inference to be drawn from the evidence is that, whether the employer realised it at the time or not, race was the reason why he acted as he did.

The case of *Nagarajan* was perhaps the first explicit establishment in law the idea of *unconscious bias*: that we hold prejudices and opinions that we might act on without ever being consciously aware of them. Nobody likes to think of themselves as prejudiced: in fact, most of us would be extremely offended if someone suggested that in interviewing someone, or considering an employee for a promotion, we discriminated against them for any reason at all – but perhaps especially for some bigoted reason like an objection to their class, age, gender, race or sexuality. But the fact that we find such ideas unpalatable doesn't mean that bias, conscious or unconscious, does not bleed into all areas of our lives, from job interviews to the choices we make on dating apps.[4] While we may mean well, we all have a subconscious bias that influences our treatment of others; be that in the way we recruit, the kind of person we want our daughter or son to marry, the kind of neighbours we'd like to have, the kind of person you'd prefer – *subconsciously* – to sit next to on the bus or train. Implicit bias association tests, such as Project Implicit, run by Harvard University, provide a way of testing our unconscious preferences: most people will take slightly longer to connect images of black people with positive terms than negative ones. For images of white people, the reverse is true.[5] So surprising are the results to some people, in fact, that the first page of the test asks the reader to explicitly consent to the test on that basis: 'I am aware of the possibility of encountering interpretations of my IAT test performance with which I may not agree. Knowing this, I wish to proceed.'

Other results from Project Implicit reveal unconscious biases in favour of light skin, thin people and straight people: overall, unsurprisingly, biases tend to be in favour of the kind of people well-represented in positions of power.[6] We've already discussed affinity bias, the preference for 'people like us' that comes into play in interviews, promotions and networking, and which reinforces the status quo. But unconscious bias is often the result of learned biases, the type we pick up during the course of our lives; from the communities we grow up in, the films we watch, the books we read, our lived experiences – good and bad –which then fold into our specific worldview in a way that we may not be fully conscious of. Whether based on affinity bias (or its absence) or the set of preconceptions that we absorb from the world around us, it's a fundamental fact of life that those in a position of power to hire and fire, to promote or ignore, to encourage or dismiss, can end up penalising people on the grounds of gender, class or race, or on any other irrational basis, without ever really grappling with *why*.

Not recognising our own unconscious biases is a problem not only because, well, it means we're biased, but also because research has shown a link between self-perceived objectivity and judgemental bias: essentially, 'when people feel that they are objective, rational actors, they act on their group-based biases *more* rather than less'.[7] If you believe or perceive yourself to be 'fair' and 'objective' and 'rational', that's when you're most likely to make mistakes, and this goes some way towards explaining why, despite personal and institutional pressures towards *avoiding* bias, it still flourishes in workplaces up and down the country.[8] All this means that, when a person walks into an interview room, a judgement may already have been formed in milliseconds; before the door behind them has shut, before they have sat down, before they've uttered a single word.

One of the things I want to argue in this chapter is that we are *all* prejudiced in some way: we need to be brave enough to say that our processes, mental as well as societal, however well-intentioned and well thought-through, are ridden with the flaws of human nature, contaminated by decades-long conditioning – our judgements will never be perfectly objective. Whether we've benefited from an accident of birth, or been dealt a harder hand to play, we emerge into a society riddled with a million subtle ways in which to discriminate against one another, between classes, between and within genders and sexualities, between those who went to university and those who didn't, and so on. Indeed, we may be able to work out what some of our unconscious biases are, and acknowledging that they exist is the starting point.

Lord Justice Singh, the first Lord Justice of the Court of Appeal from a minority background, has pointed to a 'frustration that the equality legislation in this country has not brought about the equal society that it appeared to promise', partly because there are 'limits on what the law alone can achieve'.[9] If we are to change things, we can't rely on external structures like legislation and diversity statements to do the work for us: we have to take personal responsibility not only for our own actions, but for the motivations that we might not even be fully conscious of. The first step is acknowledging they exist: unconscious bias training should be as much a part of workplace life as health and safety. At the same time, we need to provide a framework that allows people to understand why and how such biases exist. A good place to start would be teaching history in such a way that it both more accurately reflects the role played by people of colour in Britain's past, and considers the background to the social and racial divisions that exist in our world today: colonialism, the civil rights movement, the slave trade, the legacy of empire. But at the same time, space must be left for the people on the other side to grow and to change their views: to get things wrong, be tactless, ask stupid or obvious questions. It is not, of course, the responsibility of the socially mobile to educate those around them, and no one should feel entitled to ask them to do so. But at the same time, debate, conversation and communication are essential ways to convey what life is like for you, and they are stifled if bad faith is always assumed on the part of others.

This is the case for discrimination being the result of unknown, unacknowledged biases. But, sadly, I'm not convinced that it's the whole story. It remains highly taboo to be racist in our society, but it doesn't follow that we therefore have no direct racism. There was a remarkable rise in reported hate crime after the Brexit referendum, following a campaign that had deliberately stoked existing anxieties about immigration and competition for resources like access to the NHS.[10] It seems unlikely that previously blameless citizens were suddenly provoked by the referendum into criminal harassment of minorities. Instead, it seems clear that something emboldened people to blurt out in public what they were already thinking in private. Getting a straight answer about a subject as complicated and personal as prejudice is difficult, and often distorted by yet another form of bias known as social desirability bias: a desire to provide an answer that the interviewee imagines to be, in the mind of the interviewer, the correct one. In consequence, the results of surveys are often distorted by lies, misrepresentations, evasions, underreporting and so on. To get around this, American data scientist Seth Stephens-Davidowitz, author of *Everybody Lies*, looked at people's internet searches, via which, when performed in the comfort of their own homes and with only their keyboards for company, 'people confess the strangest things ... [often] because they *don't* have consequences: people can unburden themselves of some wish or fear without a real person reacting in dismay or worse'.[11] When we go in search of information, we are often forced to display what we might otherwise have preferred to keep hidden, even from ourselves. Stephens-Davidowitz points to the number of Google searches made every year in America for the word 'nigger': seven million. Searches for the words 'nigger joke' are seventeen times more common than for searches that combined other racial slurs with the word 'jokes'. Perhaps, Stephens-Davidowitz asks, the answer to why African Americans overwhelmingly report experiences of racial prejudice, despite the fact that very few white Americans describe themselves as racist, is not that everyone is in the grip of unconscious bias: 'it is the fact that millions of white Americans continue to do things like search for "nigger jokes".'[12]

This casts an interesting light on the results of a survey carried out by The National Centre for Social Research (NatCen) and Runnymede in 2017.[13] They found that, despite a general trend in favour of greater tolerance, 26 per cent of people admitted to being prejudiced against others, based on their race. Twenty per cent of respondents thought that some ethnicities are born less intelligent, and a far larger number, 40 per cent, agreed that some ethnicities are born lazier. The real number is likely to be, if anything, higher. It's shocking – but not likely to be surprising to many people reading this book. The semi-hidden nature of many of these prejudices – whether classist, racist, sexist or any other kind – is rarely invisible to those affected by it, who may find their complaints dismissed as fantasy, 'chippiness' or over-sensitivity.

* * *

Perhaps all this really does is to prove that the old adage told to immigrant children – that you have to work twice as hard just to be considered equal – is alive and kicking in modern Britain. But well before you come into contact with this kind of conscious or unconscious prejudice, there are structural problems that limit entry for applicants from 'non-traditional' backgrounds. Take the Bar for example. As I've mentioned, to become a barrister, you first do the Bar vocational course (as it was called when I did it), and then a year of training called a pupillage. For a long time, the pupillage was unpaid (indeed at one point *you* paid the chambers for the pleasure), limiting the pool of applicants to those who could afford to work for free for a year. But, just as sets of chambers were being forced to pay their trainees a decent sum they could live on, the many and generous scholarships available to do the Bar vocational course were diminishing. The result was a perfect storm: while you were now promised a decent salary for the year you were being trained, the financial barrier that had to be hurdled before you could get that salary was getting ever higher. The work experience that you need – mini pupillages at the Bar, or vacation placements in solicitors firms – are largely unpaid and therefore discriminate against kids who have to hold down a part-time job at the same time as studying, or those who can't afford the travel fare to come to London, which is where the vast majority of barrister chambers are. The rage provoked by these sorts of unpaid internships – which are rife not only in law but in many other industries, from journalism to publishing to film – is an expression of the fact that they are unfair on two levels: they exploit the young people working for free, and they are a classic example of opportunity hoarding, cutting off access to all but the already privileged. The majority of the public supports a legal ban against them,[14] but don't hold your breath: even a ban won't stop the informal networks where a parent in one profession will swap opportunities with another senior executive without ever passing through official channels. This trade in opportunities can be difficult to avoid, however much you disapprove – ironically, especially if you are not well-connected within the profession yourself, you may find an offer of, say, an introduction to a very important client difficult to turn down.

Even once you're at the Bar – technically already within an elite profession – some of the structures of inequality persist for years after qualification. Take for example the fact that barristers are mostly self-employed, and usually living pay cheque to pay cheque. We rely on chambers to assist in getting us some work, and the clerks who distribute the work are enormously powerful. Some senior barristers will 'bring you in' on matters, but a lot of it you have to drum up yourself. Some of it is based on your reputation (which takes time to build up) but a lot of it is, quite literally, touting for business. You are expected to give seminars to clients for free, you attend conferences in your spare time, you write articles and papers on the latest developments in the law, post pictures of how much fun you're having discussing some dull legislation on LinkedIn, attend multiple dinners, lunches and events, attempting to schmooze people, and you even, sometimes, take on cases, without charge, in order to get to know clients and build relationships. A lot of people want to feel like they know you before they can entrust you with work, which of course is fair enough. However, all of this costs time and money: time lost while you could be making money, time lost from working on cases that will *actually* pay you. If you are neither independently wealthy, nor have any safety net, and you're not able to rely on the bank of mum and dad for a tax-free loan of £70,000 to put down on a mortgage, for instance, then you will have to make a choice between your financial security and your career. By contrast, those who can afford to spend quality time on building relationships, connecting with clients, and investing time to get their name known, will in a few years' time reap major dividends, produce better-quality work, and have the benefit of a following wind.

As mentioned before, it's not just law that has conditions of entry that actively penalise people without a strong financial backing. Take the creative industries, a broad term covering two other sectors that have formed part of my career: journalism and publishing. Like law, job opportunities are overwhelmingly concentrated in metropolitan centres, and especially London and its commuter belt, something that has led to what the Social Mobility Index calls 'a new geography of disadvantage in England', with even other major cities performing poorly in terms of opportunities for young jobseekers.[15] The dominance of London is itself a barrier to social mobility: leaving your home in search of better opportunities takes money regardless, and, if your family can't provide a financial safety net if it all goes wrong, it can feel like an enormous leap of faith. But moving to London, with its housing crisis and spiralling living costs, is another ball game entirely. Even more so than in the law profession, journalism and publishing rely on an informal network of mainly unpaid internships and work experience placements: applicants for an entry-level job in publishing might have as much as six months of unpaid internships on their CV, while young journalists are often expected to publish work for free in return for 'exposure'. They are socially homogeneous industries: 43 per cent of employees come from middle-class backgrounds against 12 per cent of employees from working-class origins.[16] They also place a high value on cultural capital: an in-depth knowledge of the kind of books, art and places that often form the background to a middle-class childhood. Candidates will be expected to have a grasp of current affairs, a love of film or literature, which in practice often translates as sharing the interests of the narrow sector of society already represented within the industry. As part of their research for *The Class Ceiling*, Sam Friedman and Daniel Laurison conducted interviews at a TV studio, where numerous interviewees talked about the existence of an intellectual and aesthetic highbrow 'monoculture', which meant that, as one person put it 'if you make a slightly populist suggestion ... people just sort of recoil'.[17] Entry-level jobs in

creative industries are typically poorly remunerated compared to other industries such as banking – again, something that's easier to come to terms with if you have the
kind of financial background that means you don't have to
choose between a career you love and owning a house or
being free of student debt. The lack of diversity in the creative industries matters hugely, first because it's not fair,
but also because those sectors create a record of our society
and culture: through books, news programmes, film and
TV, and the adverts that shape what we eat and where we
go on holiday.

* * *

And yet, all that said, these professions are not impenetrable bastions. I found myself both in law and broadcasting, despite being a young person from a disadvantaged
background with not much in the way of cultural or social
capital. When I started, I was living hand-to-mouth, knew
very little about the world, and nothing at all about my
chosen professions. I certainly knew nothing about planning: only years later did I discover that something I had
always assumed was a quirk of fate – that wherever my
family moved, there was always a park nearby for us to play
football in – was in fact linked to urban planning policies that seek to provide for open green spaces. If you are
seeking to make the same journey I did, you should be
aware of the challenges you face – but you should also be
aware that there are ways around them.

In the summer of 2007, I had a life-changing idea. I had
just left university and was unsure what my future would
look like – but I had an inkling that I wanted it to be either
the civil service, the legal profession or journalism. I did
not know anyone in any of these professions. I didn't have

any work experience to speak of; I didn't even know where to start. But I was hungry to succeed, I was determined to make something of my life, I was sure I could find a way through. And I was prepared to try as many unconventional ways as possible. I understood, even then, in my early twenties, that if I stuck to 'the rules' or the 'normal' parameters within which people pursue a career, I would undoubtedly come up short. I had a burning desire to simply not allow my circumstances, which had so clearly determined my past, to dictate my future.

So I wrote a speculative letter to Peter Barron, then editor of *Newsnight*, the flagship BBC Two news programme, asking to learn more about its inner workings. I told him a little about my background and cheekily added that two years earlier I had swapped watching MTV for *Newsnight* and had never looked back. Amazingly, it worked. Peter invited me to spend some time with the programme, and my horizons were opened to a professional world I had known little about at a crucial time in my life.[18] I had a brilliant year at the BBC, somewhere I would return to many years after qualifying as a barrister, to reconnect with the friends I had made, and to make use of the contacts I had cultivated before leaving. I thought then, and still do now, that I would never have made it through a formal recruitment process: those processes are geared towards identifying certain people, measured through certain metrics, appealing to the whims and the formats that are managed by similar people. It was an extremely lucky break, and, despite the initiative that I had shown, there is no doubt that it required someone like Peter – who himself was an outsider, having moved to London from Northern Ireland when he was young – to recognise another outsider who needed a leg up.

The fact is that luck sometimes matters as much as

talent; sometimes you can make your own luck by taking more risks, never thinking that something 'isn't for you'. It doesn't have to be a huge leap. My younger sister Shukri, when she was sixteen and looking for a part-time job, turned up to a random cinema near where we lived, armed with copies of her CV and boldly asked to speak to the manager. The manager, startled and bemused, came out to ask what the issue was. She replied that there wasn't a problem, but that she was wondering when they would next recruit; not for some months yet, came the answer. There and then she handed him her CV, and suggested that they sit down and do an informal interview so that when the next round came up, he can, if he likes her, ring her up first. The manager, impressed by her chutzpah, took up the offer, and called her up the following weekend to ask when she could start. No one told Shukri to do this, but it's basically the same impulse as my email to Peter: when the odds are stacked against you, you need to think laterally. Of course, don't keep hammering away when you've had a clear answer (that's a waste of your time as well as theirs) – but don't accept that you have to do things 'the way they've always been done' either. Whether you're walking around London Liverpool Street or Fleet Street, with a sandwich board seeking work,[19] or sending a speculative letter to circumvent the hiring process, the way you make your approach can itself be an advert of your talents. In my experience, people usually react well. It shows tenacity, initiative, bravery, a willingness to see beyond the boundaries – all qualities that someone would want in their organisation. And don't be afraid to point out why you being you is an advantage rather than a disadvantage: the fresh perspective you can bring, the new insights you might have.

The next thing to remember is *be realistic*. In his book

Success and Luck, Good Fortune and the Myth of Meritocracy, Robert H. Frank, a professor of economics, explains why so many people underplay or underestimate the importance of luck in their own success.[20] Successful people especially are more likely to overestimate their personal role in why they have done well, and in convincing themselves that they have control over their own destiny. The example Frank gives is of cycling into a strong headwind: when the wind is against you, you're acutely aware of it, as you try to pedal harder to fight it. If you then turn the corner, and have the wind behind you, things are completely different: now you're bowling along with very little effort needed. And yet, most of us will only notice the change for the first few moments, after which you will forget the role of the wind completely. As Lynsey Hanley puts it in *Respectable*, 'The further up the social ladder you are, the more external influences are set up to favour you and your kind, to the extent that privilege becomes invisible and so weightless that – literally – you don't know how lucky you are.'[21] The failure to acknowledge the role of luck in our lives (combined with the obsessive English habit of self-deprecation), often damages peoples' true understanding of where others are actually starting from. Frank points out how, in a world increasingly dominated by winner-take-all markets, chance opportunities and trivial initial advantages often translate into much larger ones. He gives the example of Bill Gates, who was one of a handful of children in his generation who had access to an early model computer, allowing him to spend countless hours learning to programme.[22] Jeff Bezos, the founder of Amazon and one of the world's richest people, had his parents invest $250,000 into Amazon in 1995; if that's not lucky then I don't know what is.[23] Donald J. Trump, the 'self-made' billionaire president, talked about the 'small loan' of $1 million from his parents; investigations have shown the amount to have been considerably more.[24] And yet the stories we tell about these people always focus on early struggles: we talk about how Gates dropped out of Harvard, how Trump is a hustler and a dealmaker, or how Amazon was founded in a garage. These stories, told in this way, are damaging to the morale of the majority of people consuming them; they do not help us learn about what it means to be 'self-made', and they only perpetuate unrealistic expectations.

However, what is also important is to recognise what your own tailwind might be. The role of chance and chance encounters in my own life, and their impact on my success, has been immeasurable. These are things I have been lucky with: I've always been healthy and physically active; I have siblings who could provide for the family (in modest terms) when I was unable to do so, to give me time to study; and I have never had the kind of debilitating mental health problems that might have been expected given our circumstances. I had the luck to encounter those particular teachers and friends mentioned in previous chapters. I come from a culture that prizes speech and debate and discussion, and I inherited a facility with languages and a strong work ethic. Coming from another culture as I did meant that a lot of the internalised norms of British society – about what sort of life is for what sort of person – simply passed me by. Of course, I also worked hard – but it would be wholly wrong to suggest that it was all *me*. You will have your own patchwork of good and bad luck: make sure you're able to see the whole picture. And don't take others at their own estimation when they appear to suggest that their success has been seamless and easy. I am a strong believer in the adage that if it sounds too good to be true, it probably is.

Be realistic, also, about your own abilities. Don't fall

victim to imposter syndrome, that feeling of not being enough, or being in danger of being found out and sent back where you belong, which artist Grayson Perry has described as like 'the ghost of a working-class past' whispering 'What are you doing here, you oik? These places ain't for the likes of you.'[25] Imposter syndrome is common enough that most 'class travellers', as Perry puts it, will have experienced something like this, and the trick is to know how to address it. Take a clear look at your accomplishments: they might not be the same as those of other people, but you might have talents they've never even thought about. Put yourself in other's shoes: their effortless confidence or even hostility might conceal frantic paddling just to stay afloat. Make sure that you have settled any lingering issues – about identity, for example – which are preventing you from being comfortable in your own skin. Be proud of what your background has taught you, embrace skills you've developed, be the person who can walk into an interview room with the kind of swagger that says 'I deserve to be here'. Rather than asking for acceptance and special treatment, ask for respect and equal treatment. This will be expressed in how you come across, how you conduct yourself, what kind of verbal and non-verbal communication you send out. As Perry puts it, learn to turn to your imposter syndrome and say: 'Would you mind awfully and please shut the fuck up?'[26]

The third thing is to *have a plan. Any* plan. I am always staggered at how many times I meet a recent graduate who says, 'I've got the degree, I did everything I was supposed to do, and now I am applying for jobs and getting no responses.' I understand how frustrating that feels. But at the same time, often no real foresight has gone into precisely why they have studied a particular subject at university; why they didn't spend their holidays – provided they could afford to – doing more (or any) work experience, and trying to expose themselves to new people and environments in order to learn new ideas and ways of doing things. The magnitude of the challenge they face is often lost on them. They haven't researched the statistics they face in the profession they wish to enter, or thought about the characteristics of the people they wish to one day call colleagues. Who knows, they may not like them, they may really get on with them; but they don't know, they *couldn't* know, not having made any enquiries. Having a plan, even if it does not work out, is paramount: at the very least you have something to work towards. Of course, many middle-class kids are equally clueless to begin with, but they are more likely to have the blueprint for success placed in their hands, provided through careful schooling, parents and networks. To compensate, I remember working every weekend throughout my undergraduate degree, looking for work experience every summer and every winter holiday, while working at Sainsbury's stacking shelves. I knew that a degree by itself wouldn't cut it. I literally imagined my CV without the degree, and tried to build something that would really make me stand out.

Understanding what you're good at and what you simply do not like or excel at is also critical. There is no point in enduring three, four or even seven years of full-time education, only to discover at the end that you were only doing it because of your parents. My grandmother would often say to us when we were children: 'You were in the womb alone, and came out alone, and in the end you're going to be buried alone – and in the bit in the middle you're only useful to anyone once you've been useful to yourself first.' Your plan should reflect your personal circumstances and needs: the socially mobile must not only make strategic decisions early on, but also look after themselves, both financially and in terms of mental health. When entering the legal profession, for example, I knew that I needed a field that would provide a decent income, because not only was I without any kind of financial safety net, I was responsible for a large number of dependents as well. That meant that I couldn't choose the criminal Bar, which was in a sorry state and crippled by legal aid cuts. Instead, I picked planning and environment law – the world of commercial litigation – which I judged to be a good source of steady and recession-proof work: this country is *obsessed* with bricks and mortar. It happened to be something that I also had an interest in – the green spaces and parks of London were a revelation to me after Eastleigh, and I had plenty of personal experience of the effects of bad and inadequate housing – but at least as important was the fact that it allowed me to plan for my future, as well as supporting my family in their own journeys, paying for furniture, rental deposits, driving lessons, rewards for successes, emergencies of all kinds. There were, of course, also trade-offs (there always are). Planning and environment work, especially public inquiries, is virtually incompatible with starting a family, or even with having a relatively stable home life. For the first six years of my practice, in fact to this very day, I spend an enormous amount of time on the road, moving from one hotel to the next.

I often meet kids from disadvantaged backgrounds, studying law, who go through their undergraduate degree, oblivious of the fact that they need to plan for their future. They arrive for work experience convinced that their calling is human rights, helping people and wanting to make a difference. I applaud their noble thoughts, but I also worry: anyone who has struggled to get this far should be aspiring to find a path where they will be challenged but also well remunerated, and – crucially – in a position to change their own lives. The field of human rights is hotly competitive, and often poorly remunerated. A large advantage, as ever, goes to those who don't have to worry about money; that is, more affluent kids who have had the opportunities and foresight to have considered what areas of law they want to get into (backed up by the right networks), having weighed future income potential against other factors, including their own passions. Ultimately, of course, it is a matter of choice. Maybe working in the field of human rights is the only thing that matters to you – in which case, that's great, the world needs people like you. But equally, a socially mobile person should not feel ashamed about putting themselves, and their own future, first.

In summary, write your own story. Dream big and be bold. Make the effort: to learn the unwritten codes of society, and to find out what makes people tick, and what makes that particular world you wish to be part of turn. It takes time to pick up these skills, which everyone has had to do, even if they had a head start. Look – carefully and closely – for the opportunity that is there for you to exploit. It wasn't the case for me, and still less for those who came before me, but this time history is on your side: the number of organisations, institutions, entities and individuals who are willing to help, want to help, want to fund you today is bewildering. Find them, use their resources, and make the most of it. Society has never been more aware of the issues being explored in this book; there has never been a moment during which such a large number of people have been focused on trying to make a difference; and there has never been a moment more ripe to make the most of it.

* * *

Ten years after my initial contact with Peter Barron, I went back to ask him why he had bothered to respond to me. He said that it was impossible to answer all the emails he received, but that mine had caught his eye. It was well written, it was compelling, and he remembered leaving the room after our meeting and thinking *'we've got to do something here, we've got to find a way to hire him.'* The young man Peter met was a shadow of the person I am today: I was by no means the perfect candidate. But something made Peter think that I had potential. So often, employment is about what you could *become* rather than what you actually are.

Peter believes in hiring wild cards:

> I think you've just got to do it. You can talk about it forever, you can put mechanisms, schemes and structures in place to try and encourage it, but the danger of course is that you end up in a situation where you expose a wider pool of candidates to the process, but it's always just going to end up with the white person from the public school background who makes it in the final analysis.[27]

Peter is right. The formalised recruitment processes that would have made it hard for someone like me to make it through have been put in place in order to prevent nepotism, bias and judgements based on gut instinct and personal prejudice. In other words, it is sometimes the case that the very noble adjustments to the formal processes, which are there to make a difference, may not be adequate after all.

But I want to show how things could be better: how changes could be made by the only people who are currently in a position to do so. Go to any company's website right now, or their recruitment page, and search for their 'Equality and Diversity' policy statement. You will find something like this:

> [ORGANISATION] is committed to encouraging equality and diversity among our workforce, and eliminating unlawful discrimination.
>
> The aim is for our workforce to be truly representative of all sections of society and our customers, and for each employee to feel respected and able to give their best.[28]

Although by law we are mandated not to discriminate, unlawfully, against anyone based on gender, race, creed, sexuality or religion, it's well established that a CV with a foreign name attached to it will get noticeably fewer responses than one with a 'White British' name.[29] Clearly, these diversity statements are attempting to address a genuine problem, but do they actually make things better? In America, evidence has shown that job adverts that have an 'E&D' statement attached to them actually attract fewer BAME applicants, especially if they're well qualified. One of the major factors appears to be the fear of 'tokenism', or being seen as a 'diversity hire': window dressing for a company that wants to be seen as progressive and open, but doesn't back it up with support and respect.[30] The American actress Mindy Kaling has said, about joining NBC via a diversity programme, that 'for a long time I was really embarrassed about that. No one said anything to me about it, but they all knew and I was acutely aware of that. It took me a while to realise that I was just getting the access other people had because of who they knew.'[31] Feeling like you're only somewhere because of what you look like, and not because of the work you do, can be profoundly dispiriting.

So, lip service to diversity isn't enough: as this study shows, it often fails to reassure the very people it should be helping, while the equally common 'diversity networks' set up to connect LGBTQI people, or women, or BAME people, often end up pushing the responsibility for fixing the problem on to the very people who need help the most. First-generation professionals should be concentrating on getting on; why should they have to sit in endless meetings, acting as unpaid consultants whose job it is 'to fix the diversity problem'? Although in some areas this is changing, diversity requirements rarely take account of class or the intersectionality of different identities. As the writer Sathnam Sanghera put it,

> the diversity agenda, as propounded by corporations, values some differences more than others. Things such as class, geographical background, education, accent and personality don't matter. But things such as race, gender, disability and sexuality matter so much that they have become synonymous with the very word 'diverse'.[32]

So, what practically can be done? In truth, we need to start thinking about changing our workplaces from the ground up. Too often, employers are allowed to get away with presenting recruitment as a process of making a choice between finished products. I myself have been approached by employers who clearly did not want to take a risk on me when I was young and raw, but who are very interested in me now that I've been trained, polished, and given experience by a different organisation. But those who are socially mobile and are seeking to transform their lives may well come across as unpolished, in terms of how they present, both on paper and in person, in how they speak and in how they're able to 'sell themselves'. Expecting schools alone to educate and raise young people, and for universities to then turn them into adults in three years, is unrealistic; as is expecting them to rectify the damage caused by a lack of basic funding for struggling families and the school system. The transition from university life to a work environment, from young person to full-blown adult, remains one of the hardest for any prospective worker; but it's perhaps particularly difficult for someone who's also attempting a social mobility journey. Both universities and potential employers need to ensure that students make as smooth a transition as possible; a deeper collaborative approach between the two is well overdue. But employers, who stand to gain the most, must make more of the running: looking beyond the obvious, being willing to take on a rough diamond, and taking more responsibility for training and developing than they might be used to.

While leadership may set the direction of travel, the ethos and the values, recruitment will usually sit within HR. As an indication of how serious an organisation is about access and best practice, see how many people staff that department. Is it a well-resourced, well-trained team, with a good retention rate? What do they look like, where have they come from, what kind of training have they had? Instead of putting token references to inclusivity on their websites, companies need to take practical steps, for example following 'name-blind' recruitment strategy (now practised by the British government, along with a number of large corporations, such as HSBC, Deloitte, the BBC and the NHS);[33] considering candidates without a degree; and adopting strategies such as contextual recruitment, which uses big data to place a candidate's qualifications in the context of their background. (The company who came up with the concept claims that significantly more disadvantaged candidates were selected when organisations began using their recruitment system.)[34]

When it comes to selection, interviewers need to be conscious of their own biases and prejudices, and test ability and talent rather than 'fit' and existing knowledge. I'll never forget an interview that I did for my own chambers. At the time, my previous pupillage hadn't worked out, and I badly needed to find something else. As the panel of three interviewers took me through the questions, I was aware that I hadn't given the right answer to one of them: I could feel that it was a bad mistake from their reactions. But at the end of the interview, one of the panel stopped me, and asked the same question again, using a different example: this time I got it right, and I could feel the atmosphere relax. Sometimes, it's about giving someone just one more chance, of making the effort to see their potential, despite the chaotically put together CV, despite the first impressions, despite your own expectations. The raw abilities may be hidden due to the pressure of the situation, stress, lack of confidence, nervous disposition, and much more besides. As an interviewer, it is up to you to create the right environment, within the right team, to allow for those qualities to shine through. Again, this is not easy. It will take time, and cost money and resources. Make a conscious effort to question things that have 'always been done that way': if you think that your interview format gives too much scope for affinity bias, then make it part of a number of assessments, some of which should be task-based. Think about the period during which you recruit. For law firms and some blue-chip companies, and even the civil service Fast Stream, this often begins in the second year of university, when some youngsters are simply not ready – indeed, are still making up lost ground. If you overlook this, you'll end up recruiting from the small minority who are likely to be well informed, and who know what they want early in their lives, while missing those, like me, who don't really wake up to all the possibilities until around their mid-twenties. Likewise, don't wait to fill a post until the situation is urgent and you need someone who can hit the ground running: build in a couple of months for training.

This is not just about widening the talent pool because it is the right thing to do; it also makes business sense. An organisation that does not reflect its clients, the society it claims to serve, and its consumers, in a more global and globalised world, will become irrelevant. Several times during the research for this book, HR managers have privately confided in me that there have been many occasions when they have found the right candidate, only for them to fall at the last hurdle when the question is posed; *could I put this person in front of the client?* Ridiculous things, like aesthetics, accent, presentation or social skills, or even mannerisms, end up disqualifying an otherwise capable candidate – someone who deserved that job. People are afraid to admit it, but these factors do play a role in our day-to-day decision-making process. This must stop: our society must reflect the people in it, even if it means challenging clients to think differently or, bluntly, take their business elsewhere. It is important that such actions are driven by a genuine drive to not only seek out and recruit new and talented faces, but to offer the support and training required to keep them there, to see them one day leading the organisation or institution. This is likely to inject a new sense of creativity, for a homogeneous workforce is only likely to bring forward predictable answers to the challenges of tomorrow.

* * *

This last point is an important one: our world is changing fast, and we must make sense of social mobility in the workplace against a rapidly evolving context. The kind of jobs that are available today, for example, simply did not exist twenty years ago. Advances in technology, the dominance of the internet, the rise of social media: all these things have given opportunities to young people today that could scarcely have been imagined by their parents. There is ample opportunity to write your own story via a career as a blogger, citizen journalist, app developer, tech entrepreneur and so on.[35] But these opportunities come with disadvantages of their own. While they open up opportunities to young people, and offer them a level of freedom and control that might help them circumvent some of the traditional barriers to social mobility, they also expose them to unprecedented job insecurity and risk of exploitation. In the background, the dangers of automation rumble away, threatening to hollow out whole industries in ways that will almost certainly worsen inequality. In an article for *The Guardian*, the physicist Stephen Hawking wrote:

> The automation of factories has already decimated jobs in traditional manufacturing [and] the rise of artificial intelligence is likely to extend this job destruction deep into the middle classes ... [accelerating] the already widening economic inequality around the world. The internet and the platforms that it makes possible allow very small groups of individuals to make enormous profits while employing very few people.[36]

Whether this bleak prediction will come to pass, or is already here, we are yet to fully appreciate: panics about technology replacing human workers have happened before. Perhaps the larger threat is that, unless we have overall economic growth, accompanied by the creation of well-paid, high-status jobs,[37] which are catered for by a well-organised, well-funded education system with the foresight to produce the future employees required to fill those jobs, there will simply never be enough room 'at the top'. This situation – absolute mobility, in other words – has not been experienced since the post-war boom, a social and economic phenomenon that is unlikely to be repeated. We must come to terms with the fact that upward mobility will have to be balanced by movement downwards. If there is less room at 'the top', it is more likely that, in a race between wealthy families and the state, the state will lose.

Much of what determines whether the socially mobile thrive in the workplace is down to individuals: from HR directors to interviewers to each of us interrogating our own biases, we all have our part to play. But, in a changing world, we also need to have faith in our leaders: that they understand the challenges, and that empty promises will no longer cut it.

Conclusion

May the road come up to meet your feet
May the sun shine ever on your face
May the wind blow always at your back
May the rain fall softly on your fields
And till we meet again
Rest safe in the palm of God's hand.

Unknown

If a writer is to tell his own story – to tell it slowly, and as if
it were a story about other people – if he is to feel the power
of the story rise up inside him, if he is to sit down at a table
and give himself over to this art, this craft, he must first be
given some hope.

Orhan Pamuk, 'My Father's Suitcase', The Nobel Lecture, 2006

This book has been deeply painful to write. There were
moments when I had to stop writing because the tears
flowing down my face made it hard to see the screen, or the
paper on which I was attempting to put down some memories. I tried my best to continue but often it was simply
futile, not least because there was no telling when these
moments would happen, in public or in private. I wanted
to stop many times. It was often triggered by pain built up
over the years: all the sorrow, the tragedies, all the missed
opportunities, the mistakes, all the sleepless nights, the

humiliation, the rejections, all the needless family feuds – and how so much of it was avoidable. And yet, at the same time, it was all necessary. Any story about social mobility – but particularly the kind in this book – was never going to be easy to tell. We may measure social mobility in different ways, but it is ultimately a story about hope, and of wanting to take control of your own destiny; even if, in reality in this country, most of it has already been quickly settled on your behalf before you've properly understood any of this. There are hardly any second chances.

The writing process has helped me to close a chapter of my life in the best possible way, but it has come at a personal cost. This is relevant to the social mobility story; it is never just about equalling or bettering the opportunities that your contemporaries have. You need to learn: to give yourself the time to pause, reflect, make sense and proceed slowly to the next juncture. As if 'making it' was not hard enough, if the journey is to be enduring, it needs to be properly understood first, then built upon. This is why this book, for me, has been so necessary.

While memory is by definition flawed, I have tried my best to corroborate much of what I recall, especially where it has involved other members of my family, friends or people who've impacted my life. I am sure that my understanding of parts of what happened is very different to others who saw the same picture from a different perspective. That's the nature of life, I suppose: but any mistakes are mine. While writing Chapter 3, 'Painting the Room Blue', I made contact again with Ms Adler. My own memories were supplemented with her own: she told me that the school was much worse than I remembered, that the circumstances were much more grim (and also, on a more positive note, that we had painted the Eiffel Tower, among other things, in our form room!). I found a perverse kind of hope in knowing that, despite how bad things were, I chose to remember better, which perhaps speaks to a deeper sense of optimism that I believe exists in us all. Some things may only seem worse in hindsight; for if you did not know any better at the time, how could you possibly know that which was missing?

At the start of the book I was filled with anxiety. I knew I could never put together something that had *all* the answers to some of the most intractable issues of our time. I chose to explore the subject through the framework that one might take in life; to understand the legacy that my background gave me, and how best to reconcile it with the place I now call home: Britain. I have explored some well-trodden paths, like the role of education in social mobility, or the power of mentoring to transform lives. I hope that my contributions will help better inform policies – or at least the understanding of the people who make the policies. I have tried to tackle topics that are hard to define but that were nonetheless critical to me and my own experiences as well as to the wider social mobility story: concepts such as *confidence* and *imagination*, the ability to visualise for yourself the kind of future about which you know nothing, and yet wish to realise nonetheless. Language – prose, poetry and the power of words – has been incredibly important to me, and will undoubtedly remain so. I find that it is also, as I hope to have shown here, central to the social mobility story, in sometimes unanticipated ways. And finally, while employment might be seen as the fulfilling or natural aim of this journey, I hope that it is clear from my analysis that this is far from the primary objective. There are always new challenges that present themselves, even at what might previously have been considered the end of a long and hard-fought race.

* * *

While my own story is an anomaly, the reality today is that the circumstances to which you're born in Britain will overwhelmingly determine what kind of future you're likely to have. My story is not and can never be construed as contradicting this: in many ways, it only reinforces it. At the time of writing, towards the end of 2018, the Social Mobility Barometer published research, from a survey of over 5,000 people nationwide, which showed some alarming findings. Nearly half of people anticipate (correctly) that 'where you end up in society is determined largely by who your parents are'; just '15 per cent of eighteen- to twenty-four-year-olds think that their generation has the best chance of moving up in society'. On this, the generational and geographical divide is significant.[1] A staggering 75 per cent of people say there is a 'large gap between social classes in Britain, with 30 per cent believing that the gap is "very large"'.[2] While successive governments have sought to realise a 'classless society', the reality is that we have created its opposite: a caste-based society where privilege and wealth is concentrated in the hands of the very few.

As we confront a chaotic and broken parliamentary system, profound inequality and a potentially disastrous Brexit, it is hard to think of a more challenging time for our deeply divided country. Most people will agree that a stable home and starting point followed by a decent education and the chance to pursue a fulfilling and stimulating career should be attainable for most if not all. And, the place where people look for answers on the issue of social mobility is interesting. Over half of people surveyed think that central government should be 'doing more on social mobility; and 36 per cent think that employers should be doing more'. (I would love to meet the 5 per cent who think that enough is being done.) It is quite telling that nearly half (46 per cent) think that 'schools are best equipped to tackle social mobility, followed by employers (37 per cent) and then central government (34 per cent)'. Together, the overwhelming majority of people think that the answers to these intractable issues lie with our elected officials and with policy, and those who create and sustain jobs. If this is not a cry for a new consensus to be built, then I don't know what is.

Ultimately, the promise made by 'social mobility' in the way that we understand it today is a false one. The elevation of individual stories as examples of what is possible gives a misleading impression: our society is complex, and the simple notion that your talents should be able to take you as far as you like, or that 'working hard and doing the right thing' (an essentially vacuous slogan) will lead inexorably to success, just won't cut it. The situation we have now only works for a tiny few, leaving the rest of us scrambling around, prepared to fight to the death for the remaining scraps. This is not only unsustainable; I would go as far as to say that the convulsion we are seeing in major Western societies is partly because people have realised that the pie has never been cut fairly, and the idea that wealth would eventually 'trickle down' was only ever a pipe dream. Brexit was triggered partly by the conviction held by many that, in the face of finite resources, they were not getting their fair share; the social contract is being rescinded. If the promise of social mobility is to mean something we need to be honest with ourselves; the status quo not only does not work – it never really did.

The reality remains that for a young refugee boy, who buried his father at the age of nine, arrived in Britain without his mother, and was brought up in poverty and among profound deprivation, the chances that you would be writing a book like this one are minuscule. Not impossible, but highly improbable. In that context, what politicians should really be saying is this: The chance of you succeeding in Britain today is down to many factors: the wealth and profession of your parents; the kind of school you attended; your mental and physical health; and the quality of your early environment, in terms of stability and attention. You'll need to work harder than you ever imagined – and hope that whatever talents you have, given the fast-paced development of automation, are going to still be needed when you grow up. You'll need a lot of luck as you go; and let's hope that, along the way, someone explains the unwritten rules of the world you want to join. And you'll need to make it through all that with your belief in yourself – and your vision for the future – still intact. And then – maybe – you'll make it.

It's a bit of a mouthful but it is a damn sight more honest than anything with the word 'meritocracy' in it.

* * *

And so thank you for taking the time to read this book. Please share it. Question it. Think about it from another perspective. It would make everything I've talked about here that much more worth it. But above all else, if you take anything from this story, let it be that you should focus on writing your own story: become the actor, writer, director and producer of your own epic. Know that it is hard, and there will be many false starts, but I promise it will be worth it.

Notes

Introduction

1. 'A qualitative evaluation of non-educational barriers to the elite professions', Social Mobility Commission, 2015. Access at: assets. publishing.service.gov.uk/government/uploads/system/uploads/ attachment_data/file/434791/A_qualitative_evaluation_of_non- educational_barriers_to_the_elite_professions.pdf
2. These figures include those, like me, who went to Oxbridge for postgraduate studies.
3. Though I am not convinced that access to Oxbridge is a measure by which to judge the progress, or not, that we are making in modern-day Britain.
4. Dr Philip Kirby, 'Leading People 2016: The educational backgrounds of the UK professional elite'. Access at: www. suttontrust.com/wp-content/uploads/2016/02/Leading-People_ Feb16.pdf
5. The Sutton Trust Cabinet Analysis 2019. Access at: www.suttontrust.com/research-paper/ sutton-trust-cabinet-analysis-2019/
6. But, as Professor John Goldthorpe of Nuffield College, Oxford, found, the increase in opportunities at the top effectively plateaued in the early 1990s, around the time of my arrival in Britain. As a consequence, this has led to more movement *downwards*, something we seldom acknowledge or discuss.
7. Gregory Clark, *The Son Also Rises: Surnames and the History of Social Mobility*, 2014
8. Owen Jones, 'Social mobility is a dead end', *The Guardian*, 2011. Access at: www.theguardian.com/commentisfree/2011/mar/01/ social-mobility-dead-end
9. Chris McAndrew with Ahmed Roble, 'How I made it from a

Brixton comp to Eton', *The Times*, 2016. Access at: www.thetimes.
co.uk/article/how-i-made-it-from-a-brixton-comp-to-eton-
fxrstvd5j

10. 'Here's why you didn't get that job: your name', World Economic
Forum, 2017. Access at: www.weforum.org/agenda/2017/05/job-
applications-resume-cv-name-descrimination/

1 Three Hashis: Origins and Starting Points

1. This chapter needs to be read alongside the map on p. 24.
2. Records from this period are notoriously non-existent, outside
the few administrations at the time, but due to my grandfather's
status in the police force, documents do give the exact birth date
of my father.
3. Incidentally, our mother, at Shukri's age, had already given birth
to eight children.
4. Afua Hirsch, 'Meghan Markle, Prince Harry and the myth of royal
purity', *The Guardian*, 2 November 2016
5. Christopher Wilson, 'Now that's upwardly mobile! How in 150
years, Meghan Markle's family went from cotton slaves to royalty
via freedom in the U.S. Civil War... while her dad's ancestors
included a maid at Windsor Castle', *Daily Mail*, 2017. Access at:
www.dailymail.co.uk/femail/article-5130473/Meghan-Markles-
upwardly-mobile-family.html
6. Ruth Styles, Shekhar Bhatia, 'Harry's girl is (almost) straight outta
Compton: Gang-scarred home of her mother revealed – so will
he be dropping by for tea?', *Daily Mail*, 2016. Access at: www.
dailymail.co.uk/news/article-3896180/Prince-Harry-s-girlfriend-
actress-Meghan-Markles.html
7. Sam Friedman and Daniel Laurison, *The Class Ceiling: Why it Pays
to be Privileged*, 2019, p. 57
8. Toby Young, 'The fall of the meritocracy', *Quadrant*, 7 September
2015. Access at: quadrant.org.au/magazine/2015/09/fall-
meritocracy/
9. Siddhartha Mukherjee, *The Gene: An Intimate History*, 2017, p. 73
10. Ibid., p. 75
11. Ibid., p. 67
12. Victoria Brignold, 'The eugenics movement Britain wants to

forget', *New Statesman*, 2010. Access at: www.newstatesman.com/
society/2010/12/british-eugenics-disabled

13. Mukherjee, *The Gene: An Intimate History*, op. cit., p. 23

14. Alison Pilnick, *Genetics and Society*, 2002, p. 19.

15. Mukherjee, *The Gene: An Intimate History*, op. cit., p. 67

16. Tanith Carey, 'Why having FIVE children is suddenly the
ultimate middle-class status symbol', *Mail on Sunday*, January
2019. Access at: www.dailymail.co.uk/news/article-6561055/Why-
having-FIVE-children-suddenly-ultimate-middle-class-status-
symbol.html

17. Ziada Ayorech et al., 'Genetic Influence on Intergenerational
Educational Attainment Psychological Science' 2017. DOI:
10.1177/0956797617707270

18. M. Ramsay, 'Genetic reductionism and medical genetic practice',
in A. Clarke, ed., *Genetic Counselling: Practice and Principles*, 1994,
p. 258

19. Friedman and Laurison, *The Class Ceiling*, op. cit., p. 10

20. Ibid., p. 12

21. Social Metrics Commission 2019 Report, 29 July 2019; https://
socialmetricscommission.org.uk/new-report-on-poverty-from-
independent-commission-highlights-scale-of-challenge-facing-
new-prime-minister/

22. Brigid Francis-Devine, Lorna Booth, Feargal McGuinness,
'Poverty in the UK: statistics', House of Commons Library,
September 2019. Access at: researchbriefings.parliament.uk/
ResearchBriefing/Summary/SN07096#fullreport

23. James J. Heckman, Henry Schultz, 'Invest in the
Very Young', 2007. Access at: www.researchgate.net/
publication/255601449_Invest_in_the_Very_Young

24. Michael Marmot, Peter Goldblatt, Jessica Allen , et al., 'Fair
Society, Healthy Lives: The Marmot Review', 2010. Access at:
www.instituteofhealthequity.org/resources-reports/fair-society-
healthy-lives-the-marmot-review/fair-society-healthy-lives-full-
report-pdf.pdf

25. Lee Elliot Major and Stephen Machin, *Social Mobility and its
Enemies*, 2018, p. 157

26. Social Metrics Commission 2019 Report, op. cit.

27. Nissa Finney, Dharmi Kapadia and Simon Peters, 'How are

poverty, ethnicity and social networks related?', Joseph Rowntree Foundation, 2015. Access at: www.jrf.org.uk/report/how-are-poverty-ethnicity-and-social-networks-related

28. John Lanchester, 'Good New Idea' *London Review of Books*, Vol 41, No. 14, 5 November 2019. Access at: www.lrb.co.uk/v41/n14/john-lanchester/good-new-idea

29. NHS Health Scotland, 'Tackling the attainment gap by preventing and responding to Adverse Childhood Experiences (ACEs)', 2017. Access at: www.healthscotland.scot/media/1517/tackling-the-attainment-gap-by-preventing-and-responding-to-adverse-childhood-experiences.pdf

30. Leon Feinstein, 'Inequality in the early cognitive development of British children in the 1970 cohort', 17 November 2003. Access at: onlinelibrary.wiley.com/doi/abs/10.1111/1468–0335.t01-1-00272

31. Friedman and Laurison, *The Class Ceiling*, op. cit., pp. 15–16

32. 'Middle-class parents actively foster children's talents, opinions, and skills: enrolling children in organized activities, reasoning with children (i.e., answering questions with questions), and closely monitoring children's experiences in institutions such as schools.' Quote taken from Annette Lareau; see sociology. sas.upenn.edu/sites/sociology.sas.upenn.edu/files/Lareau_Question&Answers.pdf

33. Friedman and Laurison, *The Class Ceiling*, op. cit. p. 16

34. Lareau, sociology.sas.upenn.edu/sites/sociology.sas.upenn.edu/files/Lareau_Question&Answers.pdf

35. Val Gillies, 'Childrearing, class and the new politics of parenting', *Sociology Compass*, vol. 2, no. 3, April 2008

36. Lareau, sociology.sas.upenn.edu/sites/sociology.sas.upenn.edu/files/Lareau_Question&Answers.pdf

37. Ibid.

38. Ibid.

39. Kwame Anthony Appiah, *The Lies that Bind: Rethinking Identity*, 2018, p. 172

40. Boris Johnson, 'What Would Maggie do Today?', speech to the Centre for Policy Studies, November 2013. Full text accessible at: www.telegraph.co.uk/news/politics/london-mayor-election/mayor-of-london/10480321/Boris-Johnsons-speech-at-the-Margaret-Thatcher-lecture-in-full.html

41. James Lyons, 'Boris Johnson: Millions of people too STUPID to get on in life', *The Mirror*, November 2013. Access at: www.mirror.co.uk/news/uk-news/boris-johnson-millions-people-stupid-2859024

42. Theresa May, 'Britain, the great meritocracy: Prime Minister's speech', September 2016. Access full text at: ww.gov.uk/government/speeches/britain-the-great-meritocracy-prime-ministers-speech

43. Gordon Brown, 'We can break the glass ceiling', *The Guardian*, 15 January 2010. Access at: www.theguardian.com/commentisfree/2010/jan/15/aspiration-mobility-middle-class-labour

44. Michael Young, quoted in Appiah, *The Lies that Bind*, op. cit., p. 171

45. Friedman and Laurison, *The Class Ceiling*, op. cit., p. 34

2 Getting On and Getting Along: Race and Class

1. George Orwell, 'England Your England' Access at: orwell.ru/library/essays/lion/english/e_eye

2. Race Disparity Audit: Summary Findings from the Ethnicity Facts and Figures Website, Cabinet Office, 2017, p. 8. It should be noted, however, that this doesn't mean that the total proportion of white people went down significantly: the combined total of people identifying as 'White British' and 'White Other' remained stable at around 86 per cent.

3. 'The perils of perception and the EU', 9 June 2016. Access at: www.ipsos.com/ipsos-mori/en-uk/perils-perception-and-eu

4. Omar Khan and Faiza Shaheen, ed., 'Minority Report Race and Class in post-Brexit Britain', Runnymede Trust, p. 22, 2017. Access at: www.migrantsrights.org.uk/wp-content/uploads/2017/03/Race-and-Class-Post-Brexit-Perspectives-report-v5-1.pdf

5. Chris Curtis, 'The demographics dividing Britain', April 2017. Access at: yougov.co.uk/topics/politics/articles-reports/2017/04/25/demographics-dividing-britain

6. Race Disparity Audit: Summary Findings from the Ethnicity Facts and Figures Website, 2017, p. 9

7. Ibid., p. 8

8. Ibid., p. 10

9. Boston Consulting Group, for The Sutton Trust, *The State of Social Mobility in the UK* 2017, p. 14

10. Omar Khan and Faiza Shaheen, ed., 'Minority Report Race and Class in post-Brexit Britain', Runnymede Trust, p. 22, 2017. Access at: www.migrantsrights.org.uk/wp-content/uploads/2017/03/Race-and-Class-Post-Brexit-Perspectives-report-v5-1.pdf

11. Ibid., p. 25

12. Friedman and Laurison, *The Class Ceiling*, op. cit., pp. 42–43

13. Ibid., p. 43

14. Demos, 'Why are British Indians more successful than Pakistanis?', 2015. Access at: demos.co.uk/blog/why-are-british-indians-more-successful-than-pakistanis/

15. Friedman and Laurison, *The Class Ceiling*, op. cit., p. 40

16. Figures from a 2011 census: 2.7 million Muslims in England and Wales; 4.8 per cent of population; 33 per cent aged fifteen or under; 68 per cent of Asian descent; 8 per cent are of white ethnicity; 47 per cent born in Britain, 36 per cent in the Middle East and Asia; 6 per cent say they are struggling to speak English; 37 per cent of Muslims live in London; 20 per cent are in full-time employment (compared to 35 per cent of the general population); see www.bbc.co.uk/news/uk-31435929

17. 'British Muslims in numbers', The Muslim Council of Britain, pp. 16–17, 26, 37; www.mcb.org.uk/wp-content/uploads/2015/02/MCBCensusReport_2015.pdf –

18. Ibid.

19. Runnymede Trust, *Minority Report: Race and Class in Post-Brexit Britain*, 2017, p. 6

20. Caitlin Moran, 'Isis bride Shamima Begum's image problem', *The Times*, 1 March 2019

21. 'Universal credit: Brown says benefit rollout could lead to "poll-tax-style chaos"', BBC, October 2018. Access at: www.bbc.co.uk/news/uk-politics-45811239

22. More information on the Education Maintenance Allowance (EMA) at: www.gov.uk/education-maintenance-allowance-ema

23. Amanda Platell, 'Can't you show a scintilla of gratitude, Stormzy?', *Daily Mail*, February 2018. Access at: www.dailymail.

co.uk/debate/article-5429041/Platells-People-Stormzy-gratitude.
html

24. Dina Nayeri, 'The Ungrateful Refugee: "We have no debt to
    repay"', *The Guardian*, 2017. Access at: www.theguardian.com/
    world/2017/apr/04/dina-nayeri-ungrateful-refugee

25. Nick Bailey, Anna Haworth, Tony Manzi, Primali Paranagamage
    and Marion Roberts, 'Creating and sustaining mixed income
    communities: a good practice guide', published for the Joseph
    Rowntree Foundation by the Chartered Institute of Housing,
    2006. Access at: www.jrf.org.uk/sites/default/files/jrf/migrated/
    files/9781905018314.pdf

26. Dina Nayeri, 'The Ungrateful Refugee: "We have no debt to
    repay"', *The Guardian*, 2017. Access at: www.theguardian.com/
    world/2017/apr/04/dina-nayeri-ungrateful-refugee

27. Credit Suisse, Global Wealth Report 2018. Access at: www.credit-
    suisse.com/corporate/en/research/research-institute/global-
    wealth-report.html

28. Afua Hirsch, *Brit(ish): On Race, Identity and Belonging*, 2018

29. Ibid., p. 8

3 Painting the Room Blue: Education

1. Richard Adams, 'One in four teachers "experience violence from
   pupils every week"', *The Guardian*, April 2019. Access at: www.
   theguardian.com/education/2019/apr/20/one-in-four-teachers-
   experience-violence-from-pupils-every-week

2. Tony Blair, speech on education, 2001. Full text available at: www.
   theguardian.com/politics/2001/may/23/labour.tonyblair

3. Social Mobility 2017 Summit Report: The Sutton Trust 20th
   Anniversary Summit 2017, p. 9

4. Elliot Major and Machin, *Social Mobility and its Enemies*, op. cit.,
   p. 124

5. Tara Westover, *Educated*, 2018, p. 377

6. Sally Weale, 'London state school says 41 students offered
   Oxbridge place', *The Guardian*, January 2019. Access at: www.
   theguardian.com/education/2019/jan/15/london-state-school-
   brampton-manor-41-students-offered-oxbridge-place

7. Ibid.

8. Ibid.

9. Office for National Statistics, 'How has the student population changed?'. Access at: www.ons.gov.uk/ peoplepopulationandcommunity/birthsdeathsandmarriages/ livebirths/articles/howhasthestudentpopulationchanged/ 2016–09–20

10. Elliot Major and Machin, *Social Mobility and its Enemies*, op. cit., p. 115

11. Ibid., p. 117

12. Ibid., p. 124

13. Ibid., p. 92

14. Ibid.

15. Ibid.

16. Social Mobility and Child Poverty Commission, *State of the Nation 2015: Social Mobility and Child Poverty in Great Britain*, p. 47

17. Ibid., p. 4

18. Friedman and Laurison, *The Class Ceiling*, op. cit., p. 38

19. Sean Clare, 'London teens sent to Africa to escape knife crime', BBC, May 2019. Access at: www.bbc.co.uk/news/uk-48353960

20. Robert Joyce, 'Child poverty in Britain: recent trends and future prospects', The Institute for Fiscal Studies (IFS), October 2014. Access at: www.ifs.org.uk/uploads/publications/wps/WP201507. pdf

21. Hannah Richardson, 'Child poverty: Pale and hungry pupils "fill pockets with school food"', BBC, April 2018. Access at: www.bbc. co.uk/news/education-43611527

22. Elliot Major and Machin, *Social Mobility and its Enemies*, op. cit., p. 120

23. Natasha Onwuemezi, '"Staggering" £25m fall in libraries spending revealed', *The Bookseller*, December 2016. Access at: www. thebookseller.com/news/cipfa-library-figures-446101

24. Boston Consulting Group, for The Sutton Trust, *The State of Social Mobility in the UK 2017*, p. 13

25. Some efforts have been made, like extending school hours from 8 a.m. to 6 p.m. every day, but of course this is always subject to the available resources.

26. Julie Henry, Social Mobility 2017 Summit Report: The Sutton Trust 20th Anniversary Summit, July 2017, p. 14

27. Boston Consulting Group, for The Sutton Trust, *The State of Social Mobility in the UK 2017*, p. 15

28. Donald Hirsch, *Experiences of Poverty and Educational Disadvantage*, Joseph Rowntree Foundation, 2007

29. Ibid.

30. Val Gillies, 'Raising the "Meritocracy": Parenting and the Individualization of Social Class', Sage Publications on behalf of the British Sociological Association, 2005. Access at: journals. sagepub.com/doi/abs/10.1177/0038038505058368

31. Hirsch, *Experiences of Poverty and Educational Disadvantage*, op. cit., p. 5

32. Ibid., p. 4

33. Tammy Campbell, 'Stereotyped at seven? Biases in teacher judgement of pupils' ability and attainment', *Journal of Social Policy*, 2015. Access at: discovery.ucl.ac.uk/id/eprint/1474027/1/ Campbell%202015%20-%20Stereotyped%20at%20Seven%20-%20 accepted%20manuscript.pdf See also *Experiences of Poverty and Educational Disadvantage*, Op. Cit. p5.

34. Val Gillies, 'Raising the "Meritocracy": Parenting and the Individualization of Social Class', Sage Publications on behalf of the British Sociological Association, 2005. Access at: journals. sagepub.com/doi/abs/10.1177/0038038505058368

35. Department for Education, 'Permanent and fixed-period exclusions in England: 2008 to 2009'. Access at: assets.publishing. service.gov.uk/government/uploads/system/uploads/attachment_ data/file/218896/sfr22-2010.pdf

36. '"They Go the Extra Mile": Reducing inequality in school exclusions', Office of the Children's Commissioner, March 2013. Access at: www.childrenscommissioner.gov.uk/wp-content/ uploads/2017/07/They_Go_The_Extra_Mile-.pdf

37. 'Permanent and Fixed Period Exclusions in England: 2016 to 2017', Department for Education, July 2018. Access at: assets.publishing. service.gov.uk/government/uploads/system/uploads/attachment_ data/file/726741/text_exc1617.pdf

38. Whitney Crenna-Jennings, 'A black Caribbean FSM boy with SEND is 168 times more likely to be permanently excluded than a white British girl without SEND. Why?', *Times Education Supplement*, December 2017. Access at: www.tes.com/news/

black-caribbean-fsm-boy-send-168-times-more-likely-be-permanently-excluded-white-british-girl

39. Julia Belgutay, 'Former Met chief: exclusions contributing to rise in knife crime', *Times Education Supplement*, March 2019. Access at: www.tes.com/news/former-met-chief-exclusions-contributing-rise-knife-crime

40. Office of the Children's Commissioner, 'Keeping kids safe: Improving safeguarding responses to gang violence and criminal exploitation', February 2019. Access at: cscp.org.uk/wp-content/uploads/2018/04/Childrens-Commissioner-Report-Keeping-kids-safe-gang-violence-and-CCE.pdf

41. Independent Schools Council research. Access at: www.isc.co.uk/research/

42. Dr Philip Kirby, 'Leading People 2016: The educational backgrounds of the UK professional elite'. Access at: www.suttontrust.com/wp-content/uploads/2016/02/Leading-People_Feb16.pdf

43. Rebecca Montacute, Tim Carr, 'Parliamentary Privilege – The MPs 2017', The Sutton Trust, 2017, Access at: www.suttontrust.com/research-paper/parliamentary-privilege-the-mps-2017-education-background/

44. The Sutton Trust, 'Almost Two-Thirds of New Cabinet Attended Independent Schools', July 2019. Access at: www.suttontrust.com/newsarchive/almost-two-thirds-of-new-cabinet-attended-independent-schools/

45. Alan Bennett, 'Fair Play', *London Review of Books*, Vol 36. Ed. 12, November 2019. Access at: www.lrb.co.uk/v36/n12/alan-bennett/fair-play

46. Francis Green and David Kynaston, *Engines of Privilege: Britain's Private School Problem*, 2019, p. 8: 'In 2017, the proportion of private school students achieving A*s or As at A level was 48 per cent, compared to a national average of 26 per cent.'

47. Camilla Turner, 'Exam results gap between state schools and private schools is narrowing, figures show', *The Telegraph*, August 2017. Access at: www.telegraph.co.uk/education/2017/08/25/exam-results-gap-state-schools-private-schools-isnarrowing-figures/

48. Rachael Pells, 'State schools outshine Eton in science A-levels',

The Independent, July 2017. Access at: www.independent.co.uk/news/education/education-news/eton-state-school-science-gsce-results-public-boarding-league-table-ranking-your-life-a7826696.html

49. Elliot Major and Machin, *Social Mobility and its Enemies*, op. cit., p. 144

50. Appiah, *The Lies that Bind*, op. cit., pp. 172–73

51. Chris Belfield, Christine Farquharson and Luke Sibieta, '2018 Annual Report on Education Spending in England', Institute for Fiscal Studies and Nuffield Foundation, September 2018. Access at: www.ifs.org.uk/uploads/publications/comms/R150.pdf

52. 'Jess Phillips MP in Baby Shark protest over Birmingham school hours', BBC, March 2019. Access at: www.bbc.co.uk/news/uk-england-birmingham-47538926

53. James Tapper, 'Burned out: why are so many teachers quitting or off sick with stress?', *The Observer*, May 2018. Access at: www.theguardian.com/education/2018/may/13/teacher-burnout-shortages-recruitment-problems-budget-cuts

54. Allana Gay, 'BAME teachers are still marginalised in a system that refuses to change', *The Guardian*, March 2018. Access at: www.theguardian.com/teacher-network/2018/mar/20/fight-bame-teachers-senior-positions-diversity

55. Mayor of London, Annual London Education Report 2017, p. 6

56. Ibid.

57. Teddy Wolstenholme, Larushka Ivan-Zadeh, Celia Thursfield and Alice Rose, 'The Tatler guide to the best state secondary schools', *Tatler*, January 2018. Access at: www.tatler.com/article/best-state-secondary-schools-uk-2018

58. Nicky Burridge, 'The premium parents pay for a home near a top school', August 2018. Access at: www.primelocation.com/discover/property-news/top-state-schools-drive-house-price-premiums/#8SeHYTP9sEBegbj4.99

59. The social mobility index sets out the differences between where children grow up and the chances they have of doing well in adult life. Access at www.gov.uk/government/publications/social-mobility-index

60. Social Mobility Commission, 'State of the Nation 2017: Social Mobility in Great Britain 2017' p. iv

61. Ibid., p. 16
62. Ibid.
63. Ibid., p. 14
64. Ibid., p. 47
65. Ibid., p. iv
66. Ibid., p. iv
67. Social Mobility Commission, 'Ethnicity, Gender and Social Mobility', December 2017. Access at: assets.publishing.service. gov.uk/government/uploads/system/uploads/attachment_data/ file/579988/Ethnicity_gender_and_social_mobility.pdf
68. Ibid.
69. Social Mobility Commission, 'State of the Nation 2017: Social Mobility in Great Britain, op. cit. p1
70. Ibid.
71. Mayor of London, Annual London Education Report 2017, p. 4–5
72. Ibid., p. 5
73. Ibid.
74. 'The Met's Trident unit loses its gun murders brief', BBC, March 2013. Access at: www.bbc.co.uk/news/uk-england-london-21773275
75. 'What is county lines?', The Children's Society. Access at: www. childrenssociety.org.uk/what-is-county-lines
76. Ibid.
77. *County Lines Violence, Exploitation & Drug Supply 2017*, National Briefing Report, National Crime Agency, November 2017. Access at: www.nationalcrimeagency.gov.uk/who-we-are/publications/ 234-county-lines-violence-exploitation-and-drug-supply-2017/file

4 In Pursuit of Purpose: Confidence

1. 'What are my chances of getting into Oxford or Cambridge?', Oxbridge Applications. Access at: oxbridgeapplications.com/ blog/what-are-my-chances-of-getting-into-oxford-or-cambridge/
2. Darren McGarvey, *Poverty Safari: Understanding the Anger of Britain's Underclass*, 2017, pp. 26, 27, 28
3. Reni Eddo-Lodge, *Why I'm No Longer Talking to White People About Race*, 2017, pp. 57–84
4. J. D. Vance, *Hillbilly Elegy: A Memoir of a Family and Culture in Crisis*, 2016, p. 212

5. Friedman and Laurison, *The Class Ceiling*, op. cit., p. 25

6. James Ball and Andrew Greenway, 'The bluffocracy: how Britain ended up being run by eloquent chancers', *The Spectator*. Access at: www.spectator.co.uk/2018/08/the-bluffocracy-how-britain-ended-up-being-run-by-eloquent-chancers/

7. Ibid.

8. Sathnam Sanghera, 'I Learnt A Lot. But I Never Felt I Belonged', *The Times*, May 2018. Access at: www.suttontrust.com/wp-content/uploads/2018/04/The-Times-I-learnt-a-lot.pdf

9. Ibid.

10. 'List of prime ministers of the United Kingdom by education', Wikipedia. Access at: en.wikipedia.org/wiki/List_of_prime_ministers_of_the_United_Kingdom_by_education

11. Claire Kendall, 'Being a Young Carer', BBC, September 2018. Access at: www.bbc.co.uk/news/resources/idt-sh/Being_a_young_carer

12. Annette Lareau, *Unequal Childhoods: Class, Race, and Family Life* (Second Edition), 2011

13. Malcolm Gladwell, *Outliers: The Story of Success*, 2008, pp. 103–104

14. See both 'REACH: An independent report to Government on raising the aspirations and attainment of Black boys and young Black men', REACH Group, 2007 – access at: dera.ioe.ac.uk/6778/1/reach-report.pdf – and 'Gangs and young people How you can help keep children and young people safe', NSPCC. Access at: www.nspcc.org.uk/preventing-abuse/keeping-children-safe/staying-safe-away-from-home/gangs-young-people/

15. Ibid.

16. 'Single parents: facts and figures', Gingerbread. Access at: www.gingerbread.org.uk/what-we-do/media-centre/single-parents-facts-figures/

17. David Lammy, 'Tottenham past and present – a memoir', *The Guardian*, 18 November 2011

18. Stephen Bush, 'On the Tube, I saw the father I'd never met – and was happy to find that I had nothing to say to him', *New Statesman*, December 2017. Access at: www.newstatesman.com/politics/uk/2017/12/tube-i-saw-father-i-d-never-met-and-was-happy-find-i-had-nothing-say-him

19. Trevor Noah, *Born a Crime: Stories from a South African Childhood*, 2016

20. The list includes Washington, Jefferson, Hamilton, Lincoln, Clinton, Hitler, Gandhi and Stalin, just to name a few. See David Brooks, *The Social Animal; A Story of How Success Happens*, 2012, p. 132.

21. Ibid., p. 132

5 What Is and What Could Be: Imagination

1. Peter Walker, 'White working-class boys should be more aspirational, says Labour minister', *The Guardian*, January 2018. Access at: www.theguardian.com/education/2018/jan/03/white-working-class-boys-should-be-more-aspirational-says-labour-minister

2. Nick Chambers, Jordan Rehill, Dr Elnaz T. Kashefpakdel, Christian Percy, 'Drawing the Future: Exploring the career aspirations of primary school children from around the world', Education and Employers, January 2018. Access at: www.educationandemployers.org/wp-content/uploads/2018/01/DrawingTheFuture.pdf

3. Ibid., p. 32

4. Peter Walker, 'White working-class boys should be more aspirational, says Labour minister', *The Guardian*, January 2018. Access at: www.theguardian.com/education/2018/jan/03/white-working-class-boys-should-be-more-aspirational-says-labour-minister

5. 'Young people's career aspirations versus reality', Office of National Statistics, September 2018. Access at: www.ons.gov.uk/employmentandlabourmarket/

6. The Sutton Trust, 'Factsheet: Social Mobility', Access at: www.suttontrust.com/wp-content/uploads/2018/01/Socialmobility_SuttonTrust_Factsheet_.pdf

7. Romelu Lukaku, 'I've Got Some Things to Say', The Player's Tribune, June 2018. Access at: www.theplayerstribune.com/en-us/articles/romelu-lukaku-ive-got-some-things-to-say

8. Carol S. Dweck, *Mindset: The New Psychology of Success*, 2006

9. Ibid.

10. Dweck, *Mindset*, op. cit., p. 33: 'Even in the growth mindset,

failure can be a painful experience. But it doesn't define you. It's a problem to be faced, dealt with, and learned from.' See also fs.blog/2014/09/mistakes/

11. Louise Reynolds, Jonathan Birdwell, 'Rising to the Top', Demos, October 2015. Access at: demos.co.uk/project/rising-to-the-top/

12. Francis Fukuyama, *Identity: Contemporary Identity Politics and the Struggle for Recognition*, 2018, chapter 11

13. Fukuyama, *Identity: Contemporary Identity Politics and the Struggle for Recognition*, op. cit., p. 107

14. Tom Payne, 'Group of advertising executives claim they lost their jobs because they are "white, male, straight and British" after director announced plans to "obliterate" the Mad Men culture', *Daily Mail*, November 2018. Access at: www.dailymail.co.uk/news/article-6386683/Sacked-white-straight-male-advertising-executives-claim-discrimination.html

15. Elliot Major and Machin, *Social Mobility and its Enemies*, op. cit., p. 27

16. Ibid., pp. 38–39

17. 'The Scale of Economic Inequality in the UK', The Equality Trust. Access at: www.equalitytrust.org.uk/scale-economic-inequality-uk

6 Filling in the Blanks: Mentoring

1. Kate Fox, *Watching the English: The Hidden Rules of English Behaviour*, 2014, p. 93

2. Joanne Moore, Louise Higham, Anna Mountford-Zimdars, Dr Louise Ashley et al., 'Socio-Economic Diversity in Life Sciences and Investment Banking', The Social Mobility Commission, July 2016. Access at: assets.publishing.service.gov.uk/government/uploads/system/uploads/attachment_data/file/549994/Socio-economic_diversity_in_life_sciences_and_investment_banking.pdf

3. Rob Davies, 'How well-heeled City types leave you brown and out in finance', *The Guardian*, September 2016. Access at: www.theguardian.com/business/2016/sep/02/city-of-london-dress-code-brown-shoes-finance

4. Vance, *Hillbilly Elegy*, op. cit, p. 217

5. Vance, *Hillbilly Elegy*, op. cit., p. 220

6. 'Why the myth of meritocracy hurts kids of color', *The Atlantic*, 2017. Access at: www.theatlantic.com/education/archive/2017/07/internalizing-the-myth-of-meritocracy/535035/

7. E. B. Godfrey, C. E. Santos and E. Burson, 'For better or worse? System-justifying beliefs in sixth-grade predict trajectories of self-esteem and behavior across early adolescence', *Child Development*, 2017. Access at: onlinelibrary.wiley.com/doi/full/10.1111/cdev.12854

8. 'Why the myth of meritocracy hurts kids of color', op. cit.

9. John T. Jost, 'A theory of system justification: Is there a nonconscious tendency to defend, bolster and justify aspects of the societal status quo?'. Access at: www.apa.org/science/about/psa/2017/06/system-justification.aspx

10. 'Why the myth of meritocracy hurts kids of color', *The Atlantic*, op. cit.

7 What Does it Sound Like? Language

1. Before this, as early as the thirteenth century, there were unsuccessful attempts to use the Arabic script, and then in the 1920s a script resembling the Ethiopian system was tried.

2. 'Why Somali is harder than your language', Loving Language, March 2013. Access at: lovinglanguage.wordpress.com/2013/03/17/why-somali-is-harder-than-your-language/

3. Ibid.

4. Safia Aidid, 'The Cafe Talkers of Somalia', Popula, August 2018. Access at: popula.com/2018/08/01/the-cafe-talkers-of-somalia/

5. Or is it luck? Perhaps the Somalis simply make good lawyers. I was amused to come across a letter written in 1953 by a Somali soldier of the British Army named Ibrahim Haji Hassan, who complained of Somali 'Coffee Shop Lawyers' who undermined the colonial government with their constant debating and gossiping.

6. Albert Shanker Institute, 'The Early Language Gap is About More Than Words'. Access at: www.shankerinstitute.org/audio-visual/early-language-gap-about-more-words-o

7. CAN and the Royal College of Speech and Language Therapists (RCSLT), 'Bercow: Ten Years On', 1 October 2018. Access at: www.

bercow10yearson.com/wp-content/uploads/2018/03/337644-ICAN-Bercow-Report-WEB.pdf

8. UCL Institute of Education and the Communication Trust, 'What are Speech, Language and Communication Needs (SLCN)?'. Access at: www.thecommunicationtrust.org.uk/media/600984/ite_resource_2.pdf

9. Ibid.

10. Michael Marmot, Peter Goldblatt, Jessica Allen , et al., 'Fair Society, Healthy Lives: The Marmot Review', 2010. Access at: www.instituteofhealthequity.org/resources-reports/fair-society-healthy-lives-the-marmot-review/fair-society-healthy-lives-full-report-pdf.pdf

11. Green and Kynaston, *Engines of Privilege*, op. cit., p. 101

12. Emily Schutzenhofer, 'Evaluating the Effects of Refugee Experiences on Cognitive and Social-Emotional Development in Refugee Children in the Primary Care Setting', July 2018. Access at: med.virginia.edu/family-medicine/wp-content/uploads/sites/285/2018/08/Schutzenhofer_IFMCProjectFinal080818.pdf

13. I CAN and the Royal College of Speech and Language Therapists (RCSLT), 'Bercow: Ten Years On', October 2018. Access at: www.bercow10yearson.com/wp-content/uploads/2018/03/337644-ICAN-Bercow-Report-WEB.pdf

14. Sally Weale, 'Trainee teachers from northern England told to modify their accents', *The Guardian*, May 2016. Access at: www.theguardian.com/education/2016/may/12/trainee-teachers-from-northern-england-told-to-modify-their-accents

15. For examples, see *The Story of British Pathé*, BBC Four, August 2011. Access at: www.bbc.co.uk/programmes/p00jzm14

16. ITV Tonight Regional Accents Survey, ComRes, September 2013. Access at: www.comresglobal.com/polls/itv-tonight-regional-accents-survey-2/

17. Professor Sophie Scott, 'Prejudice about regional accents is still prevalent in Britain', UCL News, www.ucl.ac.uk/news/2017/dec/prejudice-about-regional-accents-still-prevalent-britain

18. Ze Wang, Aaron Arndt, Surendra Singh, Monica Biernat and Fan Liu, '"You lost me at hello": How and when accent-based biases are expressed and suppressed', *International Journal of Research in Marketing*, vol. 30, no. 2, 2013, pp. 185–96. Access at: portal.

idc.ac.il/en/main/research/ijrm/documents/frthcoming per cent20ijrm per cent20d-12–00014_wang per cent20et per cent20al per cent20.pdf

19. David Crystal, January 2013. Access at www.davidcrystal.com/?id=3106

20. Rosemary Bennett, 'Brummie accent is perceived as "worse than silence"', *The Times*, April 2008. Access at: www.thetimes.co.uk/article/brummie-accent-is-perceived-as-worse-than-silence-9m2xmdgcqjq

21. Daniel Lavelle, 'The rise of "accent softening": why more and more people are changing their voices', *The Guardian*, March 2019. Access at: www.theguardian.com/society/2019/mar/20/ugly-rise-accent-softening-people-changing-their-voices

22. Professor Sophie Scott, 'Prejudice about regional accents is still prevalent in Britain', UCL News, www.ucl.ac.uk/news/2017/dec/prejudice-about-regional-accents-still-prevalent-britain

23. Sally Weale, 'Trainee teachers from northern England told to modify their accents', *The Guardian*, May 2016. Access at: www.theguardian.com/education/2016/may/12/trainee-teachers-from-northern-england-told-to-modify-their-accents

24. Louise Tickle, 'Accent snobbery boosts demand for elocution lessons', *The Guardian*. Access at: www.theguardian.com/small-business-network/2016/oct/14/accent-snobbery-boosts-demand-elocution-lessons

25. Kit de Waal, ed., *Common People: An Anthology of Working-Class Writers*, 2019

26. Lillian May, Krista Byers-Heinlein, Judit Gervain, and Janet F. Werker, 'Language and the Newborn Brain: Does Prenatal Language Experience Shape the Neonate Neural Response to Speech?', *Frontiers in Psychology*, April 2011. Access at: www.ncbi.nlm.nih.gov/pmc/articles/PMC3177294/ See also Katherine D. Kinzler, Kristin Shutts et al., 'Accent trumps race in guiding children's social preferences', Social Cognition, August 2009. Access at: www.ncbi.nlm.nih.gov/pmc/articles/PMC3096936/

27. Appiah, *The Lies that Bind*, op. cit.

28. Lynsey Hanley, *Respectable: Crossing the Class Divide*, 2016, p. 42

29. Hugh Muir, 'Izzit or innit in our best interests?', *The Guardian*,

2013. Access at: www.theguardian.com/uk-news/2013/nov/24/
izzit-innit-black-culture-doesnt-depend-on-slang

30. Friedman and Laurison, *The Class Ceiling*, op. cit., p. 128

31. Appiah, *The Lies that Bind*, p. 218

32. A portmanteau of 'fake' and 'Jamaican', because it was perceived
to be based on the English spoken by Caribbean immigrants.

33. Benn Quinn, 'David Starkey claims "the whites have become
black"', *The Guardian*, August 2011. Access at: www.theguardian.
com/uk/2011/aug/13/david-starkey-claims-whites-black

34. Ibid.

35. Lisa O'Carrell, 'David Starkey's Newsnight race remarks:
hundreds complain to BBC', *The Guardian*, August 2011. Access at:
www.theguardian.com/media/2011/aug/15/david-starkey-newsinght-
race-remarks

36. Urszula Clark, 'You are what you speak'. Access at: www2.aston.
ac.uk/research/research-impact/case-studies/you-are-what-you-
speak

37. Will Millard and Amy Gaunt, 'Speaking up: The importance of
oracy in teaching and learning', *Impact*, May 2018. Access at:
https://impact.chartered.college/article/millard-importance-
of-oracy-in-teaching-learning/

38. https://www.tes.com/news/call-teachers-learn-about-oracy

8 Be Useful to Yourself First: Employment

1. Bridge Group, *Socio-economic Background and Early Career
Progression in the Law*, Summary Report, September 2018, https://
static1.squarespace.com/static/5c18e090b40b9d6b43b093d8/t/5
cd180d73cfb160001436429/1557233888333/03+Research+2018+Pr
ogression+law.pdf. The data gathered related to over 2,800 early
career professionals and interviews with current and former
employers from eight leading UK law firms, including Magic
Circle firms: Allen & Overy, Clifford Chance, Linklaters, Bryan
Cave Leighton Paisner, Dentons, Hogan Lovells, Holman Fenwick
Willan, and Pinsent Masons.

2. Bridge Group, *Socio-economic Background and Early Career
Progression in the Law*, op. cit.

3. Robert Booth and Aamna Mohdin, 'Revealed: the stark evidence
of everyday racial bias in Britain', *The Guardian*, December

2018. Access at: www.theguardian.com/uk-news/2018/dec/02/revealed-the-stark-evidence-of-everyday-racial-bias-in-britain

4. 'Modern love: the internet has transformed the search for love and partnership', *The Economist*, 18 August 2018, https://www.economist.com/leaders/2018/08/18/modern-love

5. Project Implicit is accessible at: implicit.harvard.edu/implicit/takeatest.html

6. Ibid.

7. Eric Luis Uhlmann and Geoffrey L. Cohen, '"I think it, therefore it's true": Effects of self-perceived objectivity on hiring discrimination', *Organizational Behavior and Human Decision Processes*, vol. 104, no. 2, November 2007. Access at: www.sciencedirect.com/science/article/pii/S0749597807000611

8. Ibid., conclusions

9. Lord Justice Singh, Sir Mota Singh Memorial Lecture, November 2018. Full text available at: www.judiciary.uk/wp-content/uploads/2018/11/speech-lord-j-singh-racial-equality-and-the-law-lecture-13-nov2018.pdf

10. 'Hate crime: the facts behind the headlines', October 2016. Access at: www.civitas.org.uk/content/files/hatecrimethefactsbehindtheheadlines.pdf

11. Seth Stephens-Davidowitz, *Everybody Lies: Big Data, New Data, and What the Internet Can Tell Us about Who We Really Are*, 2017, p. xi

12. 'Everybody lies: how Google search reveals our darkest secrets', *The Guardian*, 9 July 2017. Access at: www.theguardian.com/technology/2017/jul/09/everybody-lies-how-google-reveals-darkest-secrets-seth-stephens-davidowitz

13. 'Racial prejudice in Britain today', September 2017, http://natcen.ac.uk/media/1488132/racial-prejudice-report_v4.pdf

14. 'Unpaid internships are damaging to social mobility', Social Mobility Commission, October 2017. Access at: www.gov.uk/government/news/unpaid-internships-are-damaging-to-social-mobility

15. The Social Mobility Index, The Social Mobility Commission. Access at: assets.publishing.service.gov.uk/government/uploads/system/uploads/attachment_data/file/496103/Social_Mobility_Index.pdf

16. Dave O'Brien, 'Why class is a far bigger problem in publishing than you think', *The Bookseller*, March 2019. Access at: www.thebookseller.com/blogs/why-class-far-bigger-problem-publishing-you-think-979436

17. Friedman and Laurison, *The Class Ceiling*, op. cit.

18. I wrote about the experience in an article for *Prospect* magazine, April 2017. Access at: www.prospectmagazine.co.uk/politics/the-case-for-a-wild-card

19. Sarah Butcher, 'Student with sandwich board seen seeking employment outside Liverpool Street Station', eFinancial Careers, June 2012. Access at: news.efinancialcareers.com/uk-en/104328/student-with-sandwich-board-seen-seeking-employment-outside-liverpool-street-station

20. Robert H. Frank, *Success and Luck: Good Fortune and the Myth of Meritocracy*, 2016; and see 'The role of luck with Robert Frank', at www.youtube.com/watch?v=IaphLWikHbo

21. Hanley, *Respectable*, op. cit., p. xi

22. In *Outliers*, Malcolm Gladwell spends a great deal of time on the particular focus on 10,000 hours.

23. Avery Hartmans, 'Jeff Bezos' parents invested $245,573 in Amazon in 1995 – now they could be worth $30 billion', Business Insider, July 2018. Access at: www.businessinsider.com/jeff-bezos-parents-jackie-mike-amazon-investment-worth-2018-7?r=US&IR=T

24. Susanne Craig, Russ Buettner, David Barstow and Gabriel J. X. Dance, '4 Ways Fred Trump Made Donald Trump and His Siblings Rich', *The New York Times*, October 2018. Access at: www.nytimes.com/interactive/2018/10/02/us/politics/trump-family-wealth.html

25. Grayson Perry, 'If you have ever felt a class apart, this column is for the likes of you', *The Guardian*, January 2010. Access at: www.theguardian.com/commentisfree/2010/jan/31/grayson-perry-social-mobility

26. Ibid.

27. This is a transcript from the documentary: www.bbc.co.uk/sounds/play/b081h7gf

28. This example comes from ACAS, the conciliation service that seeks to provide resolutions to disputes between employers and employees.

29. Zack Adesina and Oana Marocico, 'Is it easier to get a job if you're Adam or Mohamed?', BBC's *Inside Out*, February 2017. Access at: www.bbc.co.uk/news/uk-england-london-38751307

30. Ibid.

31. Hadley Freeman, 'Mindy Kaling: "I was so embarrassed about being a diversity hire"', *The Guardian*, May 2019, www.theguardian.com/film/2019/may/31/mindy-kaling-i-was-so-embarrassed-about-being-a-diversity-hire

32. Sathnam Sanghera, 'I'm no role model for diversity', *Financial Times*, May 2005. Access at: www.ft.com/content/4372301c-c30a-11d9-abf1-00000e2511c8

33. 'Who, What, Why: What is name-blind recruitment?'. Access at: www.bbc.co.uk/news/magazine-34636464

34. More about Contextual Recruitment can be found at: contextualrecruitment.co.uk/index.php

35. 'We're doing jobs that didn't exist 20 years ago', BBC, Access at: https://www.bbc.co.uk/bitesize/articles/z6rkscw

36. Stephen Hawking, 'This is the most dangerous time for our planet', *The Guardian*, December 2016. Access at: www.theguardian.com/commentisfree/2016/dec/01/stephen-hawking-dangerous-time-planet-inequality

37. That is, not the kind of low-paid, insecure transient jobs that have made up the majority of new jobs in the past decade.

Conclusion

1. Social Mobility Barometer, 'Public attitudes to social mobility in the UK', December 2018. Access at: assets.publishing.service.gov.uk/government/uploads/system/uploads/attachment_data/file/762966/Social_Mobility_Barometer_2018_report.pdf

2. Just 22 per cent of those aged twenty-five to forty-nine think that their housing situation is better than that of their parents compared to 60 per cent of those aged sixty-five.

Bibliography

Books

Appiah, Kwame Anthony, *The Lies that Bind: Rethinking Identity*, 2018

Brooks, David, *The Social Animal; A Story of How Success Happens*, 2012

Clark, Gregory, *The Son Also Rises: Surnames and the History of Social Mobility*, 2014

De Waal, Kit, ed., *Common People: An Anthology of Working-Class Writers*, 2019

Dweck, Carol S., *Mindset: The New Psychology of Success*, 2006

Eddo-Lodge, Reni, *Why I'm No Longer Talking to White People About Race*, 2017

Elliott Major, Lee, and Machin, Stephen, *Social Mobility and its Enemies*, 2018

Fox, Kate, *Watching the English: The Hidden Rules of English Behaviour*, 2014

Frank, Robert H., *Success and Luck: Good Fortune and the Myth of Meritocracy*, 2016

Friedman, Sam, and Laurison, Daniel, *The Class Ceiling: Why it Pays to be Privileged*, 2019

Fukuyama, Francis, *Identity: Contemporary Identity Politics and the Struggle for Recognition*, 2018

Gladwell, Malcolm, *Outliers: The Story of Success*, 2008

Green, Francis, and Kynaston, David, *Engines of Privilege: Britain's Private School Problem*, 2019

Hanley, Lynsey, *Respectable: Crossing the Class Divide*, 2016

Hirsch, Afua, *Brit(ish): On Race, Identity and Belonging*, 2018

Lareau, Annette, *Unequal Childhoods: Class, Race, Family Life* (Second Edition), 2011

McGarvey, Darren, *Poverty Safari: Understanding the Anger of Britain's Underclass*, 2017

Mukherjee, Siddhartha, *The Gene: An Intimate History*, 2017

Noah, Trevor, *Born a Crime: Stories from a South African Childhood*, 2016

Pilnick, Alison, *Genetics and Society*, 2002

Ramsay, Maureen, 'Genetic reductionism and medical genetic practice', in A. Clarke, ed., *Genetic Counselling: Practice and Principles*, 1994

Stephens-Davidowitz, Seth, *Everybody Lies: Big Data, New Data, and What the Internet Can Tell Us about Who We Really Are*, 2017

Vance, J. D., *Hillbilly Elegy: A Memoir of a Family and Culture in Crisis*, 2016

Westover, Tara, *Educated*, 2018

Academic Journal articles

Aston University, 'You are what you speak', https://www2.aston.ac.uk/research/research-impact/case-studies/you-are-what-you-speak

Chartered College of Teaching, 'Speaking up: the importance of oracy in teaching and learning', https://impact.chartered.college/article/millard-importance-of-oracy-in-teaching-learning/

Feinstein, Leon, 'Inequality in the early cognitive development of British children in the 1970 cohort', 17 November 2003, https://onlinelibrary.wiley.com/doi/abs/10.1111/1468-0335.t01-1-00272

Gillies, Val, 'Childrearing, class and the new politics of parenting', *Sociology Compass*, vol. 2, no. 3, April 2008

Godfrey, Erin B., Santos, Carlos E., and Burson, Esther, 'For better or worse? System-justifying beliefs in sixth-grade predict trajectories of self-esteem and behavior across early adolescence', https://onlinelibrary.wiley.com/doi/full/10.1111/cdev.12854

Hirsch, Donald, *Experiences of Poverty and Educational Disadvantage*, Joseph Rowntree Foundation, 2007 https://www.jrf.org.uk/sites/default/files/jrf/migrated/files/2123.pdf

Jost, John T., American Psychological Association, 'A theory of system justification: Is there a nonconscious tendency to defend, bolster and justify aspects of the societal status quo?', https://www.apa.org/science/about/psa/2017/06/system-justification.aspx

Orwell, George, 'England Your England', http://orwell.ru/library/essays/lion/english/e_eye

Sir Mota Singh Memorial Lecture, Lincoln's Inn, Racial Equality and the Law, 13 November 2018, https://www.judiciary.uk/wp-content/uploads/2018/11/speech-lord-j-singh-racial-equality-and-the-law-lecture-13-nov2018.pdf

Uhlmann, Eric Luis, and Cohen, Geoffrey L., '"I think it, therefore it's true": Effects of self-perceived objectivity on hiring discrimination', *Organizational Behavior and Human Decision Processes*, vol. 104, no. 2, November 2007, https://www.sciencedirect.com/science/article/pii/S0749597807000611

Wang, Ze, Arndt, Aaron, Singh, Surendra, Biernat, Monica, and Liu, Fan '"You lost me at hello": How and when accent-based biases are expressed and suppressed', *International Journal of Research in Marketing*, vol. 30, no. 2, 2013 http://portal.idc.ac.il/en/main/research/ijrm/documents/frthcoming per cent20ijrm per cent20d-12-00014_wang per cent20et per cent20al per cent20.pdf

Other articles

The Atlantic, 'Why the myth of meritocracy hurts kids of color', https://www.theatlantic.com/education/archive/2017/07/internalizing-the-myth-of-meritocracy/535035/

Ball, James, and Greenway, Andrew, *The Spectator*, 'The bluffocracy: how Britain ended up being run by eloquent chancers', https://www.spectator.co.uk/2018/08/the-bluffocracy-how-britain-ended-up-being-run-by-eloquent-chancers/

The Economist, 'Modern love: the internet has transformed the search for love and partnership', 18 August 2018, https://www.economist.com/leaders/2018/08/18/modern-love

Mohamed, Hashi, *Prospect*, April 2017, https://www.prospectmagazine.co.uk/politics/the-case-for-a-wild-card

National Crime Agency, *County Lines Violence, Exploitation & Drug Supply 2017*, National Briefing Report, November 2017, http://www.nationalcrimeagency.gov.uk/who-we-are/publications/234-county-lines-violence-exploitation-and-drug-supply-2017/file

Office for National Statistics, 'How has the student population changed?' https://www.ons.gov.uk/peoplepopulationandcommunity/birthsdeathsandmarriages/livebirths/articles/howhasthestudentpopulationchanged/2016-09-20

Prime Minister's Speech, 'Britain, the great meritocracy', 9
September 2016; https://www.gov.uk/government/speeches/
britain-the-great-meritocracy-prime-ministers-speech

The Shanker Institute, 'The early language gap is about more
than words', http://www.shankerinstitute.org/audio-visual/
early-language-gap-about-more-words-0

Social Mobility Commission, 23 October 2017, https://www.gov.uk/
government/news/unpaid-internships-are-damaging-to-social-
mobility

The Social Mobility Index, https://www.gov.uk/government/
publications/social-mobility-index

University College London, 'Prejudice about regional accents is still
prevalent in Britain', 18 December 2017, https://www.ucl.ac.uk/
news/2017/dec/prejudice-about-regional-accents-still-prevalent-
britain

World Economic Forum, 'Here's why you didn't get that job: your
name', https://www.weforum.org/agenda/2017/05/job-
applications-resume-cv-name-descrimination/

Young, Toby, *Quadrant*, 'The fall of the meritocracy', 7 September
2015, https://quadrant.org.au/magazine/2015/09/fall-meritocracy/

Reports

Boston Consulting Group, for The Sutton Trust, *The State of Social
Mobility in the UK 2017*

Bridge Group, *Socio-economic Background and Early Career Progression
in the Law*, Summary Report, September 2018 https://static1.
squarespace.com/static/5c18e090b40b9d6b43b093d8/t/5cd180d73
cfb16000143 6429/1557233888333/03+Research+2018+Progression+
law.pdf

Credit Suisse, Global Wealth Report 2018; https://www.credit-suisse.
com/corporate/en/research/research-institute/global-wealth-
report.html

Department for Education, 'Permanent and fixed-period exclusions
in England: 2008 to 2009', https://assets.publishing.service.gov.
uk/government/uploads/system/uploads/attachment_data/
file/218896/sfr22-2010.pdf

Department for Education, 'Permanent and fixed-period exclusions in
England: 2016 to 2017', https://assets.publishing.service.gov.uk/

government/uploads/system/uploads/attachment_data/
file/726741/text_exc1617.pdf

Education and Employers Report, 'Drawing the future: exploring the career aspirations of primary school children from around the world', https://www.educationandemployers.org/wp-content/uploads/2018/01/DrawingTheFuture.pdf

The Equality Trust, https://www.equalitytrust.org.uk/scale-economic-inequality-uk

'Hate crime: the facts behind the headlines', October 2016, https://www.civitas.org.uk/content/files/hatecrimethefactsbehindtheheadlines.pdf

'How are poverty, ethnicity and social networks related?', Joseph Rowntree Foundation, https://www.jrf.org.uk/report/how-are-poverty-ethnicity-and-social-networks-related

The Marmot Review. 'Fair Society, Healthy Lives'; http://www.instituteofhealthequity.org/resources-reports/fair-society-healthy-lives-the-marmot-review

Mayor of London, Annual London Education Report 2017

The Muslim Council of Britain, 'British Muslims in numbers', https://www.mcb.org.uk/wp-content/uploads/2015/02/MCBCensusReport_2015.pdf –

Poverty in the UK, 5 September 2019, https://researchbriefings.parliament.uk/ResearchBriefing/Summary/SN07096

Race Disparity Audit: Summary Findings from the Ethnicity Facts and Figures Website, Cabinet Office, 2017

'Racial prejudice in Britain today', September 2017, http://natcen.ac.uk/media/1488132/racial-prejudice-report_v4.pdf

Runnymede Trust, *Minority Report: Race and Class in Post-Brexit Britain*, 2017

Social Metrics Commission 2019 Report, 29 July 2019; https://socialmetricscommission.org.uk/new-report-on-poverty-from-independent-commission-highlights-scale-of-challenge-facing-new-prime-minister/

Social Mobility 2017 Summit Report: The Sutton Trust 20th Anniversary Summit 2017

Social Mobility and Child Poverty Commission, *State of the Nation 2015: Social Mobility and Child Poverty in Great Britain*

Social Mobility Barometer, 'Public attitudes to social mobility in the UK', December 2018: https://assets.publishing.service.gov.uk/government/uploads/system/uploads/attachment_data/file/762966/Social_Mobility_Barometer_2018_report.pdf

Social Mobility Commission, *State of the Nation 2017: Social Mobility in Great Britain* 2017

Sutton Trust Report, https://www.suttontrust.com/wp-content/uploads/2016/02/Leading-People_Feb16.pdf

Acknowledgements

My friend, the late Tessa Jowell, used to say, *'we'd get so much more done if everyone wasn't trying to take the credit'*. Nothing can prepare you for writing a book like this; you just have to start it and see how it goes. Two years after starting, in addition to holding a full-time job as a practising barrister, and attempting to 'have a life', I am very proud of what has emerged. But it is also undoubtedly a collaborative process.

Stephen King, the famous and successful author, once remarked that *'to write is human, to edit is divine'*. I only fully appreciated the truth of this once I started writing myself. None of this would have been possible without my editor, Cecily Gayford. It was she who first approached me directly, and who subsequently planted the seed of writing a book. Cecily helped introduce me to a wholly alien process. She helped re-order my sometimes disparate ideas and disordered thoughts into a coherent narrative, by challenging me, by asking me to do more, by asking me to think again, to find a new level of clarity. I will be eternally grateful to her.

I have nothing but gratitude to all the team at Profile Books, for having invested so much in my first book and for all the continued support provided by the incredible people who work there. To Susanne Hillen, my sub-editor, for all her help and sharp attention to detail. Many thanks also to my agent Niki Chang, who from the outset believed in this book.

I want to thank Zainab Moallin in particular for her enormous assistance, for synthetisation of reports, for her attendance during numerous meetings, for her attention to detail and for her ability to highlight quickly the most pertinent information. My sister Shukri Hashi and my paternal uncle Ibrahim Hashi were immensely resourceful when it came to researching the brief family history and information I needed. Thanks to Beheshteh Engineer, Penny Rabiger, and all those who helped me with research queries and often gave up their evenings to tell me about their jobs and experiences. I want to particularly thank Sam Friedman and Daniel Laurison, whose timely book *The Class Ceiling* (2019), informed so much of the analysis in this book; especially to Sam and his colleague Aaron Reeves for making the time to meet me and answer my numerous questions.

Whilst writing can be a lonely experience, it leaves you often with little perspective. It is therefore critical to have a network of friends and individuals who are generous with their time; time spent looking over drafts of various chapters, testing ideas, questioning angles and the premise of an argument; all of which informs the book. For this, I am enormously indebted to James Corbet Burcher, Emily Wilsdon, Arzoo Ahmed, Salim Rachid, Elizabeth Rantzen, Kathy Gee, Stephen Ashworth, Hugh Levinson, Michael Speer and Samuel Hunt, who all spent their precious time reading different drafts.

To my family, there are no words to describe fully and appropriately what I feel. I have put so much of our personal lives in the public domain and I was conscious throughout the writing process of doing so responsibly. I may have chosen to tell my own story so publicly, but none of you chose to put yourselves out there; and I sincerely hope that you will all think that I have done our struggle and journey so far some justice, without negative repercussions. I hope that in reading it many of you, some of whom have even better stories, will embark on your own journey storytelling, of reconciliation, of redemption and renewal. The Hashi clan is made of tough stuff, and I am confident the future is bright.

To all my friends, wherever you are on the globe. I have found in you what I didn't have elsewhere; if, as they say, you can't choose your family but you can choose your friends, I have chosen the best I possibly could. To my mentors, personal and professional, to all those who took a risk on me; I hope that the book you've just finished reading has brought you some pride in what you've given me; if it was not apparent already, it has made, and continues to make, a huge difference to me. Thank you so very much.

As I stated in the introduction, the trigger for this book was the Radio 4 documentary broadcast in April 2017. It was commissioned by Mohit Bakaya, from a proposal I put together with the help of Hugh Levinson, the Head of BBC Radio Current Affairs. Hugh is also the reason why I have something of a Radio 4 'career' if I can even call it that. In putting together the documentary, my producer Rosamund Jones was also a source of perspective, clarity and wisdom. Arguably, this book would not have happened without all their support. Thank you.

To Leila, the woman who really got to know me during the time I was writing this book, as she read draft after draft, surprised, shocked and proud at different times. You make me a better man every day.

Finally, to all of you I may never get to meet or perhaps encounter from afar, thank you for your time, thank you for reading this and please share it widely.

Hashi Mohamed
December 2019

Index